COCKATOOS
in Aviculture

COCKATOOS
in Aviculture

Rosemary Low

BLANDFORD

A BLANDFORD BOOK

First published in the UK 1993
by Blandford, a Cassell imprint
Villiers House, 41/47 Strand, London WC2N 5JE

Distributed in the United States by
Sterling Publishing Co., Inc.
387 Park Avenue South, New York, NY 10016–8810

Distributed in Australia by
Capricorn Link (Australia) Pty Ltd
P.O. Box 665, Lane Cove, NSW 2066

*A catalogue entry for this title is available
from the British Library*

ISBN 0–7137–2322–X

Typeset by Cambrian Typesetters, Frimley, Surrey
Printed and bound in Great Britain by Bath Press
Colourbooks Ltd., Glasgow

Contents

Appendices

Acknowledgements

My grateful thanks are extended to the following people who so readily complied with my requests for information:

Australia: Ray Akroyd, Victoria; John Beardmore, Queensland; Neville and Enid Connors, New South Wales; John Courtney, New South Wales; Stacey Gelis, Victoria; David Judd, Victoria; Ian and Rose Langdon, Victoria; Ian Rowley, Western Australia; Graham Taylor, Pearl Coast Zoo
France: Marc Boussekey
Germany: Thomas Arndt; Dr F. Janeczek; Dr R. Peters and Roland Wirth
Netherlands: Catherine King, Rotterdam Zoo
Sweden: Ulf Rohlin
UK: Mrs F. Behrens, Henley; John Heath; Dr M. Jones; John and Pat King; Frank Lambert, IUCN; Stuart Marsden and Dr R. Wilkinson, Chester Zoo
USA: Sheldon Dingle; J. R. van Oosten; Mike Taylor, Florida

Special thanks are due to Simon Joshua and Professor J. Parker of Reading University for contributing the chapter on phylogenetic studies and to Stacey Gelis for helping to compile some of the weight tables.

Photographs
I am indebted to the following friends who contributed photographs: Armin Brockner, Germany (p. 39); Sheldon Dingle, USA (p. 169); R. H. Grantham, UK (pp. 199 and 201); Simon Joshua, Reading University, UK (p. 133 and 135); David Judd, Australia (p. 156); Rod Morris, Natural History and Science Unit, Television New Zealand (p. 136); Peter Odekerken, Australia (pp. 196 and 224); Dr Robert Peters, Germany (p. 189); Ulf Rohlin, Sweden (p. 195); Stan Sindel, Australia (p. 141); Dr R. Wilkinson, Chester Zoo, UK (p. 170); Graham A. Wood, Australia (p. 244).
All other photographs are by the author.

Introduction

In August 1699, William Dampier, an English explorer, sailed around part of the coast of Australia. He described the birds seen on an offshore island, which included: 'a sort of white parrot, which flew a great many together'.

They were Bare-eyed Cockatoos, or Little Corellas, possibly the first species of Australian parrot to be observed and reported by a European. It is likely, however, that cockatoos had previously been observed in the wild and, indeed, had probably already reached Europe – species from Indonesia or the Philippines. At the first sight of these distinctive members of the parrot family, naturalists would have observed how they differed from other parrots. Approximately 330 species are recognized (one cannot be precise as taxonomists differ on whether some forms are species or sub-species), of which 17 are cockatoos and all have crests. But only one other species of parrot is crested. The cockatoos are a highly distinctive group – some would say *the* most distinctive of the parrots. They differ not only in having a crest but in being either basically black or mainly white (with a couple of exceptions).

Little was recorded about parrots in captivity (and even less about them in their natural habitat) until the nineteenth century, by which time not only had all the species been exported to Europe, but two Australian species were among the most widely kept of all pet birds. They were popular mainly because of their intelligence, often affectionate behaviour and their ability to mimic. Those which proved amenable to training often became cherished and spoilt pets. W. T. Greene in his three-volume classic, *Parrots in Captivity*, published in the 1880s, described a Slender-billed Cockatoo (Long-billed Corella) which was a greater mimic of sounds *and* actions than of words. One of its favourite performances was that of pouring tea:

> The sugar is first put into the cups – the action of putting it in, you understand – and then the tea is poured out; his beak being the spout of the tea-pot, and he makes the noise of pouring exactly, while pretending to do so. . . . One morning, from an old ladder that is devoted to his use in the garden, he watched the gardener clipping the laurels, and when he came in, we had the whole performance of clipping laurels gone through exactly, giving his head a little jerk with each snap of the shears – his beak was of course supposed to be those implements – and the sound was exact.

While perhaps few cockatoos are as clever as this bird was, this account demonstrates certain characteristics which many cockatoos possess and which makes them such appealing pets – their acute powers of observation, intelligence and perhaps, above all, an ability to reason. I believe that few birds possess this latter ability to a greater degree than cockatoos. These features of their personality, plus their beauty, has unfortunately given them great appeal as house pets and aviary birds. Although they have been popular as pets since the early nineteenth century, when they decorated Worcester and Meissen porcelain, and were considered perfect adornments for the rooms of literary salons (which seems strange, given their vocal 'accomplishments'), it was not until the 1970s that this popularity started to threaten the very existence of some species.

During the course of a century there has been a drastic, and latterly tragic, change in regard to cockatoos and the pet trade. Not a lot happened, except the prohibition of the commercial export of Australian cockatoos and other fauna in 1959, until the 1970s. Then, in the last part of that decade, trade in cockatoos from Papua New Guinea and Indonesia gained momentum. By the late 1980s it was so intense that at least one species, the Moluccan Cockatoo, was quite suddenly found to have been trapped from the wild almost to the point of extinction. By this time, although substantial numbers of cockatoos were being reared by aviculturists, the number was but a small fraction of that which had been exported from their native countries and islands.

Mass export was, in part, due to deforestation, especially on certain Indonesian islands where logging rights had been purchased, resulting in the destruction, in a handful of years, of nearly all the forested habitats. So, almost overnight, it was realized that the Moluccan Cockatoo – and, almost certainly this will not prove to be the only example – was far more numerous in captivity than in the wild. Their trade had been a scandal, discovered too late to effect a halt.

Many parrots reproduce very freely in aviaries but there are a number of problems associated with rearing cockatoos, some of which result from the nervous temperament of most species. Can aviculturists ever produce enough cockatoos for the pet trade now that their export has virtually ceased? And, more importantly, can they breed birds suitable for reintroduction to their original habitats? In these pages, these important questions are discussed – and many more relating to the welfare of captive cockatoos and the conservation of their wild counterparts.

Part I
The Cockatoo in Aviculture

1

Introducing the cockatoo

Parrots are perhaps the best known group of birds in the world. Although there are more than 330 species, which differ widely in appearance, they are easily recognizable because of the shape of their beak and because most have brightly-coloured plumage.

Classification

The parrots form a distinct order of birds, the Psittaciformes. Within an order, further divisions are made to indicate the relationship of various groups of species. These are: families (whose names end in 'idae'), and sub-families (whose names end in 'inae'). Cockatoos belong to the sub-family Cacatuinae. Sub-families are further divided into tribes (whose names end in 'ini'). There are three cockatoo tribes: Calyptorhynchini (black cockatoos), Cacatuini (white cockatoos, Galah and Gang Gang) and Calopsittacini (Cockatiel).

The Cockatiel is the smallest and most distinctive member of the three tribes; its size and long tapering tail give it the proportions of a parrakeet. To this day, many birdkeepers find it difficult to accept that it is a member of the cockatoo family. But this is indubitably the case. Because of the ease with which it breeds in captivity, resulting in a large number of mutations being established, and due to the fact that it makes an appealing pet, the Cockatiel is bred in countless thousands in many countries – in fact, wherever aviculture is practised. Breeders do not regard it as a cockatoo but as a 'fancy' in its own right, like the Budgerigar or Canary. More books have been written about it than any other member of the parrot family, with the exception of the Budgerigar. The Cockatiel is therefore covered less comprehensively in this book than the other cockatoos.

EVOLUTIONARY LINEAGES

The order Psittaciformes is well defined morphologically (by its form or appearance) but the primary evolutionary lineages within it are not so clear-cut. However, in all studies, two distinct assemblages have been recognized: the cockatoos and the lorikeets (Christidis et al., 1991).

There are several methods by which the biochemical distance between species and genera of parrots are judged. One of these is protein electrophoresis. Using this method it has been found that genetic distances are greater between cockatoos and the remaining parrots than between other groups of parrots, at values ranging between 0.80 and 1.65. To put this in perspective, genera of Australian broad-tailed parrots (Platycercinae) are separated from each other by distances of 0.20 or less (*Platycercus*, *Barnardius*, *Lathamus*, *Purpureicephalus* etc.).

Genetic distances between major lineages of the cockatoos (*Cacatua* and *Calyptorhynchus*) are as great as between tribal groupings in other parrots, suggesting that their lineages are ancient rather than rapidly evolving. The cockatoos are probably one of the oldest lineages of the order. Lorikeets, in contrast, are little differentiated; they evolved more recently. Chromosome karyotypes further stress the division between cockatoos and other parrots. Christidis *et al.* state that, whereas nearly all parrots have a diploid complement of 60–72 chromosomes, cockatoos have 72–80 (see Chapter 12). When taken into account with the many morphological and behavioural differences between the cockatoos and other parrots, these data lend support for recognizing the cockatoos as a family.

Characteristic features of cockatoos

PLUMAGE COLORATION AND CRESTS

If parrots are the most distinctive group of birds, cockatoos are the most readily discernible group of parrots – or, more accurately, of the white species. Cockatoos possess a feature which is unique among the parrots – an erectile crest. Only one other parrot is crested – the Horned Parrakeet (*Eunymphicus cornutus*) from New Caledonia. Some of this parrot's crown feathers are elongated to form a crest but it is not erectile. No other sub-family of parrots can be defined so succinctly: they have movable crests! However, there are several types of crest formation, from curved and highly conspicuous (even when not erected), as in the Sulphur-crested Cockatoos, to the type which lays flat and is not apparent until erected, as in the Goffin's Cockatoo.

Parrots are known for their bright colours, yet probably only two or three cockatoo species would be described as brightly coloured by most people. The brilliant plumage colours of parrots are of two types: structural and pigmentary. The former result from the structures of the barbs and barbules of the feathers, which vary due to different formations of the keratin cylinders within the barbs. Then, various pigments exist, such as melanin (responsible for black and brown) and carotenoids (responsible for red and orange). There is another type of pigment, of unknown composition, in which the pigment is pale yellow

Erupting feathers of a young cockatoo, including powder-down feathers. The latter grow continuously, producing the white powder which protects and cleans the feathers. This is very well developed in the *Cacatua* cockatoos, so much so that they give off a cloud of white dust whenever they ruffle their plumage.

in visible light and fluorescent yellow-gold, sulphur-yellow or green in ultraviolet light. This type of pigment is found in the crests of some *Cacatua* species. Cockatoos are white because of the composition of the feather barbs, which lack the Dyck texture (a structural feature which produces colours by the back-scattering of light). However, some nestling *Cacatua* exhibit the odd grey feather. This adds weight to the theory that they evolved from grey-plumaged birds because nestling plumage often exhibits some atavistic feature. Most people think of cockatoos as being white or predominantly so, but this is true of only one of the three tribes.

THE BEAK

A cockatoo's beak is a powerful tool, capable of feats which no man can achieve unaided. It is particularly effective when combined with the intelligence of its owner – especially when that species is the Greater Sulphur-crested Cockatoo. Then the combination is awesome. A cockatoo's beak is designed to destroy wood, which it does with consummate ease. I know of someone who allowed his Umbrella Cockatoo the freedom of the room for a while every day. After the cockatoo had destroyed all the wooden furniture, he was forced to replace it with steel! It speaks volumes for the endearing nature of many cockatoos that such destructiveness is tolerated!

The beak of the Palm Cockatoo is the largest, in proportion to its body size, of any parrot; that of the sub-species *Probosciger aterrimus goliath* is larger even than that of the Hyacinthine Macaw (*Anodorhynchus hyacinthinus*), the largest of all parrots. The strength of the Palm's beak enables it to feed on the fruits of the *Pandanus*, each segment of which contains a kernel which is covered in fibrous flesh up to 10 cm (4 in) thick. Nothing else can open them.

The beak has evolved to its shape and size for a particular reason (see pp. 232 and 234). In each species of *Calyptorhynchus*, for example, it is different. Forshaw (1981) described the beaks of three as follows: *C. funereus* has a narrow, protruding beak, with the tip of the upper mandible elongated and pointed, enabling it to extract wood-boring insect larvae from timber and to prise seeds out of deep, woody fruits; *C. banksii* has a broad, blunt beak, for crushing seeds and hard nuts,

The pointed tip of the upper mandible of the Yellow-tailed Black Cockatoo (*Calyptorhynchus funereus*) enables it to extract wood-boring larvae from timber.

i.e. it is suitable for breaking, not extracting; *C. lathamus* has a protruding, bulbous beak, with an exceptionally broad lower mandible, an adaptation for tearing apart *Casuarina* cones.

The lower mandible of the Gang Gang Cockatoo, which has a marked central identation, is an adaptation for opening eucalyptus seed capsules, and the elongated bill of the Western Long-billed Corella assists it in digging up roots and corms, especially those of onion grass (*Romulea longifolia*), which constitutes a large part of its diet.

Roland Wirth (1990) points out that the Indonesian cockatoos have different beak sizes.

This is by no means a whim of nature; it is in effect the birds' adaptation to the different variety of plant food available on each specific island. So it becomes apparent that birds which originally appeared in great numbers, such as the Moluccan Cockatoos, must have exerted some influence on the propagation of those plants they prefer for their diet, be it in the negative sense by consuming their seeds, or in the positive sense by excreting undigested seeds and thus spreading them over large areas.

With their strong beaks, Moluccan Cockatoos are possibly the only animals on the island of Seram capable of cracking the hard shell of some nuts, and the survival of certain types of trees may well depend on the seed-spreading activities of these birds. Consequently, the gradual extermination of these birds, could, in the long run, bring about a change to the rainforest flora, or even result in the disappearance of certain types of trees, with the subsequent inevitable extermination of other animal and plant species.

CHEEK FEATHERS

Cockatoos are able to move their cheek feathers to partly cover the beak, in a manner unknown in other parrots. Wood (1988), who watched Palm Cockatoos in the Iron Range, recorded that, when aware of being observed, they would retreat some distance, 'conceal themselves in thick foliage and use their cheek feathers to conceal their red cheek patches'. They also did this during cold winds or rain, no doubt to prevent the loss of body heat from this area of bare skin.

THE FEET

The degree to which parrots use their feet as 'hands' varies among parrot species. All the larger parrots are adept at this, none more so than the cockatoos. Only the Cockatiel lacks this ability (normally). Cockatoos really do use the foot as a hand, in that they are adept at grasping objects, not merely holding them. A *Cacatua*, for example, will often put the whole length of its leg through the cage and reach for an object it wants. Cockatoo-owners must never leave anything – plants, electric cables, curtains, etc. – within reach, as part of it is liable to end up in the bird's crop, perhaps with fatal consequences. Cockatoos have very strong feet. As chicks, the feet are the first part of their anatomy to grow to full size. Sometimes they seem to have difficulty in coping and literally fall over their feet! As in all parrots, the feet are zygodactyl, i.e. two toes point forwards and two backwards. The nails wear with use and grow continuously throughout their lives, just as in human beings. However, if the entire nail is lost as the result of an injury, it will not grow again.

Behaviour

MIMICRY

In captivity, some cockatoos learn to mimic a few words; others never do, even though they have been hand-reared and kept in close proximity to people. Judged against the large parrots in general, cockatoos are not considered to be good 'talkers', although they may mimic various sounds, including those of other birds. The ability to mimic is in no way related to intelligence. Indeed, one of the best 'talkers' of the family is the Cockatiel, which may acquire a large vocabulary.

INTELLIGENCE AND POWERS OF REASONING

The Concise Oxford Dictionary defines 'intelligent' as 'having or showing (usually a high degree of) understanding; clever, quick of mind'. In my opinion, cockatoos are among the most intelligent of parrots; indeed, some are remarkable and, in this respect, must rank very highly in the whole of the bird kingdom. While it is difficult to define intelligence in birds, powers of reasoning must surely be important, and so must tool-using. This is the term given to an action by any animal which involves the use of an inanimate article. Very few animals are known to use tools, the most notable being the chimpanzee, which is renowned for its intelligence. Among birds, there are few species which have this ability.

In captivity, a few species of parrots, including Amazons and macaws, can use an object, such as a spoon or a twig, to scratch the head. Boswall (1983) recorded the case of a Moluccan Cockatoo which regularly used twigs, a piece of wire and other items. It would also grab one of its primary feathers with the foot, bend it and use the end to scratch the lower part of the head. Many cockatoo-keepers could relate similar instances.

However, there are few reports of tool-using in wild birds, probably because there is rarely anyone to record them. In New Guinea, two Sulphur-crested Cockatoos were observed screeching at two passive Bat Hawks (*Machaerirhynchus alcinus*) sitting on a lower branch. The cockatoos continued their vocal harrassment but the hawks did not move. Then one of the cockatoos flew to a branch about 4 m (13 ft) above the hawks, 'snapped off small twigs containing several leaves and dropped them on to the hawks with a sideways flick of its head . . . it proceeded to rain leafy twiglets up to six inches in length' until the hawks flew off, pursued by the cockatoo (Finch, 1982).

The best known tool-using species of parrot is the Palm Cockatoo which uses a 'tool' in its display – a stick with which it makes a drumming sound (see pp. 240 and 244).

★ ★ ★

As described, cockatoos have a number of remarkable qualities which set them apart from other parrots. One of them is their distinctive beauty. It is no wonder that they have long captured the imagination of artists, sculptors, toy-makers and designers of greetings cards, stamps and fabrics.

Aviculturists who come to know very well the personalities of cockatoos – or the owner of a single bird – are fascinated, enchanted, entranced and sometimes momentarily infuriated by these extraordinary birds. Cockatoos are capable of great tenderness and gentleness towards the object of their affection, be it human or their own kind. They can teach us so much – even that deep affection, long retained, is not the prerogative of the human race. Perhaps by watching cockatoos we can learn to treat captive birds with greater respect, as the realization dawns that many species have the same emotional needs as ourselves. Careful observation of a compatible pair of cockatoos over a long term will make this abundantly clear.

2

Cockatoos in the wild

Range and distribution

Cockatoos occur in Australia, New Guinea and the islands of Indonesia, the Solomons and the Philippines. The map (opposite) shows their natural range. In Australia they reach their zenith in number of species, flock sizes and ubiquity. It would be almost impossible to go to Australia and not see any cockatoos in the wild. In contrast, one could spend months or even years in South America and never see a wild macaw. It is easier to observe parrots 'down under' than anywhere in the world – and it would be almost as impossible *not* to see such noisy, conspicuous, widespread and common birds as cockatoos as it would be to miss feral pigeons in most large cities. One can even see them in suburbia – Sulphur-crested, Galahs (Roseate or Rose-breasted Cockatoos) and Bare-eyed Cockatoos and, if one is fortunate, even the beautiful little Gang Gang.

Cockatoos are found throughout Australia and in Tasmania. There have been enormous changes in their distribution and habitat since the first white men colonized Australia in 1788. Much of the native vegetation has been cleared to grow cereal crops. This has adversely affected some species and benefited others. For example, the Galah was once found only within flying distance of tree-lined water courses, but the provision of water troughs for cattle has enabled it to colonize almost the entire continent. Unlimited food and adequate nesting facilities have resulted in its population increasing out of all proportion to its former numbers. On the other hand, the original inhabitant of the cleared areas, the Leadbeater's (Major Mitchell's) Cockatoo, has decreased, despite the fact that, in one area where a study was carried out, annual productivity and survival of fledged young was actually better than that of the Galah.

Humans and cockatoos

COCKATOOS AS AGRICULTURAL PESTS

Because cockatoos are large, conspicuous and noisy birds, they have gained the reputation of being agricultural pests where they occur in areas where cereal crops are grown. Sometimes this reputation is

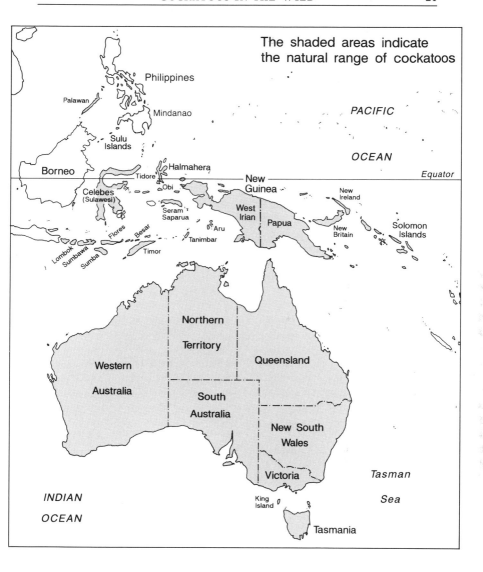

The shaded areas indicate the natural range of cockatoos

Philippines

Palawan

Mindanao

PACIFIC

Sulu
Islands

OCEAN

Borneo

Halmahera

Tidore
Obi

New
Guinea

Equator

Celebes
(Sulawesi)

New
Ireland

Seram
Saparua

West
Irian

Aru

Papua

New
Britain

Solomon
Islands

Flores

Besar

Tanimbar

Lombok
Sumbawa

Timor

Sumba

Northern

Territory

Western

Australia

Queensland

Australia

South

Australia

New South

Wales

INDIAN

Victoria

Tasman

King
Island

Sea

OCEAN

Tasmania

justified – but not always. When the cockatoo controversy was at its height, a leaflet produced by a group of Australians – who called themselves 'A Better Alternative' – claimed that many growers were reluctant to sow crops because of attacks by the four 'pest' species of cockatoos, the Galah, the Long-billed Corella and the Bare-eyed and Greater Sulphur-crested Cockatoos. It claimed that the costs and labour to patrol a 40-hectare crop (about 100 acres) was as follows:

Loss in production	A$ 4,000
1,000 cartridges	A$ 500
3,000 km travel, fuel and running costs	A$ 1,000
350 man-hours lost	A$ 5,250
TOTAL:	A$10,750 per 40 hectares

It claimed that these four species, which include the Galah, were 'causing severe undue hardship for both urban and rural dwellers right across Australia'. Not until studies of several cockatoo species were commenced by the CSIRO (Commonwealth Scientific and Industrial Research Organization) was it found that claims against cockatoos were often unjustified or exaggerated, or no longer applied.

Rowley (1990) pointed out that conflict between Galahs and the farming community was intense during the first half of the twentieth century. During this era, wheat was transported in sacks and storage bins, and railway trucks were primitive in their design, allowing cockatoos to help themselves. Modern machinery and concern over weevil damage in silos have resulted in less waste and spillage. These days, grain that cockatoos find would never have reached the silos. However, cockatoos are a pest of growing crops, such as sunflower and sorghum.

Poor farming practices often worsen the situation. Rowley (1990) stated that the ripe crop is often left standing in the paddock for weeks before being harvested, allowing the number of birds recognizing and using the food source to increase. This is relevant because the period can extend into the winter when food for Galahs is most scarce. During this period they exist on a wide variety of weeds. A seven-year study in Western Australia (Rowley, 1990) concluded that the pest problem posed by Galahs there was 'minuscule' and that:

. . . complaints by farmer were largely restricted to accusations that Galahs kill trees. The advice of experienced foresters suggests that the cause of tree-death is usually salting due to injudicious over-clearing of native vegetation.

One study revealed that, far from being pests, cockatoos were actually performing a service to the farmer. In south-western Australia there were complaints that Banksian (Red-tailed Black) Cockatoos were feeding on crops. However, careful observation revealed that they come to the ground to feed on double-gee (*Emex australis*), a harmful introduced weed in pastoral districts.

No such claims can be made for the white cockatoos, unfortunately. In view of the threat to the livelihood of many farmers, it is permitted to control the four 'pest' species. Farmers are allowed to shoot them or to call on the services of a licensed trapper. Since about 1950 Ray Akroyd has been trapping cockatoos at the request of farmers in New South

Wales and Victoria. Farmers often shoot them but he states that this 'does not reduce the population and is cruel'. Eastern Long-billed Corellas are shot at their roosts at night. The other three species are killed as they feed, the fields echoing to the sound of the shot gun and afterwards littered with blood-stained white bodies. One farmer employed a man to shoot cockatoos for six hours daily.

Even worse, many farmers use an illegal and inhumane form of control – poisoned grain. Cockatoos and other species eat the grain and die an agonizing death. This method shows the measure of the farmers' desperation, says Mr Akroyd, as they risk heavy fines or even imprisonment. Not until 1991 was a more humane method of killing employed – by the State Government of Western Victoria. A lure-bird and grain are used to attract cockatoos. Then a radio-controlled trap-net is operated. As the cockatoos are removed from the net, they are thrown into a 200-litre (44-gallon) drum with a rubber-sealed lid. Into this is piped carbon dioxide. The birds quickly become unconscious and die within 2–3 seconds.

Comparatively speaking, this seems to be the most humane method employed to date. Now let man exercise his ingenuity by replacing poisoned bait with grain treated with a substance which causes temporary infertility. It would need to be used for only a few weeks of the year.

It is not only in Australia that cockatoos are considered to be agricultural pests. In Indonesia, on the island of Bacan in the northern Moluccas, crop damage was blamed on Umbrella Cockatoos. But numbers of this species there had been so severely reduced by over-trapping for export that it was no longer seen in flocks. The raiding birds were white Imperial Pigeons (*Ducula bicolor*). There again, crop losses due to avian depredation could have been substantially reduced by better management. Garden plots, instead of being located in the middle of the forest, should have been situated close to human habitation. Losses of ripe crops immediately before harvesting could have been avoided by placing someone to frighten off the birds early in the morning (Milton & Marhadi, 1987).

TRADE IN INDONESIAN COCKATOOS

With regard to the status of Indonesian cockatoos, in most species any assessment made prior to 1985 can now be considered invalid. The scale of trapping and export which occurred during the 1980s, compounded on some islands by massive deforestation, changed the status of some cockatoo populations from common to near extinction. This trade was among the most scandalous which has occurred in the history of parrot export, notwithstanding even that of Spix's Macaw (*Cyanopsitta spixii*). I make this statement because Spix's is, by nature, a rare bird – but all the Indonesian cockatoos were thriving until the tree-fellers and the trappers started work. The Convention on International Trade in Endangered Species of Wild Flora and Fauna (CITES) which was designed to protect all fauna from excessive trade, failed dismally in respect of these cockatoos. The almost inevitable result is that at least one species will become extinct in the wild within the next one or two decades unless a massive effort is launched before the mid-1990s.

Behaviour

FEEDING

Different species exploit food sources of varying types and in different locations. The Galah feeds mainly on the ground on a wide variety of items, whereas the *Calyptorhynchus* species are arboreal feeders. One species, the Glossy Cockatoo, is a specialist, feeding almost entirely on the seeds of *Casuarina* trees. Among parrots, ground-feeding species are not adept at using the foot as a hand, thus the Galah does this much less than the other cockatoos (except the Cockatiel, in which such behaviour is very rare). All other cockatoo species have this ability and use the foot, while feeding, much more than most other parrots. Forshaw (1981) commented of the Gang Gang:

> Each seed-capsule or berry is removed, split open and pressed firmly against the foot while the seeds are extracted. If the cluster is too cumbersome, the bird will hold it down against the perch under the right foot and will bite off smaller sections. I know of no other Australian parrot in which the foot-holding technique is so highly developed.

[Notice that mention was made of using the right foot to tether the food. This is because most parrots are 'left-footed'.]

Ground-feeders have different methods of working. Galahs take seeds which are visible on the ground, or they make a sideways raking movement with the beak to disturb seeds or grain just below the surface. They rarely dig deeply. In contrast, the Eastern Long-billed Corella digs up corms of the introduced onion grass (*Romulea longifolia*); it also digs up newly sown grain.

Cockatoos seldom feed alone. They are usually part of a small group, or a flock which could, in some species, number 1,000 or 2,000 birds. In his detailed study of the Galah, Rowley (1990) found that, in any foraging flock, only about 25 per cent of the cockatoos are mated pairs from a nearby roosting or nesting area; the remainder are young or unmated birds which have no territorial ties and are free to move over a

Greater Sulphur-crested Cockatoos (*Cacatua galerita galerita*) usually feed in open country such as on the crops on this farm in New South Wales, Australia.

large area in search of optimal feeding conditions. This area could be as large as 1,000 km^2 (386 sq miles).

The amount of time cockatoos spend feeding is linked to food availability. Rowley recorded that, on 25 August 1976, a pair of marked Galahs was watched throughout the day under conditions of minimal plant growth after poor winter rains. The spent eight of the 11 hours of daylight foraging over old stubble. Clearly, food was scarce. On 28 and 29 August, 94 mm (3¾ in) of rain fell and plant growth responded rapidly. On 15 September, the pair was again watched all day. This time they foraged for only four hours.

DRINKING

In the wild, cockatoos probably normally drink only twice daily, in the morning and in the evening. In Australia they often utilize artificial sources, such as stock troughs and pipes; elsewhere they drink at the edges of rivers or pools. Among parrots, the method of drinking varies according to the species. Cockatoos sip; they dip the bill into water, fill it, then lift up the head and swallow, aided by the tongue. This method of drinking is probably unique to the cockatoos.

Drinking is a dangerous activity for birds as it leaves them momentarily vulnerable to predators. Some seem to be very aware of this and approach water with great caution. Saunders (1979) described how Galahs and Bare-eyed Cockatoos fell victim to a feral cat which waited under a stock trough. The cat caught the cockatoos as they landed directly above it. Black cockatoos did not fall prey to the cat as they have a different method of approach – landing a distance away and walking to the water.

HYBRIDIZATION

Cockatoo hybrids sometimes occur in wild populations in Australia. Rowley and Chapman (1991) described how this can occur. Galahs, for example, in contrast to Leadbeater's Cockatoos, roost near their nest throughout the year and visit it nearly every evening. Sometimes a pair takes over a hollow which has been used by Leadbeater's Cockatoos; the latter species does not start to re-visit its nest site until August (in the Western Australian wheat belt), at which time some pairs find Galahs in residence. Leadbeaters usually win disputes regarding nest ownership but, on occasions, the Galahs were evicted, leaving eggs which were incubated by the Leadbeaters along with their own. If both species hatched and were reared, the Galahs associated with, and eventually mated with, the species which had reared them.

Mortality

Rowley (1990) reported deaths of nestling Galahs from a wasting syndrome. Symptoms were: weight loss, failure to develop normally, diarrhoea and a near-continuous whining call. The parents continued to feed them but many died; a few recovered and fledged later than normal. In 1972, in one locality, 79 per cent of nestlings died and, in 1975, 84 per cent. However, it was not a widespread epidemic. Investigation into this disease was carried out by Ken Richardson of the School of Veterinary Studies, Murdoch University, Western Australia, in conjunction wih the CSIRO. At Kellerberrin, 200km (124 miles) east of Perth, 61 nest hollows were monitored, commencing in 1988. In 1989, body weights, crop contents, faecal samples and blood samples were obtained from 42 nests. A total of 109 nestlings hatched, of which 14 died from disease. Autopsies were carried out on nine of these. Five had a viral infection, located in the duodenum and jejunum, one appeared normal and the cause of death was not established in the others. It was concluded that the virus responsible could be enterovirus and/or papovavirus. It resulted in liver malfunction and malabsorption in the duodenum. Weight loss, poor muscle tone and oil present in the faecal samples could be attributed to the damage to the duodenum and to the liver malfunction indicated by the plasma analyses.

The growth of hundreds of Galah chicks was monitored during the seven-year study of this species. However, only 59 per cent of chicks hatched survived to leave the nest (and 45.3 per cent of eggs laid produced fledglings).

Mortality in the wild is high among young birds and lower among adults. Studies have shown, for example, that adult Western Long-billed Corellas have an annual mortality of 8 per cent. Immature birds stay together in a flock until they breed at three to five years of age, at which time only 20–35 per cent are still alive (CSIRO, 1982).

Rowley (1990) marked many nestling Galahs with tags. Of these, the tags of 154 were returned after they died. Thirty died before the age of 2 months, 34 between 2 and 4 months, 15 between 4 and 6 months, 21 between 6 and 12 months, 20 between 12 and 18 months, four between 18 and 24 months, 11 between 24 and 30 months, five between 30 and 36 months, three between 36 and 42 months, three between 42 and 48 months, one between 48 and 54 months, one between 54 and 60 months and none between 60 and 66 months. This clearly indicates that mortality is highest during the first two years. However, it should be pointed out that mortality among wing-tagged birds must be higher than normal because the tags make the birds conspicuous and therefore they are more likely to be targets for hunters with guns or for birds of prey.

Rowley and Chapman (1991) wing-tagged 155 Leadbeater's Cockatoos in the nest at the age of 42 days. One month later, 125 had survived; three months later 95 were alive, and six months later 90 were alive. This study was made at Yandegin Hill, Western Australia. They also tagged breeding birds in the same area, a total of 81 males and 79 females. A season later 76 males (94 per cent) were alive and 64 females (81 per cent). Mean annual mortality for breeding males and females was 12 per cent and that for independent immature birds was 34.5 per cent.

Mortality among White-tailed Black Cockatoos (*Calyptorhynchus latirostris*) in the south-west of Western Australia was even higher. The annual survival rate at two study sites was between only 60.6 per cent (females at Coomallo Creek) and 69 per cent (males at Manmanning). Mortality among young birds was very high, with only 14.8 per cent surviving at the end of the first year. All these figures related to tagged birds (Saunders, 1982).

The cause of death was known in 35 of these birds. Four (two males and two females) were hit by cars, two females were shot, 26 were taken by Wedge-tailed Eagles (18 females, two males and six juvenile birds) and three (two females and one juvenile) died in other accidents (caught in a tree or drowned).

A lasting memory

To most Australians, the sight of cockatoos in the wild is too familar to cause any excitement. But to those from overseas, even if they have scant knowledge of birds, cockatoos provide a lasting memory. For the cockatoo-enthusiast, they will in many cases be the highlight of the visit – their sheer numbers, their beauty in flight and, above all perhaps, their *joie de vivre*, which some species express in an exuberant flight which has no connection with travelling from one point to another. Watching birds in the wild is so different from observing them in captivity. You never truly know a species until you have seen it in its natural habitat. I will never forget the pleasure of focussing a spotting scope on the heads of a pair of Yellow-tailed Black Cockatoos as they sat atop a bare tree in early morning drizzle, and minutely studying their faces and actions. Or watching a flock of Leadbeater's Cockatoos foraging on the ground, so absorbed in their task of food gathering. Or being in the midst of a chirruping, chattering, deafening mass of 2,000 Cockatiels. I would urge anyone with an interest in the Cacatuinae to grasp any opportunity which presents itself to get to know these magnificent birds, so fascinating when seen in their true domain.

3

Australian cockatoos – their present and future status in aviculture

Status in Australia

The status of native cockatoos in Australian aviculture has been summarized (Courtney in press) as follows:

> . . . with the exception of the Palm Cockatoo which has reached the point of extinction in Australian aviculture, and the shy-breeding members of the *funereus* complex, all Australian cockatoos are being bred in reasonable numbers, in proportion to the limited number of people seriously keeping them. The unfortunate reticence of Australian aviculturists in publishing their breeding results has contributed to the mistaken impression that cockatoos are seldom bred. Many erroneously feel that only "first" or "rare" breedings are worthy of publication, when in fact the incubation and nestling periods, and chick development in even the most common species, are so poorly known that all carefully kept records would add considerably to knowledge, and ought to be published in one of the avicultural journals.
>
> Finally, it is stressed that a high level of care for cockatoos in captivity is not only important for the well-being and health of these birds (essential for a successful breeding programme) but is necessary also to maintain the good public image that will enable aviculture to survive into the future.

There are two very valid points. First, aviculturists *must* be more scientific, must keep careful notes and good photographic records, and then must publish the result in a well-established avicultural journal (see also Low, 1991a).

Secondly is the mention of 'the good public image that will enable aviculture to survive into the future'. In a number of countries there are groups of people, known as animal rights activists, who are against the keeping of animals in captivity. Keeping birds in an inadequate manner adds fuel to their argument. While a small finch kept in a small cage may not outwardly look different to one kept under excellent conditions, the same is not true of cockatoos. They are among the most sensitive and nervous of all parrots; they are also highly social. If deprived of companionship or frequently stressed, they will soon resort to self-plucking.

In Australia the three most common species of native cockatoos, Galahs, 'Cockies' (Greater Sulphur-cresteds) and Bare-eyed Cockatoos, cost a few dollars each. To construct a breeding aviary for such destructive birds costs many times the price of even a single bird. This adds to the temptation to house them badly. When you see, for example, a pair of 'Cockies' in an aviary which cost several hundred dollars, you know without any doubt that their owner is a real bird-lover. A well-known breeder of black cockatoos in New South Wales told me that he kept Greater Sulphur-cresteds 'because they are so beautiful'.

Alas, too few see beauty in something so familiar. Outside Australia this species is rare and extremely expensive. Because of its rarity, it costs more than the specimens of *Cacatua galerita* from Indonesia. There are few breeding pairs of *C. galerita galerita* outside Australia and probably fewer still within Australia. Seldom will people there devote an aviary to a pair of birds whose offspring are almost valueless when the same aviary could be producing young of a much more expensive species – Leadbeater's, for example. So the Australian Greater Sulphur-crested will continue to be rare as an aviary bird. Or will it? There are those who believe that, if enough pressure is put on the Australian Government, it will relent and permit the export of perhaps a few thousand annually.

The slaughter of 'pest' species of cockatoos in Australia is an issue which has caused tempers to flare in many countries throughout the world. It was brought to the attention of many people in 1988 when licensed bird-trapper Ray Akroyd clubbed cockatoos to death in front of a government building. Television news footage of this event was seen on countless TV stations throughout the world. In fact Mr Akroyd was staging a protest, by doing publicly what he normally carried out as part of his job as a government licensed trapper. He believed, however, that the birds should be trapped and exported under an approved management programme – not killed.

This opinion is held by many people – especially aviculturists overseas – but I believe that they have not considered the implications. Let us briefly look at some of the arguments put forward on both sides of this debate.

The four species classified as pests, which are allowed to be killed by a licensed trapper where they attack crops are: the Galah, the Long-billed Corella and the Greater Sulphur-crested and Bare-eyed Cockatoos.

'A Better Alternative' (from Bringelly, New South Wales) placed before the government a plan to establish an export industry in these species, claiming that:

(1) It would 'reduce the illegal smuggling of Australian native species'. Legal export would, of course, put an end to the smuggling of these particular species, but it is illogical to believe that it would stem the illegal demand for other cockatoos (such as the black species and Gang Gangs) or for other rare Australian parrots.

(2) It would 'provide an immediate downward trend in pest cockatoo numbers'. However, the total populations of the four species are so large that millions of cockatoos would have to be exported if, as the leaflet states, the combined populations add up to 'hundreds of millions'.

I am not aware of any studies which have estimated total populations of these abundant and widespread birds but, supposing that the total population is tens of millions rather than hundreds, it would be necessary to capture and export several million cockatoos annually to have any impact on wild populations. Could avicultural and pet demand worldwide really absorb such immense numbers? The answer to this question is undoubtedly 'No'.

Just consider what happened in the case of Goffin's Cockatoos from the Tanimbar Islands of Indonesia. During the years 1981 to 1985 inclusive, the minimum numbers of Goffin's Cockatoos legally exported were as follows: 1,710, 3,327, 9,233, 8,832 and 1,045; total: 24,147. They went to the USA, Europe and elsewhere. However, supply soon far exceeded demand and, during the mid-1980s, Goffin's was the least expensive of any cockatoo available. They were commonly seen in pet shops. This is the smallest of the cockatoos so, theoretically, might be the most suitable as a house pet. At that time, very few captive breedings had occurred. But I was breeding this species – my pair bred once or twice a year – and it was always with difficulty that I could find homes for the young.

If a five-year average export of less than 5,000 per year resulted in supply exceeding demand, what would happen when millions of Australian cockatoos were suddenly unloaded on to the market? Just because they were exported *en masse* they would not be cheap. Air transport of all birds must adhere to the regulations of the International Air Transport Association (IATA), and each bird must be contained in a box of specified dimensions. Because of their nervous disposition, which often results in one bird attacking another when closely confined, cockatoos must be transported individually boxed. If this was not done the death rate would be high and export would quickly be criticized and halted. Add to this the high cost of air freight (especially expensive in the case of the Greater Sulphur-crested because of its large size and the great strength of its beak, which enables it to dismantle any wooden box with ease) and the expenses of the mandatory quarantine period, plus various other expenses, including taxes, the cost would at least equal that of the Indonesian cockatoos.

Because most of these birds would be adults, they would be unsuitable as pets, therefore potential buyers would be limited. Sindel and Lynn (1989) described what happened in Australia when state wildlife authorities legalized the trapping of Long-billed Corellas to be sold into the pet trade:

> These wild birds will usually adapt to aviary life but are totally unsuitable for pet cage birds. Most new owners persevere with their wild birds for a few weeks or months then give them up in disgust and they are pushed aside for a new toy. Often these birds are released by their owners as an easy means of ridding themselves of these ungrateful and now unwanted responsibilities, without, of course, any thought of the damaging effect on the environment.

This has resulted in feral populations of these cockatoos becoming established near some cities, often thousands of kilometres from their natural habitat.

The main point, however, is that adult birds do not adapt to the close confinement of a cage. If mass export was allowed, many would die of stress, boredom or neglect – a long, slow torture, for relatively few people have the sympathy, patience and time needed to give cockatoos the companionship they crave in the absence of a mate. Equally few can afford a large, strong aviary for parrots with such formidable strength of beak. The best that most could hope for would be the monotonous confines of a suspended cage. Cockatoos are not finches which can endure for years a reduced quality of life. They are intelligent social animals with, as already stated, better powers of reasoning than most others. My personal belief is that it is even more cruel to let them suffer the monotony of a lonely life in a small cage than it is to kill them; for only a very small percentage would the quality of life be worthwhile. I wish I could believe otherwise – for I hate the mass slaughter of such beautiful, intelligent and appealing birds. But I do not know what the alternative is – and neither do the Australian authorities. I know only that humans created the situation by replacing what was the natural habitat of these cockatoos with millions of hectares of cereal crops, and that humans must utilize their scientific knowledge to use not poison or nets but some form of oral contraceptive for these birds in agricultural areas. Surely scientists could develop some food which is attractive to ground-feeding cockatoos which reduces their fertility? Can we, with our genius for invention, not solve this particular problem?

Status in the rest of the world

Outside Australia, prices of Australian cockatoos remain high because there has been no commercial export since 1959. A few cockatoos have left Australia legally, either as exchanges between certain zoos (in the 'non-profit-making' category, i.e. zoological societies rather than other types of zoos) or, in the case of the 'pest species', birds which belonged to ex-patriates in Australia who were returning to their home countries permanently. Fairly large numbers of cockatoos have left Australia illegally – by being smuggled out; no one can tell how many. Many of these unfortunate birds died in transit because of the methods used to try to conceal the illegal cargo. Tranquillized birds were placed in wire tubes inside suitcases – but losses were high when the tranquillizers wore off and the birds started to struggle and bite each other. Then wire tubes were replaced by lengths of plastic irrigation pipe into which dozens of holes were drilled. This was obviously time-consuming work. One smuggler anonymously telephoned Customs officials asking on which refuse tip the pipes from several seized shipments had been placed (Schooley, 1988)!

The offence of fauna smuggling is taken very seriously in Australia. Great efforts are made to apprehend those responsible, resulting in prison sentences for Australians, Europeans and Americans, among others. Some smugglers have tried to take out the eggs of cockatoos because the birds themselves are too large and noisy. In September 1991 a ranger broke an international egg-smuggling ring after observing men acting suspiciously in Victoria. As a result, at least six Americans and one Canadian were alleged to have been involved and 140 eggs were recovered. At the same time, a major effort was being made in the USA by wildlife officials to bring to justice those responsible for smuggling in large numbers of Australian cockatoo eggs. One genuine and long-standing breeder of Galahs told me that so many young of that species had hatched from smuggled eggs that the price had dropped to the point where she was retaining her young until the market had recovered.

However, smuggling has not occurred on a scale large enough to have affected prices of other Australian cockatoos. The most expensive is Leadbeater's – about twice the price of the Greater Sulphur-crested yet possibly more numerous outside Australia than the latter. Probably, up until 1990, not enough Greater Sulphur-cresteds were reared to sustain its numbers. In that year, however, New Zealand permitted the export of non-native captive-bred birds. This species was introduced to the North Island of New Zealand, where it is now well established as a feral species. Captive-bred birds apparently originate from this population. The legal entry of a few pairs into the UK and other countries since 1991 may improve the captive status of this handsome cockatoo.

The Bare-eyed Cockatoo has never been a favourite with aviculturists. It was rare in aviculture until the 1980s. I assume that the origin of most of the birds imported at that time was New Guinea, as it seems unlikely that smugglers would bother with this species when the demand and the price for Galahs and Leadbeater's Cockatoos was so much higher. Fortunately, this cockatoo breeds more readily than the Greater Sulphur-crested and Leadbeater's so, although the original stocks were not large, it seems likely that numbers are increasing.

Because of its beautiful plumage, the Galah has always been popular in aviculture. Its price is quite high but its beauty ensures that there is always a demand for it. If correctly managed (a diet low in fatty seeds is essential for breeding success), this species can be prolific, laying larger clutches than any other cockatoo. Its future in aviculture seems assured – except perhaps in the USA where the practice of hand-rearing the young and selling them as pets may prove detrimental to its long-term survival.

In Australia, where its value is a few dollars only, there is considerable avicultural interest in the Galah. It has produced a number of mutations – some very striking – which have a very high value.

The *Calyptorhynchus* cockatoos have always been rare in aviculture; indeed, it is only since the 1980s that they could be described as no longer rare within Australian aviculture. In 1960, when export of Australian fauna ceased, there were very few of these magnificent birds in Europe and the USA, and most of these were aged birds. Those which have been exported since are either legal acquisitions by certain zoos or have been smuggled out of Australia. However, their numbers remain small – and this is reflected in their high prices. The insignificant numbers being reared are increasing very slowly. The White-tailed Black, especially, has always been rare; it is not easy to breed and perhaps will never be properly established. In Western Australia, young of this species, and also of Banksian (Red-tailed Black) Cockatoos, have been taken from nests in the wild and passed off as captive-bred birds. However, the introduction of genetic fingerprinting should ensure that this regrettable practice dies out. In 1992 four breeders who claimed to have bred black cockatoos were heavily fined as a result of their false claims. Scientists were able to disprove such claims by performing a DNA scan on blood samples from the putative parents and young. Each young bird not of the designated family cost its owner A$1,000 in fines!

The status of Australian cockatoos in aviculture is unlikely to change drastically – except in the event of Australia permitting the export of the four 'pest' species. If that happened, their prices would fall at once. The incentive to breed them would then disappear overnight.

4

The future of
Indonesian cockatoos

In the past, the trade in wild-caught birds was unjustly blamed for the decline or even the endangered status of several parrot species. Unfortunately, however, it now appears that trade has dealt the final blow to a species originally threatened by habitat destruction, the magnificent Moluccan Cockatoo. Trade and deforestation have gone hand in hand to endanger other Indonesian cockatoos whereas, in the case of the Red-vented (Philippine) Cockatoo, it has been habitat destruction in the Philippines (the only group of islands on which it occurs) which has been responsible for the very serious decline in its numbers.

Status in the wild

Even as recently as the 1970s, Indonesian cockatoos were rare in aviculture, with the exception of the Lesser Sulphur-crested. This was the only species commonly available and I can recall when wholesalers in the UK offered them for as little as £8 each. Then deforestation of parts of Indonesia commenced; the Japanese acquired the timber concessions in many cases and started to extract timber on a large scale. This opened up areas which trappers had not previously been able to penetrate. In the early 1970s Goffin's Cockatoos, for example, started to appear in the avicultural trade worldwide. Previously this species was an avicultural rarity. Deforestation of its only habitat, the Tanimbar Islands had commenced. During the next 15 years or so, thousands upon thousands of Goffin's Cockatoos were exported. The number will never be known. As the total area of these islands is only 51,800 km^2 (20,000 sq. miles), it was perfectly obvious – at least to me – that the species was doomed unless deforestation or trade ceased. Yet it was not until 1992, 20 years after commercial trade commenced, that this cockatoo was placed on Appendix 1 of CITES. Clearly, CITES was not doing the job for which it was instituted.

Then there was the case of the Umbrella Cockatoo which, while not rare, had never been very common in captivity. But, during the 1980s, it became, with Goffin's, the most often imported and inexpensive cockatoo. In 1983 Umbrellas formed 15 per cent of all bird exports from Indonesia and, between 1984 and 1986 alone, 23,000 were exported officially. No doubt many more did not leave via an official route. Its habitat includes Halmahera and four small islands – a total land area of less than 28,000 km^2 (10,800 sq. miles). Obviously no cockatoo could tolerate trapping on this scale without a serious decline. The large flocks of the 1970s have gone forever and, unless the Umbrella Cockatoo is afforded complete protection, it is likely to join Goffin's on Appendix 1 of CITES.

The situation is even worse for the Citron-crested Cockatoo because it is confined to a single island – Sumba in the Lesser Sundas. The island is approximately 12,000 km^2 (4,600 sq. miles) in extent. By 1990, only about 16 per cent of the island was still under forest cover, and this figure included plantations and secondary forest. As with the Umbrella, in the early 1970s, large flocks of Citron-cresteds were seen. By 1991 it was 'rarely encountered' (Riffel & Dwi Bekti, 1991). The reason, reported the local people, was not deforestation but extensive trapping. One cockatoo-catcher stated that the inhabitants of the remote village of Tengairi caught approximately 3,000 within five years in the vicinity of the village. But, so scarce had they become by 1991, that the price paid to catchers by dealers had increased four-fold from the equivalent of US$12 in 1985 to US$50.

Until the late 1980s little field work had been carried out in Indonesia to investigate the status of cockatoos except by Messer who produced a report for PHPA (Indonesian Directorate General of Forest Protection and Nature Conservation) in 1982 and by Fred Smiet whose findings were published in the same year. Messer described Goffin's and Moluccan Cockatoos as common and Smiet (1982) reported:

> In general trade has not yet had a big impact on wild parrot populations. Most parrots, including cockatoos, have a great reproductive capacity, adapt readily to habitat alteration and profit greatly from the widespread introduction of fruit trees throughout Maluku [the Moluccan islands]. This, coupled with the fact that large stretches of original habitat occur on most islands, has helped them to maintain stable populations despite the great hunting pressure . . .

In *Endangered Parrots* (Low, 1984) I commented:

> Smiet's assessment might be considered over-optimistic. Personally, I would not consider cockatoos and other larger parrots of Maluku, such as Eclectus, to have "a great reproductive capacity". In both groups the clutch normally consists of two eggs which are incubated

for four weeks; the young fledge after three to four months . . . .
Furthermore, they occur in an area where habitat is diminishing
with every year that passes.

I warned of Goffin's Cockatoo:

> Greater efforts must be made on behalf of this delightful little
> cockatoo if it is not to become extinct in collections, as it may be in
> the wild before very long. The same holds true of the Red-vented
> Cockatoo.

But no one did anything to stem the trade, until the Moluccan was
almost trapped out of existence in its native islands. By the time it was
placed on Appendix 1 of CITES in 1989, only a few birds remained in
the wild. In 1992 Goffin's and Red-vented Cockatoos were added to
Appendix 1. By this time the Red-vented was rare in aviculture;
Goffin's and the Moluccan were still common because of the enormous
numbers which had been exported – not because of any breeding
success by aviculturists.

Although the numbers reared in captivity increase each year, and will
continue to do so as lack of wild-caught birds forces up the price of the
species, the future of Indonesian cockatoos in aviculture is to me a
source of great concern. There are many problems to be overcome if
they are to survive long-term in aviaries, as described in Chapter 7. The
main one is the very small number of captive-bred birds which are
retained for, or suitable for, breeding purposes.

Breeding success in captive Indonesian cockatoos

In 1991 I carried out a survey (Low, 1992c) among members of the
World Parrot Trust who kept Indonesian cockatoos. This resulted in
information on 35 pairs, a number too small to provide significant
results. In fact, as one might expect with such a small sample, the
results were definitely not representative of the relative numbers of
each species kept. Also, I suspect that the hatch rate figures in the data
collected are higher than average because many breeders do not
respond if they are unsuccessful, believing that their negative results
are not of interest. To obtain a clear picture, however, one needs data
on pairs which laid eggs but failed to hatch them as well as on successful
pairs. The information was received from four zoos and 15 private
breeders, nearly all in Europe. If the same survey had been conducted
in the USA, hatchability and breeding success rate would have been
higher because nearly all eggs are artificially incubated and the resulting
chicks hand-reared for the pet trade. Only egg-laying pairs were included
in the survey, the results of which are shown in Table 1 (see p. 40).

The Citron-crested Cockatoo (*Cacatua sulphurea citrinocristata*) is now critically endangered due to deforestation on Sumba, in Indonesia – the only island on which it occurs.

On the survey form I requested details of both parents because I was concerned about the long-term effect of imprinting on birds which have been hand-reared, in some cases making them unsuitable for breeding or unsuccessful as breeders. Of the 35 pairs in the survey, the origins of four pairs were unknown or unspecified. In 24 pairs, both male and female were wild-caught. One pair consisted of a hand-reared and a wild-caught bird; unfortunately, it was not stated which was the male. This was a very successful pair of Goffin's which produced 16 young in five years, of which four were parent-reared. Only two other pairs included one bird which was hand-reared – both Citron-cresteds. In one case both birds were hand-reared; the female produced four eggs in 1991, all of which were infertile. The other pair was made up of a parent-reared male and a hand-reared female. She laid only one egg in each of the three years, none of which was fertile. Obviously the number of birds sampled was too small to make any positive conclusions, but it was noted that the only pairs which were totally infertile included a hand-reared bird. (Of course there are many wild-caught birds which, for various reasons, have also proved infertile.)

If the future of Indonesian cockatoos is dependent upon parent-reared birds, I fear that most species will be effectively extinct within a few decades. Although plenty of birds will exist, they will either be very old wild-caught birds or non-breeding captive-bred ones.

Moluccan Cockatoos (*Cacatua moluccensis*) in a trapper's cage on the island of Seram, Indonesia, in 1991 – after trapping and export of this species had been prohibited.

Table 1
1991 World Parrot Trust survey of breeding in Indonesian cockatoos.

Species	No. of pairs	Eggs Laid	Eggs Known to be infertile	Eggs Hatched	Chicks reared by Parents	Chicks reared by Hand	Died
Lesser Sulphur-crested	7	49	3	29	none	27	2
Citron-crested	5	22	5	11	4	5	2
Triton	2	29	none	12	none	5	7
Blue-eyed	3	18	4	2	1	1	none
Moluccan	6	28	9	16	none	9	7
Umbrella	5	50	10	24	2	16	6
Goffin's	7	58	15	36	8	17	11
TOTAL:	35	254	46	130	15	80	35

51 per cent of eggs hatched.
Over three years, 45 pairs produced 95 young which survived, an annual productivity of 0.68 per pair. Mortality of young before independence was 28 per cent.
N.B. Sample size was considered too small to give representative results.

On the survey form I tried to obtain information on the destinies of the young reared but this was not always supplied.

Where it was, the results showed that 64 young were sold (five for breeding, 24 for pets, the rest not specified) and 11 were retained. I am afraid that this confirms what is already known – that most breeders are producing young for the pet trade with little thought of the avicultural future of the species. Unfortunately, in the case of some Indonesian cockatoos, this may be the only future they have.

The point is often made that some birds sold as pets end up in breeding aviaries. This is true, but there is no guarantee that they will breed. Many cockatoos isolated from their own kind from an early age are hopelessly imprinted on people. Some hand-reared males will not accept a female and I know of one case of a hand-reared male which killed two females and will never be given another opportunity to live with another.

However, hand-reared birds can be used for breeding if they have *always* had contact with their own species – with the possible exception of Moluccan Cockatoos. Many of these, even if hand-reared with their own species, show a strong desire only to interact with human beings.

Breeders *must* make more effort to produce at least some parent-reared young. This is discussed further in Chapter 7.

Restocking and reintroduction

Already there are, in the case of one or more species of cockatoo from Indonesia, more specimens in captivity than in the wild. This is true of the Moluccan Cockatoo and may soon apply to the Citron-crested and to other species. What will happen when they are gone, when they become totally extinct in their natural habitat? Would reintroduction from captive-bred birds be possible, assuming that enough habitat survived? This is a difficult question to answer. At the time of writing, reintroduction of former captive parrots is in its infancy. It has been attempted with only two or three species and it is too soon to say whether the result will be successful.

There are many problems to overcome – perhaps even more with cockatoos than with most other parrot species. In my opinion, a major problem would be finding *enough* captive-bred birds suitable for re-introduction. It is already known that hand-reared parrots are not suitable for this purpose. Worldwide, I would estimate that a minimum of 85 per cent of cockatoos hatched in aviaries are hand-reared. Commercial breeders would therefore be unlikely to be able to provide enough birds suitable for reintroduction.

Another problem is that of psittacine beak and feather disease (PBFD) (see Chapter 11). If this or some other viral disease now frequently found in captive birds was to be introduced to a wild population, the result would be catastrophic, especially if restocking was attempted. ('Restocking' is the term used when a wild population is so small or in-bred that it is considered necessary to augment the numbers with captive-bred birds.) Unless carefully carried out, it could bring about the extinction of a species.

I believe that the only way is to create a closed breeding programme for the specific purpose of reintroduction or restocking. Every bird used in the programme would need to be DNA blood-tested to ensure that its ancestry was pure and that the birds used were not too closely related. They would have to be screened very carefully for disease, especially PBFD. Only parent-reared young could be used. As it is useless to release small numbers, it might be years before enough birds were reared which were suitable for release. They would have to be carefully conditioned, pre-release, in a large aviary in the release area and they would have to be familiarized with native foods. Careful monitoring of released birds would be essential. Radio telemetry is normally used to do this – but would a cockatoo tolerate a 'foreign body' in the form of a transmitter?

None of these problems is insurmountable, but such a programme would be very expensive and would probably take some years to achieve. With so many bird species in desperate need of conservation programmes, it seems unlikely that the funding or personnel would ever be available except in a very special case.

5

The correct accommodation

Cockatoos have extremely powerful beaks; this, combined with their well-developed destructive urges, their intelligence and their ability to undo and manipulate, means that only a very strong cage or aviary will confine them. This adds greatly to the initial cost because an aviary for a pair may be nearly as expensive as the birds.

Suspended cages

To reduce the expense and the space required, in recent years many breeders of parrots have used suspended cages instead of the traditional type of aviary. These cages are constructed entirely of welded mesh and situated about 1m (3ft) off the ground usually on a metal frame. Some parrots, especially Greys, certain Amazons, lorikeets and conures, do very well in them. I have seen many cockatoos housed in this manner and have also kept a few pairs in this way for short periods. However, with the exception of young birds which have been hand-reared, and a few pairs of a species with a less nervous temperament (such as the Bare-eyed Cockatoo), I cannot recommend such cages for cockatoos. I am convinced that they feel more secure and are less subject to stress in normal aviaries. Even better are aviaries with solid walls in which only the front and part of the roof (or part of one side) are constructed of welded mesh. Cockatoos also like to walk and even play on the ground, to dig in sand or perhaps leaf litter. Such a surface covering a concrete floor provides them with hours of enjoyment.

It is true that suspended cages are more hygienic because the birds do not have access to stale food or old faeces. They are therefore unlikely to contract parasitic worms and it is difficult for mice and other vermin to become established. On the other hand, it is difficult to catch cockatoos in suspended cages and any attempt can be prolonged and therefore stressful.

Aviaries in enclosed areas

The quality of life for pairs of cockatoos kept outdoors is usually far superior to that of pairs kept in basements or other indoor rooms, usually in small suspended cages. (In my opinion, this is comparable to keeping chickens in battery cages.) Cockatoos love to feel rain on their plumage and to have access to sun which is not too strong. However, this is not always practical, especially in view of the fact that cockatoos are very noisy birds. Their screams may not be tolerated by neighbours and so it may be necessary to house them in a building which is at least partially sound-proof. The walls need to be solid and uninterrupted, except by the doors. To let in ample light and fresh air, windows or large areas covered by heavy mosquito netting should be located in the roof. Buildings of this type usually accommodate suspended cages but there is no reason why normal aviaries should not be used, provided that the entire base is of concrete and sloping slightly so that, when it is hosed down, the water quickly drains into channels.

The success of such a building may depend on adapting it to local conditions or problems. In Florida and California, for example, sarcosporidiosis has caused enormous losses among parrots, including cockatoos, kept in outdoor aviaries. This disease is caused by a protozoal parasite excreted by opossums. Infection may result directly from contaminated faeces, deposited on the roof of an aviary, or indirectly from the droppings of cockroaches or rats which have consumed the faeces and entered the aviary or nest box. As a result of chewing contaminated food or nest litter, the cockatoo ingests the parasites and then develops sarcosporidiosis, which is fatal (see p. 119).

Joel D. Murphy, a veterinary surgeon who experienced this problem in his Florida aviaries (resulting in the loss of all his proven pairs of Moluccan Cockatoos) recommended that, in vulnerable areas, aviaries should be located within an enclosure of 6 mm (¼ in) welded mesh (hardware cloth) and be covered in mosquito netting, with a solid floor and *completely enclosed* roof. Every three weeks, Dursban granules should be spread (not sprayed) around the outside of the building. The interior of the aviaries and nest boxes should be sprayed with pyrethrin (Murphy, 1991a).

Security is another reason for keeping cockatoos within an enclosed building. All the higher-priced parrots are at risk from thieves. In an enclosed building, an observation camera near the door or doors and monitors in permanently manned locations will help to combat the problem.

If the roof must be fully enclosed, thus denying the cockatoos the pleasure of rain on their plumage, each aviary should be equipped with a sprinkler. This can be turned on for a few minutes daily so that the birds can take a shower. White cockatoos do not normally bathe in standing water. Not only do they obtain ecstatic enjoyment from the shower, it helps to reduce the build-up of feather dust. This is a problem within enclosed buildings – and a serious problem to anyone with an allergy to dust. However, ionizers are of great assistance in taking the dust out of the air. One or two will be invaluable in a small room (including the hand-rearing room) and a number will be required in a large building.

RULES FOR AVIARY CONSTRUCTION

Several important points must be borne in mind when constructing a cockatoo aviary:

(1) Metal is the best material for the framework. This can take the form of angle iron or scaffolding poles.
(2) If wood is used, all exposed surfaces must be covered with strips of aluminium or some other metal.
(3) Make the floor escape-proof, either by concreting it or by burying welded mesh in the earth. Cockatoos will dig in earth and could escape.
(4) A greater aviary height and width than is recommended for most parrots is desirable, but not essential. Cockatoos look better and feel more secure in an aviary 2.4m (8ft) high. For species up to the size of the Citron-crested, the width should be at least 1.2m (4ft) and preferably 1.8m (6ft); for other species the width should be no less than 1.8m (6ft).
(5) Wire netting (chicken-wire) is useless; welded mesh of 16 guage or heavier is essential. For the larger and most destructive species, such as the Greater Sulphur-crested, it is necessary to use 12 gauge, obtainable only in panels, not rolls. Do not use chain link or large welded mesh, e.g. 50mm (2in) square or 75mm × 25mm (3in × 1in). These meshes will admit sparrows, mice, rats, small mammals, such as stoats, and even snakes. (In Zimbabwe, a recently fledged Citron-crested Cockatoo was taken by a python.) Some vermin, especially mice and sparrows, consume the cockatoos' food; rats and mice may take over the nest box and even eat the eggs. All vermin can be carriers of disease, such as pseudotuberculosis, which could be passed on to the cockatoos with possibly fatal consequences.

Large mesh is easier for cockatoos to destroy as it provides room for leverage. The heaviest gauge mesh, available in 12mm (½in) square, will not be destroyed by most cockatoos if large pieces of wood are available for gnawing and the perches are renewed frequently. Cockatoos unfortunate enough to be kept on indestructible perches with a metal nest site would be likely to destroy any type of welded mesh out of sheer frustration. It is worth remembering that cockatoos may make no attempt to destroy mesh that they could cut with ease if they felt inclined; if they are stressed, however, they may suddenly do so. As an example, six male Triton Cockatoos had lived for several years in a large aviary at

Palmitos Park with other cockatoos; when a seventh was added, the harmony of the aviary was disrupted and the six made a hole within a couple of days and escaped. (One was lost but the rest lived at liberty within the park, close to the aviary.)

(6) Do not use C-clips for joining lengths of welded mesh. Cockatoos can undo these with ease. Join lengths with binding wire or by stapling them to wooden supports and covering the supports in metal.

(7) The absolute minimum length aviary for any cockatoo should be 3.6m (12ft); 6m (20ft) is preferable.

(8) Although cockatoos are very hardy birds when acclimatized, and many prefer to roost in the open part of the aviary, an enclosed shelter must be incorporated into the design if neighbours are likely to complain about the noise, especially in the early morning. The birds can then be shut in the shelter at night.

It is difficult to describe the degree of destructiveness or noise of which cockatoos are capable. Much depends on the individual bird and the circumstances. It is not always the largest which do the most damage. I have kept Goffin's Cockatoos which removed staples from welded mesh with ease, worked away at 25mm × 12mm (1in × ½in) welded mesh until they had converted it into 25mm (1in) square, and could open complicated catches and, in the case of one bird, even padlocks.

PERCHES IN THE AVIARY

Cockatoos have a perpetual need to gnaw which must never be ignored. If this need cannot be met, other birds should be kept instead. Perches can be made from the branches of such trees as apple, pear, plane, poplar, beech, eucalyptus and pine. Great enjoyment is derived from gnawing the bark from fresh branches. Lengths of prepared timber are a poor substitute but many cockatoo-keepers have to use them. Perches from which the bark has been removed should not be left in the aviary for a long time as they become shiny and slippery.

SITING THE AVIARY

If observation cameras and monitors are not used, cockatoo aviaries should be located near the house. This helps to reduce the likelihood of theft; also it may be possible to observe the birds' normal behaviour when they are unaware of being observed (see p. 65). The aviaries should be located away from sources of disturbance as cockatoos are easily frightened by unknown or unexpected sounds and sights. They will not appreciate the sudden appearance of balls and children from neighbouring gardens or, at night, lights from passing vehicles. Loud

A well-designed cockatoo-breeding facility in Canada where the climate is too harsh to keep birds out of doors. Note the swivel feeders (left) for ease of feeding, and the holders which prevent the birds removing the dishes.

noises on a regular basis, such as trains, will not upset them once they are used to them.

If cockatoos are kept in a range of aviaries, it is essential to double-wire the partitions between each enclosure, leaving a minimum of 40mm (1½in) between each partition. Perches which are too long can cause the two sections of wire to be pushed together; there is then a danger of a cockatoo seriously injuring a bird in the adjoining aviary. Proper perch-holders should be made in order to prevent this. It is also advisable to avoid housing two pairs of cockatoos in adjacent aviaries which are very close. Aggression between the pairs or an interest in the neighbouring male or female, could prevent breeding.

AVIARY HYGIENE

The frequency with which the aviary floor will need to be cleaned depends on its size. Most will need to be cleaned once or twice a week, or once weekly with daily removal of uneaten food which has fallen onto the floor. Disturbance should be kept to a minimum when pairs are incubating or rearing young. Once a month, concrete floors should be thoroughly scrubbed with water containing a strong disinfectant made for use in animal cages. The concrete base beneath suspended cages should be hosed down daily or every other day and the cages themselves cleaned with a high-pressure steam machine every second week.

In a dry climate, a floor covering of sand can be used. It must be raked every few days and the faeces removed. The sand will need to be renewed about four times a year. Cockatoos enjoy walking in this and picking up the grit. Another surface which is excellent, as it keeps the occupants occupied for hours, is a covering of leaves and twigs, such as one might find on a forest floor.

Large stones or shingle can be used if the drainage facilities are good. Stones must be hosed regularly to remove faeces and stale food must be picked up daily. As it is best to avoid entering the aviary, it is a good idea to build a feeding shelf which juts out at the front of the cage, so that the waste food does not fall into the aviary. If the area in front of the aviaries is of concrete, much time is saved on cleaning; spilled food can be swept up each morning and the area hosed clean.

HARDINESS OF COCKATOOS IN AVIARIES

Whether imported or aviary-bred, cockatoos are extremely hardy birds once they are used to the climatic conditions. Needless to say, they should be transferred to outdoor accommodation only during mild weather, not during extremes of temperature. They can tolerate cold, even cold and damp when acclimatized, and will often chose to roost outside in bad weather rather than use the shelter, except when there are strong winds. Most cockatoos suffer more in hot weather than in cold and they must be protected from strong sun. Unlike some parrots, they do not normally suffer from frost-bite; if the perch is wide, their toes will be covered by the breast feathers.

Indoor cages

It is possible to buy spacious, well-designed and attractive cages for a single cockatoo which will complement the finest décor but probably only in the USA is there a good range of designs. However, such cages are very expensive. Most pet cockatoos are housed in cages which are much too small. A cockatoo should be able to open both wings simultaneously. It is worth noting that the wingspan of an Umbrella, for example, is about 82cm (33in). The alternative to a commercially-produced cage is to construct one from welded mesh. Even for someone not used to building cages, this is not too difficult. Neither is it expensive as, for indoor use, a large mesh can be used, such as 50mm (2in) square or 75mm × 25mm (3in × 1in). The following instructions are for a cage 60cm (24in) square and 90cm (36in) high, or they can be adapted to give a cage 90cm × 60cm × 60cm high (36in × 24in × 24in high). Obtain one sheet of 12 gauge welded mesh (or whatever gauge is considered suitable for the bird in question) measuring 4.5m (15ft) × 90 cm (36in), or two sheets 60cm (24in) square for the top and bottom and four sheets measuring 60 cm × 90 cm (24in × 36in) for the sides. These can be spot-welded together (a garage can do this for a small charge). Alternatively, obtain three panels of welded mesh of the requisite size. The size depends on the species involved and the space available. Bend two of these to form the sides and measure and cut the third to make the top and bottom. Spot-welding or strong binding wire can be used to join them. A section about 25cm (10in) square can be cut out for the door. This must be secured with a carefully designed fastening as cockatoos can learn to undo quite complicated catches. A gap of about 2.5cm (1in) can be left between the front and the floor to take a tray. If its appearance does not offend the eye, make 5cm (2in) legs for the cage and place sheets of newspaper below the welded mesh floor. In this way, cleaning can be accomplished without opening the cage. Place the cage where the bird will feel secure, preferably in a corner. At least one perch in the cage should be made from a fresh branch and renewed every two or three weeks.

6

Diets and food preferences

Perhaps more than any other parrots, white cockatoos enjoy eating items which they can hold in the foot. When attempting to add variety to their diet, you are more likely to be successful with items which they can hold and nibble simply because they enjoy this activity. They then taste the food and eat it instead of playing with it. Persuade cockatoos to take a wide variety of items and their enjoyment is plain to see. They need to be occupied and foods such as spray millet, seeding grasses and peas in the pod are as excellent for occupational purposes as they are for nutrition.

Some cockatoos are willing to try everything offered; others are conservative in their choice of foods. Perseverance is essential; when many wild-caught birds were available, it could take two years before they broadened their diet. Initially, captive-bred birds readily take a good variety of foods unless allowed to eat an excess of one or two favoured items.

Cockatoos must be fed at least once daily and, if possible, two or three times; different 'extras' should be offered at the later feeds. Just as we look forward to mealtimes to break up the routine of the day, so do cockatoos. At the first feed, as early in the morning as possible, fresh water should be given, plus the basic items of the diet. These usually consist of a mixture of seeds, cooked or sprouted beans, fresh fruit and vegetables and commercially prepared foods. When feeding cockatoos, at least three factors must be considered: nutrition, variety and enjoyment. Most foods offered will consist of seeds, nuts, vegetables, fruits, animal protein (e.g. mealworms or cooked meat), wild foods such as berries and weeds, and commercially prepared foods such as pellets.

Diet in general

I have purposely not recommended specific diets. So much depends on the species, circumstances, locally available foods and whether the birds are kept as pets or for breeding. Most important is individual preference. Cockatoos have marked dislikes and some foods will not be eaten no matter how many years one perseveres. The important factor is to discover which foods are acceptable and try to make up what appears to be a balanced diet, with fresh foods forming at least 20 per cent of that diet, in most cases.

One must also be willing to experiment; there is no formula that can be followed. This is especially important when pairs are rearing young. Their needs and preferences may change completely. Unfortunately, some pairs do not feed suitable foods to their young which, as a result, may become debilitated or stunted. No matter how wide the choice of items offered, such pairs will persist in feeding an unbalanced diet; in such instances hand-rearing is essential if healthy young are to be reared.

CALYPTORHYNCHUS COCKATOOS

One cannot generalize about dietary needs and preferences as this depends to some degree upon the species, as well as on the individual. Black cockatoos of the genus *Calyptorhynchus* will not accept such a varied diet as white cockatoos. The evils of feeding too much sunflower seed to parrots have been repeated *ad infinitum* in recent years. However, they do not apply to *Calyptorhynchus* cockatoos. In Australia, breeders of these birds maintain them on about 75 per cent or more sunflower seed, with the addition of silver beet, green peas, and nuts of *Banksia*, *Hakea* and *Casuarina*. In other countries, the Australian nuts are replaced by commercially available pine nuts (from Russia and China), walnuts and almonds. It would be misguided to try to force

A Yellow-tailed Black Cockatoo (*Calyptorhynchus funereus*) picking peas (its favourite food) out of a mixture.

cockatoos to eat such items as pulses, rice, etc., on which many neotropical parrots thrive. Palm Cockatoos will take a slightly more varied diet which, in my experience, includes orange, ripe banana, pomegranates and the oily nuts of the *Arecastrum* palm, whereas *Calyptorhynchus* usually show no interest in these. (See also under species in Part II). It should be noted that a basic diet of sunflower seed does *not* have a harmful effect on black cockatoos. They appear not to be susceptible to obesity. One reason for this may be that, in comparison with other parrots of similar size, they eat less. Indeed, some appear to eat less than the smaller white cockatoos.

COCKATIELS

Unlike the larger cockatoos, Cockatiels exist mainly on a mixture of seeds such as canary, white millet, oats or groats and small sunflower. In cool climates, a little hemp or niger can be added during the winter. Most of them enjoy seeding grasses, chickweed and young leaves of dandelion. As a rearing supplement, wholemeal bread and milk or a Canary egg-rearing food can be offered. Some will eat apple and other fruits.

Types of food

COMMERCIAL FORMULATIONS

Some avian nutrition experts warn against offering a wide variety of foods and allowing birds to choose, claiming that the result is often a dietary imbalance. They state that specially formulated foods, such as pellets, can provide a complete diet, with all the necessary nutrients presented in the correct proportions. If the dietary requirements of all parrots were identical this would be true, but over 200 species are kept in captivity, very few (if any) of which feed on exactly the same items in nature. It is therefore unwise to assume that all have identical needs.

Another factor is that some commercially formulated foods, such as pellets, are not very palatable. Cockatoos will chew them because they enjoy destroying things but they may be consuming little. These foods are relatively new and are constantly being improved. More imaginative and palatable items are being produced. For example, at the time of writing, an American company is offering a blend of fresh shelled canary seed, millet and sunflower mixed with peanut kernels and covered with a thick coating of vitamins, minerals and amino acids. These are made into the shape of a berry (Parrot Nutri-Berries made by Lafeber Co., Odell, Illinois). I believe that they are much more attractive than pellets from the bird's viewpoint. In my opinion, no matter how apparently excellent a commercially formulated food is from the nutritional aspect, it should not form 100 per cent of the diet of an intelligent bird like a cockatoo. It is acceptable for poultry but to expect parrots to exist solely on such foods is to rate speed and convenience above the bird's enjoyment and occupational needs. No one who cares about their birds would do so – only, I suspect, those for whom breeding the larger parrots is a commercial exercise only.

In any case, there is increasing evidence that 100 per cent pellet diet can be harmful and, in some species, even prevent breeding. In June 1988 American veterinary surgeon Joel D. Murphy began a feeding trial using pellets as 98 per cent of the diet fed to 20 pairs of parrots, including macaws, cockatoos, Amazons, Greys and Eclectus. Roudybush pellets were chosen because no other manufacturer published a complete analysis of their foods. Pellets were fed for one year. No parrot took longer than four days to adjust to the diet. After one year, all the birds appeared to be in excellent health but biochemical profiles indicated otherwise. Serum uric acid levels had increased over the year, especially in the Moluccan Cockatoos. Murphy (1989) stated:

> Elevated uric acid levels have to be evaluated cautiously because very little research has been done on the physiology of the avian kidney, let alone the psittacine kidney. The elevated uric acid levels suggest that a protein level of 20% may provide more protein than the avian kidney can secrete. All excess and metabolised protein is degraded into uric acid in the liver and kidneys, and is transported into the kidney. It is probable that over time the 20% dietary protein level overloads a parrot's ability to secrete uric acid . . .
>
> We have been seeing a very marked increase in kidney disease in aviaries that feed pellet diets primarily. This kidney disease is characterized by urate deposits in the kidney tubules with resultant kidney mineralization, kidney failure and death. We made the decision to stop the feeding trial based upon the blood chemistry results of the first year, and convert the birds to a lower protein diet.

Based on the limited research of one year, Murphy recommended feeding diets containing 10–15 per cent protein for breeding parrots and pet parrots. This level should be balanced with all the essential amino acids (not present in seeds). With pelleted foods, however, the energy level must also be considered. Less food will be consumed in diets high in calories, so the protein level theoretically should be raised.

Murphy also stated:

> An increase in kidney failure in larger hand-fed parrots makes us very suspicious that we are going to find species differences in diet requirements for psittacines.

One man related to me his attempts to convert his Galahs to a pelleted diet. They almost starved to death. For some days he refused to admit that they could not be converted to this type of food, because his other parrots were eating pellets. He was forced to revert to their original diet.

Because some aviculturists have found that their parrots stopped breeding when fed entirely on pellets, Dr Murphy carried out another experiment. He used 28 pairs of Quaker Parrakeets immediately after they were released from quarantine. They were sexed and housed in suspended cages 60cm (24in) square and 1.2m (4ft) high. After 16 months not one pair had produced eggs; therefore ten pairs were offered Cockatiel seed mixture. Within 10 days two pairs had produced eggs and within 20 days eight pairs had eggs. Then five more pairs were changed to a seed diet for 10 days, during which time three pairs produced eggs (Murphy, 1990).

I have no experience of feeding pellets to parrots but I daily experience pleasure from watching cockatoos examine the contents of their food dish to see what is on that day's menu. It should be varied daily and seasonally so that they do not become bored with their diet. Imagine how you would feel if presented with exactly the same food day in and day out! I know that anthropomorphism is frowned upon, yet the best aviculturists are those who try to put themselves in the place of their birds and consider what *they* would like if they had to change places with the birds!

SEEDS AND GRAINS

A basic mixture for cockatoos can be made up from the larger seeds and grains such as sunflower, safflower, wheat and maize. Except when the weather is hot, I prefer to give seeds and grains (except maize) which have been soaked in cold water for 12–24 hours and then left to sprout. The seed should be fed when it has just started to sprout and not when the sprouts are more than about 8 mm (⅓in) long. Soaking removes the dirt that is found even on cleaned seed and sprouting renders the food far more nutritious, increasing the vitamin content. However, in warm climates, fungus grows very quickly on soaked seed; if a small portion can be fed early in the morning and other foods reserved for later, it will be eaten before the fungus can develop, especially if this is the only sunflower seed offered.

It is advisable to carry out a germination test on all seeds fed. At least 90 per cent should germinate; if the percentage is less than 75 per cent, the seed is stale, has been mishandled or received excessive application of chemicals. It is therefore of low nutritional value and another source should be sought. A large supplier and/or importer is preferable to a local shop where the seed may be in stock for months.

Maize should be boiled until soft when it will be readily eaten by most cockatoos. Chicken 'scratch' and pigeon mixtures are sometimes fed to the birds. (I have not done this but in this way one might discover other grains which are favoured.) Among the seeds which can be offered are: canary, white millet, buckwheat, hemp, oats, paddy rice and melon seeds. They can initially be provided as a mixture (preferably in a container of their own and not mixed with larger grains such as sunflower and maize) to discover which will be eaten. Some cockatoos will not eat small seeds. Cage trials showed that Galahs, Bare-eyed Cockatoos and Long-billed Corellas preferred smaller seeds and tended to have similar preferences (Rowley *et al.*, 1989). Spray millet is a universal favourite and can be offered once a week, for amusement as well as nutrition.

Food values of seeds
When making up a mixture, keep in mind the protein, fat and carbohydrate content of each type of seed (see Table 2). The percentages shown apply to the kernel only, when fed dry. All the above (except groats, oats should be used instead) can be fed sprouted and cockatoos can be given a portion in this form daily, as well as a dry seed mixture.

Table 2
Percentage food values of seeds.

	Protein	Fat	Carbo-hydrate	Energy kcal/100g
Canary seed	15.6	5.6	65.6	379
White millet	11.5	4.1	69.4	358
Groats	14.3	6.6	67.5	393
Sunflower (striped)	21.7	33.9	41.5	556
Sunflower (white)	24.0	47.0	20.2	594
Safflower	15.2	34.6	43.2	540

After Nott (1992).

VEGETABLES AND FRUITS

The most favoured vegetable is usually fresh corn-on-the-cob or corn which has been frozen and then thawed (not cooked). As it is usually available for only a short season in many countries, those who use large amounts will find it worthwhile to stock a chest-type freezer. Corn kernels, bought tinned or frozen under the name of sweet corn, are also popular. Both are excellent rearing foods. To prevent wastage, cobs should be cut into sections about 5cm (2in) long. All the green-leaved vegetables are useful, the darker green the better; dark green cabbage has a higher Vitamin A content than white cabbage. All cabbages contain vitamins of the B complex, as well as traces of Vitamin E. Some cockatoos will eat the stalks and not the leaves, or shred the stalks, eating little. But they enjoy this, and the outer leaves may just as well be offered to the cockatoos as discarded. Cauliflower and broccoli leaves can also be offered. Different types of spinach and Swiss chard are widely fed. However, this food is said to bind calcium (i.e. to make the calcium in foods unavailable) although it is doubtful whether anyone knows what quantity would have to be fed for this to occur. It is high in carotene, vitamins and minerals. Carotene will usually be converted to Vitamin A. Kale is another excellent greenfood, and hardy enough to withstand winter conditions.

Carrot is the best of the root vegetables for palatability and carotene (Vitamin A) content. It is most likely to be eaten if cut into long pieces and pushed into the welded mesh. It can also be grated as an ingredient of a rearing food (helping to keep it moist). Celery is also popular; feed the green type for its higher vitamin content. It is rich in minerals, contains some carotene, small amounts of B vitamins and has a high fibre content. When red or green peppers are being prepared for cooking, cut out the stalks and seeds as one piece and save this as a treat for a cockatoo. Some will also eat tomatoes. Peas in the pod are a great favourite and most cockatoos also like green beans and broad beans. When peas were out of season I used to cook extra frozen peas and found that these were enjoyed fed warm on cold winter days.

Mung beans, obtainable from health-food stores, are highly nutritious when sprouted. Soak them for a few hours, wash and drain, and leave them to sprout. They should be fed when the sprouts are only about 6mm (¼in) long when they taste not unlike raw peas. Their nutritional value is then at its greatest because the embryo plant has not had a chance to utilize the nourishment. In addition to vitamins and minerals, they contain pre-digested protein which has been converted to amino acids. They are ideal for birds rearing young; mashed into a paste, they can be added to the food of older chicks, which are being hand-reared, once the food has been heated (heating kills the enzymes in the bean sprouts). For chicks at the weaning stage, remove the skins and break the beans in half.

A wide variety of fruits is accepted by cockatoos; individual preferences must be determined by trial and error. Orange, grapes and pomegranates are among the most popular. Many seasonally and locally grown fruits are also enjoyed. Where I live, in the Canary Islands, the hard oily orange fruits of the queen palm (*Arecastrum romanzoffianum* var. *australe*) are relished by many parrots, but especially by white cockatoos and Palm Cockatoos. Some fruits, such as peaches and nectarines, are enjoyed mainly for their kernels; cracking them keeps the birds occupied. All fruits can be offered except avocados and their stones (pits).

ANIMAL PROTEIN AND TABLE ITEMS

Insect larvae form an important part of the diet of several species but most cockatoos seem to benefit from animal protein. They are passionately fond of a chicken carcase with some meat adhering to it, but it is marrow bones which they enjoy most. Chop bones are also relished. Swiss aviculturist Dr R. Burkard persuaded his cockatoos to take raw minced meat as well as mice up to three days' old. Some cockatoos will kill and eat any small bird, such as a sparrow, which is unfortunate enough to enter the enclosure. Others will eat mealworms, which should be provided only in small quantities. Cooked lean meat is enjoyed by many pet cockatoos. Other table items are suitable, such as pasta, cereals, biscuits, cheese, yoghurt and cooked vegetables. Wholemeal bread is excellent, fresh or stale. However, as in all things, moderation is important; no item should be fed to excess. Rosskopf *et al.* (1992) described a case of iron-storage disease (haemochromatosis) in a nine-year-old captive-bred Citron-crested Cockatoo. Its diet had consisted largely of commercial breakfast cereals (seven or more types), plus fruits and vegetables. It had been maintained in this way for three years but previously had a seed-based diet. On autopsy it was found that the liver was massively swollen and hard and the spleen was ten times the normal size. Excessive iron in the diet, derived from the cereals, had resulted in the cockatoo's death.

WILD FOODS

Berries and weeds are the most natural foods which can be offered by most aviculturists outside Australia. Those popular garden shrubs, *Pyracantha* and hawthorn, are also found in Australia where their berries are relished by certain cockatoos. Elderberries and rose hips can be offered fresh or can be collected in the autumn and dried or frozen for use later in the year. Berries for freezing can simply be removed from their clusters, washed, drained and placed in plastic containers in the freezer. Berries growing alongside busy roads should be avoided as they may be contaminated with lead.

A number of weeds are also valuable foods for cockatoos. Waste places and arable fields which have not been sprayed with chemicals, and are not bordered by roads, are good sources. Sowthistle, chickweed, dandelion leaves and roots, and many kinds of seeding grasses are relished. In Australia, a little research and observation will show you which weeds are preferred in certain areas by the various cockatoos.

NUTS

Nuts are an excellent food if they are not fed to excess and if they are of a quality suitable for human consumption. If they have been incorrectly stored and, in the case of pine nuts, allowed to become mouldy, they could cause death. Great care must be taken in obtaining and storing peanuts as they can contain aflotoxins which could prove lethal. I pefer to feed peanut kernels which have been boiled rather than peanuts in the shell. In any case, many cockatoos destroy peanut shells and drop the kernels. Nuts which are hard to crack (some species cannot easily open walnuts or almonds) provide hours of amusement and are totally safe playthings. All cockatoos relish walnuts; one or more can be given daily per bird.

MINERALS AND SUPPLEMENTS

The lack of a small but vital component of the diet may make the difference between breeding success and failure, e.g. a dietary deficiency could result in chicks dying in the egg. The addition of powdered vitamins and minerals to the normal food may result in it being refused, and adding them to the drinking water is not effective. However, if they can be added to some soft food or rearing food, such as bread and milk, they are more likely to be accepted provided that they do not have a strong taste. I favour the use of a pleasant or mild-tasting fine powder (such as MSA made by Nekton Produkte, Germany) containing calcium, trace minerals and amino acids. A wide range of such products is advertized in avicultural magazines.

Cockatoos also enjoy coarse mineral blocks made for the larger parrots. Cuttlefish bone is an unparalleled source of calcium which is excellent for Cockatiels but usually quickly destroyed by the cockatoos.

Effects of incorrect diet

An incorrect diet can result in chicks dying in the nest. 'Country Aviculturist' (1991) related the first breeding attempt of his pair of Eastern Long-billed Corellas. When two chicks hatched, the parents were offered cooked sweet corn and silverbeet, both of which were relished, and shot wheat, lettuce and a slice of bread – none of which were enjoyed. The chicks thrived until the supply of sweet corn (frozen) was depleted. Preserved commercial sweet corn was refused. After three or four days, boiled maize was offered and accepted (any other items of the diet were not described). However, nest inspection revealed that one youngster had died. Wheat and oats were then buried in about 4cm (1½in) of sand in the cockatoos's flight in order to provide

The oily orange fruits of the queen palm (*Arecastrum romanzoffianum* var. *australe*) are relished by most cockatoos.

growing greenfood. After another 10 days the second chick was found dying.

The following season the diet was changed to:

> . . . normal seed, panicum and canary mix, 5cm of first grade sweet corn kept fresh by freezing and then allowing it to self-defrost, a quarter of a cup of good seed wheat mixed with a quarter of a cup of polished rice and one teaspoon of sugar or syrup boiled for 30 minutes until the water has evaporated, leaving just the basic wheat and rice which is then fed to the birds three times a day, together with a fresh slice of bread. Half an apple is fed daily with seeding grass or vegetables that have gone to seed such as silverbeet, carrot, lettuce, broccoli, parsnip flowers without stalks and lots of silverbeet leaves.

This diet resulted in the young being reared successfully.

Food containers

Most cockatoos will destroy food dishes and water dishes made of plastic and will smash earthenware ones by throwing them on the ground, unless some method is found of securing them. Some thought needs to be given to a cockatoo-proof method of presenting food containers, preferably before the aviary is constructed. I favour an arrangement in which the container fits exactly into a shelf or slot.

In a suspended cage, a wire tray can be fitted at the front of the cage below the floor, the welded mesh above it being cut away. The feeding tray slides in at the front and a small flap of welded mesh, secured with a dog-lead clip or similar, prevents the tray from being pushed out. Another tray can be made for the water container.

Some people place food dishes and water dishes on the floor of ordinary aviaries but some cockatoos may not be used to feeding from the floor and will not descend. In any case, this system means that one has to enter the aviary to clean and refill dishes and that the contents are more likely to be soiled by droppings or by vermin. Containers should be at eye level (not higher – one needs to see the contents at a passing glance) and on a feeding shelf which can be attended without entering the aviary. At least one spare set of dishes should be maintained so that the other set can be thoroughly cleaned daily. Harmful bacteria can breed in dirty containers, especially in hot weather.

The condition of the food and water containers can reveal a great deal about the person in charge of the collection. Those who really care for their birds ensure that they are spotless.

7

Aviary breeding

Captive breeding – a history

Until the 1970s captive breedings of cockatoos were irregular events. This had been the case for a century; although many wealthy people had aviaries, few tried to breed from their birds. The first captive success that I can trace was that by C. W. Gedney who bred the Galah in 1870. When the female of his pair died, he used a bantam to brood the chicks and chewed up maize and groats and fed the chicks from his mouth! He truly was a pioneer of hand-rearing! He recorded:

> The trouble was certainly great, but the results were perfectly satisfactory, and having previously reared a nest of English nightingales, the cockatoos were an easy matter by comparison . . . (Gedney, 1879)

Until Australia ceased to permit the export of its fauna in 1959, Galahs and some other Australian cockatoos were available at a low price. There was no embargo on the export of cockatoos from other countries, most of which were seldom available. The following dates of first recorded breedings in the UK provide some indication of availability of species, those bred in the earlier years being the most readily available: 1901 – Leadbeater's (London Zoo, also Mrs Johnstone); 1915 – Greater Sulphur-crested (Herbert Whitley); 1924 – Lesser Sulphur-crested (M. T. Allen); 1956 – Citron-crested (S. B. Kendall); 1964 – Blue-eyed (A. V. Griffiths); 1968 – Umbrella (Tropical Bird Gardens, Rode); 1975 – Moluccan (in three collections); 1977 – Goffin's (N. O'Connor, also R. H. Day); 1984 – Red-vented (Mrs Uebele); and 1984 – Palm Cockatoo (Mann/Smith).

In the 1970s, when keeping pairs of larger parrots started to become popular, success with cockatoos was still a fairly rare event but no organization was collecting data on the numbers of parrots bred. Then the International Foundation for the Conservation of Birds (IFCB) funded a survey of birds in zoos in the USA as at 31 December 1985. Responses were received from 81 zoos and 11 private collections. Data for the cockatoo species in this survey are shown in Table 3 (see p. 62). It is reproduced to give an indication of how common or rare the various species were in zoos and aviculture at that time, and their relative prolificacy. Note, however, that the proportion of Australian species was higher than would be found in private collections because some zoos – but not private collections – were able to import Australian cockatoos which had been bred in captivity in Australian zoos. Eastern Long-billed Corellas, for example, are almost unknown in private collections. Note also that the number of young hatched and reared is very low, partly because some zoos keep cockatoos in mixed parrot exhibits without the opportunity to breed. The breeding success rate in private collections is very much higher. Compare the figures for this mainly zoo census with that of the 1989 USA breeding results from mainly private collections, as detailed in TRAFFIC (USA) *Psittacine captive breeding survey*, Allen and Johnson, 1991 (Table 4).

Table 3
Cockatoos in American zoos in 1985.

Species	Males	Females	Sex unknown	Hatched	Survived
Palm	14	13	1	0	0
Red-tailed [Banksian]	4	2	2	0	0
Gang Gang	4	5	0	0	0
Galah	56	60	14	72	56
Leadbeater's	30	26	1	0	0
Lesser	20	13	3	0	0
Citron-crested	30	29	13	12	10
Timor*	1	2	0	0	0
Greater	26	19	13	5	3
Medium [Eleonora]	13	12	7	1	1
Triton	24	22	19	16	15
Moluccan	75	61	24	4	2
Umbrella	40	30	6	15	12
Red-vented	4	3	1	1	1
Goffin's	21	22	4	1	1
Bare-eyed	22	19	13	14	13
Eastern Long-billed Corella	11	8	0	4	2
Unrelated species for comparison:					
Blue and Yellow Macaw	165	163	147	139	120
Double Yellow-headed Amazon	76	66	25	44	39

* This sub-species is often not distinguished from the Lesser Sulphur-crested.

Table 4
Cockatoo breeding success rates. Comparison between USA zoos in 1985 and mainly private collections (TRAFFIC (USA) *Psittacine captive breeding survey*) in 1989.

Species	Abundance*		Total no. of birds in survey		Participants		No. of birds hatched		No. of birds weaned		Breeding success rate**	
	Z	P	Z	P	Z	P	Z	P	Z	P	Z	P
Moluccan	—	4	160	820	42	239	4	158	2	120	1	15
Umbrella	—	5	76	798	16	217	15	441	12	380	16	47
Goffin's	—	8	47	711	12	215	1	77	1	68	2	10
Lesser Sulphur-crested	—	19	36	410	18	133	0	78	0	69	0	17
Palm	—	—	28	109	7	11	0	17	0	10	0	9

Z = Zoo.
P = Private breeder.
 * Abundance: relative to the number of species in the census, e.g. Moluccan fourth out of 183.
** Breeding success rate: number of young weaned as a percentage of the number of adults.

Factors affecting breeding success

What are the most important factors which lead to breeding success? Breeders no doubt hold widely varying views but, in my opinion, they are as follows:

(1) Compatibility of male and female.
(2) A stress-free environment.
(3) Certain stimuli.
(4) An adequate diet.
(5) Sexual maturity.
(6) In the case of Yellow-tailed Black, White-tailed Black and Palm Cockatoos, an aviary of adequate size, i.e. larger than that required by the other cockatoos (see pp. 46 and 228).

COMPATIBILITY OF MALE AND FEMALE

The larger parrots differ from the smaller species in that compatibility is a major factor in breeding success, but I believe that in no species is this more important than in cockatoos and macaws. In these two groups many pairs do not attempt to breed because they are not compatible. Yet the same species can prove extremely prolific when a happy partnership is formed.

The pair bond between two cockatoos can be so strong that, if the birds are separated, one or both may show no interest in another partner. As the history of many cockatoos acquired by breeders is unknown, it is difficult to assess how common a cause of breeding failure this is. However, the following are good examples.

A well-known breeder in the USA purchased a male Umbrella Cockatoo which had been kept with a female who had become egg-bound on two occasions. (A veterinary surgeon had warned the owner that the female might not survive the next time and she had very reluctantly decided to sell the male.) Although the male seemed compatible with a new female, with which he had been placed, no breeding attempt occurred. Two years later the former owner of the male contacted the breeder, offering the original female. A new job meant that she would often be away from home. In the intervening two years, as a result of advice from the breeder, the female's diet had been greatly improved; it seemed likely that an inadequate diet had been the cause of egg-binding. The female was therefore acquired and re-united with her mate.

The breeder, Julie Atkinson, continues the story:

> What happened next was the most amazing thing I ever witnessed in my life! The female stepped from the carrier, looked around, saw the male and literally ran over to him. The greeting was instantaneous

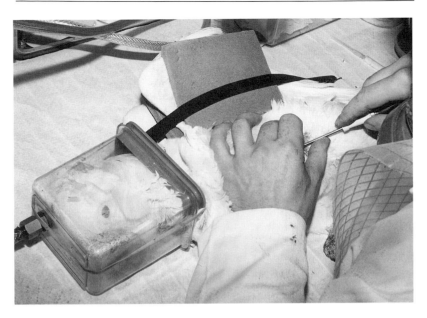

Surgical sexing not only positively identifies the sex of birds (such as this Moluccan Cockatoo, *Cacatua moluccensis*) but also provides information on the condition of the gonads (sexual organs) and whether the bird is likely to breed.

between the two. The male was moaning and clicking as he inspected every inch of her, as if to say: "Where the heck have you been for two years!" Within ten seconds the male mounted the female and they were mating right there on the ground while we all stood there with our mouths agape. Mating over, they retreated to the nest-box for some privacy. The lady cried with happiness. (Atkinson, 1989)

Within two months the female was producing fertile eggs. Many people have no idea of the strength of the devotion which exists between some male and female parrots, and especially cockatoos. I can think of no story which illustrates this better.

How does one ascertain whether or not a pair is compatible, especially in the case of very nervous Indonesian cockatoos (usually wild-caught adults) which are rarely glimpsed out of the nest box? This is very difficult without the use of observation cameras. I personally believe that camera and monitor are the finest aids to cockatoo breeding modern technology has so far produced. Cockatoos behave naturally only if they are unaware of being observed. The observation camera reveals the true nature of the relationship between a male and female.

Attacks on females

With the aid of a camera, one can observe each stage in the breeding cycle: copulation, the absence of one or both birds when eggs have been laid and, with luck, the emergence of the young from the nest and the male (or female?) feeding the offspring. The observation camera may also be the means of saving the female's life. Unfortunately, even in – or perhaps especially in – long-established breeding pairs, the male's aggression often results in the death of the female or in serious damage to her beak. The injury or the experience may scar her for life if she recovers, and render her useless for breeding. For example, a female Citron-crested with a damaged beak, the result of an attack by a male, was placed with another male but spent all her time cowering on the aviary floor. She was so stressed by his presence that to sell her as a pet was considered the kindest action to take.

The observation camera can warn of impending disaster – possibly fatal aggression on the part of the male. Behaviour may be seen which would not occur in front of a human observer, e.g. outright aggression or unusual actions, such as the female descending to the ground to escape the male. It is often suggested that, when such behaviour is either seen or anticipated, the flight feathers on one wing of the male should be cut (preferably leaving the outer feather intact); however, if the male can climb into the nest box, this action is not effective because it does not prevent the male from attacking the female in the nest – *unless it has a double exit* (see p. 71). Cutting the wing feathers has not been found to impair the male's fertility.

If aggressive behaviour is noticed, the male should be removed immediately from the aviary. It is not wise to remove the female because there is an even greater danger of attack when she is returned to his aviary (which by then, he will consider to be his territory). If the female has to be removed from the aviary – e.g. if she is sick – the male should also be moved and caged near her. This has a double advantage: the pair can be returned to the aviary at the same time and, in the case of a strongly bonded pair, they are not stressed or depressed by separation. If a female must be removed on her own, and an attack is feared on her return, both birds should be re-introduced into an aviary which neither has previously inhabited.

A male usually attacks a female because he is ready to breed and she is not. However, an attack could occur as the result of closely confining the birds or of some other action, not part of their normal routine, which results in stress.

Berry (1979) recorded: 'We have had males of compatible breeding pairs which have reared young for ten to 12 years abruptly go into sham rage and kill their partner.'

Technique for limiting effects of male aggression
At the Avicultural Breeding and Research Center in Florida a technique
for rendering an aggressive male cockatoo less capable of inflicting fatal
injury is under investigation. The tip of the bird's upper mandible is
blunted and shortened with a drill and a stainless-steel intra-osseous pin
is inserted through the mandible, with 2–3mm (approx. ⅛in) extending
on either side. Light-sensitive acrylic is applied to the tip of the beak,
covering the extensions of the pin, to form a so-called 'beak-ball'. The
acrylic is hardened with ultraviolet light. It must not be anchored around
the tip of the beak or the bird will be able to crack it. This method offers
only a temporary solution. It had been used on four species of *Cacatua*, a
total of seven birds. The length of time which the 'beak-ball' remained in
position varied between 24 and 51 days and averaged 34 days. Because
the mandible grows rapidly, the ball and pin will loosen and crack, or fall
off with growth. The bird must be monitored closely to ensure that he
can feed and initially be given large pieces of fruit and vegetables. If the
wire mesh of the aviary is less than 25mm (1in) square he may be unable
to climb or the ball may become caught in the wire (Schubot, Clubb &
Clubb, 1992).

Finding a compatible pair
How does one find a compatible pair? Very few breeders can afford to
buy a number of birds, place them in a large aviary, mark each with a
different colour on head or wing, then remove the newly formed pairs
from the aviary. It should be pointed out that, if a number of pairs are
left together, it is likely that the dominant pair will inhibit breeding in
the other birds, unless the aviary is extremely large.

Several breeders in one locality, who have pairs of the same species
which are not breeding, can co-operate either by placing several pairs in
one large enclosure until pair bonds are formed or by exchanging one
bird of each pair. Breeders involved in this kind of co-operation should
agree to each bird being first checked thoroughly by an avian veterinary
surgeon, preferably the same one. It would be very easy to introduce
disease to previously healthy birds.

An aviculturist who is isolated, or wishes to remain isolated from
other breeders, is advised to keep several pairs of the same species,
rather than one pair of each of several species. It is much easier to
change around one's own birds than to involve other keepers.

One breeder suggested pairing together cockatoos with similar
personalities:

> . . . easy-going males with sweet hens; aggressive males with
> aggressive hens, etc. I pair Sulphur-crested Cockatoos this way to
> lessen the impact of volatile male aggression during the mating
> season. (Stennet, 1988)

A STRESS-FREE ENVIRONMENT

Some stressful influence in their environment can prevent cockatoos from breeding. It could be the close presence of another pair of cockatoos or noisy and aggressive macaws. Sudden loud noises could disturb them, for example, the presence of children playing near the aviary. An enclosure with solid walls is recommended for nervous birds. I recall the case of a pair of Palm Cockatoos which had been kept for several years in an aviary about 7m (23ft) long with sides of chain link. This type of construction was used in all the aviaries in the block and so there was little privacy. The other aviaries were inhabited mainly by large, noisy macaws. These Palms never attempted to breed, neither did another five pairs kept in the same manner. One pair was moved to an aviary 17m (56ft) long and 2.5m (8ft 3in) wide. They nested a few months later and produced a chick. None of the other females laid. One cannot prove that the more private location suited them better, but it seemed likely.

As pair bonding can occur at a very early age it can be a mistake to keep siblings together for many months as it may then be difficult to persuade them to accept other partners. Robert J. Berry, former curator of birds at Houston Zoo, described what happened with three sibling Leadbeater's Cockatoos in his own collection. One male and two females were housed together compatibly until they were about eight months old. Then aggressive behaviour developed and the less favoured female had to be removed. The following spring the pair bond was intentionally disrupted and each individual was isolated from sight contact with the other. After six months the male was returned to the flight and the first female which had been removed was introduced. The two were tolerant of one another but showed no sign of pair formation. After a further six months the female was removed and the favoured female was re-introduced. The birds were clearly delighted to see each other and copulation occurred immediately (Berry, 1979).

STIMULI

My experiences in keeping and breeding cockatoos in England, where rainfall is frequent and often prolonged, and in the Canary Islands, in locations where rain is rare and of short duration, suggest that cockatoos are harder to breed in a dry climate. Sprinklers should be used to simulate rainfall for a few minutes once or twice daily, for several weeks, at a suitable time of year, just before one might want or expect the cockatoos to breed. Dennis Lofto of Prairie Aviaries, Winnipeg, Canada, related an interesting experience which bears this out (Lofto, 1992). In the spring of 1990 and 1991 there were several thunderstorms which caused flooding of his indoor breeding area (the climate is too cold to keep birds outdoors). A 'breeding frenzy' followed the flooding in both years, and after a similar time interval, the cockatoos being especially prolific. (In 1991, for example, 22 Moluccans were reared from 11 pairs.) In 1992 there were no natural floods so the floor area was flooded (all the cages are suspended) with similarly good breeding results. Another stimulus for pairs which have never attempted to breed could be the excavation of a log. One with a small cavity which needs enlarging to make a suitable nest site could trigger nesting.

Cockatoos will normally enter any nest box, but they often destroy it and appear to have no intention of using it as a nest site. Providing the right nest site can be a real challenge and various types and locations can be tried. I had a pair of Goffin's which, for seven years, ignored vertical nest boxes. When provided with a horizontal log on the ground, they nested, usually twice a year, for many years. The log was patched and repaired until only the entrance survived unaltered.

AN ADEQUATE DIET

Cockatoos which are primarily ground-feeders in the wild, such as the Galah and Greater Sulphur-crested, feed mainly on seeds and easily become overweight in captivity if fed an over-rich diet, e.g. one containing too much sunflower seed. The result in these two species is the formation of fatty lipomas (lumps), usually on the lower part of the abdomen, which can grow to an enormous size. Overweight cockatoos, especially with lipomas near the vent, are unable to produce fertile eggs. The lipoma can be removed surgically and the diet then corrected to ensure that the bird does not again become overweight.

It seems unlikely that any cockatoo would be given a diet so poor that it did not attempt to breed. However, some missing component of the diet, such as amino acids or minerals, can result in a breeding attempt failing. The death of chicks in the egg just before they are due to hatch, for example, can be the result of a dietary deficiency. Alternatively, eggs can fail to hatch because they are thin-shelled, indicating that the female lacked calcium and/or Vitamin D.

Some cockatoos can be stimulated to breed by adding animal protein to the diet. White-tailed and Yellow-tailed Black Cockatoos may respond to a sudden supply of the large type of mealworms, and other species to cooked chicken carcases.

AGE AT SEXUAL MATURITY

It would appear that most cockatoos become sexually mature between the ages of two and four years. Most of the information is derived from aviculture as there have been few studies of marked birds in the wild. However, one carried out on Galahs showed that males breed for the first time at two or three years (Rowley, 1990). It has been known for captive-bred females of this species to lay at only two years but three is probably more usual. The same applies to most white cockatoos. However, a female Moluccan in my care laid her first egg when only 24 months old.

The black cockatoos (Palm and *Calyptorhynchus*) are generally sexually mature at between three and four years. An exception appears to be the Glossy. In 1987 a female bred by R. T. Lynn laid her first egg when only 20 months old. The egg hatched. One female reared by John Courtney laid her first egg at three years and two weeks; another laid for the first time when less than three years old – and she successfully reared the chick to fledging.

Nesting

NESTING MATERIAL

All cockatoos need to line the base of their nest. Most use wood chips but two species have special needs. The Galah uses green eucalyptus leaves in the wild but, in an aviary, will utilize any non-poisonous branches. In the wild, male and female cut sprays up to 30cm (12in) long but many are accidentally dropped before they reach the nest tree (Rowley, 1990). Lining of the nest with green leaves usually commences five weeks before the first egg is laid. If eggs fail to hatch, or small chicks die, they are covered with eucalyptus sprays by the parents. Prior to nesting, Palm Cockatoos need a constant supply of fresh branches which the males fashions into splinters about 10cm (4in) long. Nest boxes for other species should contain a layer of wood shavings at least 7.5cm (3in) deep. These are usually chewed into a finer consistency. Pieces of wood can be nailed inside nest boxes to prolong the life of the box; however, one must check that the nails or screws used to keep the offcuts in position will not present a hazard when the wood has been gnawed away. A lining of welded mesh also helps to preserve the box but wood should always be available inside as gnawing and destroying this is a normal part of nest preparation.

When young are parent-reared it is advisable, in some cases, to change the wood shavings every three weeks or so, but *only* if this is possible without causing stress to the breeding pair. This is not because the shavings become very dirty but because they become very dusty from the powder down of the parents.

NEST SITES

Cockatoo nests should be left in position all the year round. This is partly because many cockatoos are not seasonal breeders and also because, for nervous birds, the nest becomes a place of refuge from stress. Nest sites offered to captive cockatoos are usually either nest boxes, tree trunks, barrels, metal dustbins (trash cans) or even a concrete 'nest' built into the back wall of the aviary. The worst, in my opinion, are metal dustbins, as they offer no protection from extremes of temperature and are made of a most unnatural material which the birds cannot gnaw. If they must be used, they should be partly or entirely lined inside with wood.

From the aviculturist's viewpoint the essential qualities of a good nest site are:

(1) Ease of inspection, preferably without entering the aviary.
(2) Resistance to destruction by the cockatoos.
(3) Protection from weather extremes.
(4) The presence of two entrances, i.e. the nest is Y-shaped with an entrance in each fork of the Y. This gives the female the opportunity to escape if attacked in the nest by the male and is important for pairs in which aggression is known or feared; it is advisable for all pairs of *Cacatua* species.
(5) Ease of positioning.

Nervous cockatoos can react with panic to anyone entering the aviary to inspect the nest. If inspection cannot be carried out from outside, breeding failure may result. In the case of very strong and aggressive cockatoos, such as Greater Sulphur-cresteds, a very serious injury can be inflicted on anyone who enters the aviary when they are nesting. A nest-box can be constructed with an inspection door in the back or side which coincides with a door in the back of the aviary.

Another idea worth considering is to build a concrete nesting chamber into the back of the shelter. At Palmitos Park this kind of nest is used for all birds except Palm Cockatoos. The front is faced with split eucalyptus logs to provide a more natural appearance. The interior is not lined because low temperatures are not experienced; in most climates concrete nests need to be lined with wood. Pieces of bark and wood are placed inside for the birds to gnaw. A large inspection door in the back opens on to the service passage of the next row of aviaries. Incidentally, some cockatoos have the habit of taking stones or walnuts into the nest and may even 'incubate' them. They should be removed in case their presence inhibits laying.

SIGNS OF NESTING

When cockatoos become noisier, bolder and even aggressive towards their keeper, the males perhaps strutting along the perch, screaming and displaying, nesting activity can be expected. Courtship feeding is rarely seen in white cockatoos. Rowley (1990) studied the Galah in the wild and, in seven years, saw an adult feed another fewer than ten times. However, closely bonded pairs indulge in long periods of mutual preening every day. In some, copulation is apparently a means of maintaining the pair bond and does not necessarily mean that laying is imminent. Mutual preening may occur between *any* two cockatoos, regardless of sex or species. Indeed, a cockatoo may befriend a parrot of a totally different genus if it has no other companion. I recall the unique sight in a German zoo in the 1970s of a Hawk-headed Parrot (*Deroptyus accipitrinus*) nestled up against a Palm Cockatoo!

Laying and incubation

Clutch size generally varies from one to four, according to the species, although up to six is known in the Galah and even up to eight in the Cockatiel. Incubation periods vary from 20 days in the Cockatiel to between 23 and 30 days in other species. A Cockatiel lays every second day; the interval in other species is three or four days, sometimes longer. Incubation is generally carried out by male and female, except in black cockatoos in which only the female incubates (except with some Palm Cockatoos).

ARTIFICIAL INCUBATION

There are two main reasons why cockatoo eggs are removed to an incubator or to foster pairs. The first is that some cockatoos break or damage their eggs; the second is the desire to increase production. Breeders should be warned, however, that hatchability of cockatoo eggs which are removed to an incubator within a few hours or days of laying is lower than hatchability of other parrot eggs thus removed, and much lower than eggs which are incubated for at least two weeks by the parents. If eggs must be removed at once because of the risk of breakage, they should ideally be placed under other large parrots which are incubating. The species is not important as long as the egg size is approximately similar. After they have been incubated for two weeks the eggs can be removed to an incubator, and a higher rate of hatchability will ensue. If no other parrots are available to incubate the eggs, pigeons or bantams can be used, but the disease risk must be considered.

A reliable brand of small-capacity incubator should be used; with valuable birds it makes no sense to economize by buying cheap incubators. The incubator should be running for at least two days at a temperature of 37°C (98.6°F) before the eggs are placed inside, and should then be kept running permanently. Eggs of different species have different humidity requirements. For parrots 50–53 per cent

Cockatoo eggs are pyriform and ovate-elliptical in shape whereas most parrot eggs are elliptical. Compare the four cockatoo eggs (left) with the more rounded macaw egg (right). Above is shown an egg of an Umbrella Cockatoo (*Cacatua alba*) (left) and a Moluccan Cockatoo (*Cacatua moluccensis*) (right). Below is an egg of a Palm Cockatoo (*Proposciger aterrimus*) (left) and a discarded shell of a Leadbeater's Cockatoo (*Cacatua leadbeateri*).

relative humidity (wet bulb 27–29°C/80.6–84°F) is often suggested. At the Hagen Avicultural Research Institute (HARI) in Canada excellent hatchability of cockatoos eggs was reported using 58–61 per cent relative humidity (wet bulb 30–30.6°C/86–87°F). Weight loss from day one to pipping of 18 Medium Sulphur-crested Cockatoo eggs averaged 9.7 per cent and of four Moluccan eggs 9.4 per cent. In contrast, weight loss of six Blue and Yellow Macaw eggs, from laying to pipping, was 12.9 per cent and of eight Double Yellow-headed Amazon eggs 13.4 per cent. Note that in some locations it might be necessary to use a dehumidifier to achieve the correct weight loss.

When the first pip mark (the crack in the shell) is seen, turning should cease and the egg should be moved to a hatcher. This could be a brooder or another incubator where turning does not occur and where the relative humidity is about 80 per cent (wet bulb 33–34.4°C/ 91.4–94°F). Hand-turning of eggs is preferable, five or more times daily. Mechanical turning devices which jar the eggs can result in the embryos dying. Incubators designed to hold eggs in an upright position should not be used for parrot eggs.

INCUBATION PROBLEMS

In all cockatoos except the black species, incubation is shared by male and female. This sometimes causes problems in captivity; in the wild, one bird would be out much of the day foraging for food, but, in an aviary, the bird not incubating may feed and then return to the nest. It may just sit alongside its incubating mate; or male and female may incubate an egg each. More rarely, the two may fight, resulting in broken eggs. Berry (1979) solved this particular problem by removing the male and found that the female will incubate and rear young well on her own.

Young in the nest

SIBLING CHICKS

As incubation usually commences on the day, or the day after, the first egg is laid, chicks hatch at intervals. In the larger species which lay two eggs, the second is probably only an insurance against failure of the first. It may hatch but, in the wild, the chick cannot compete with the older, more forceful sibling at feeding time and usually dies after a few days. In captivity, it may survive but will need to be removed for hand-rearing as soon as its growth falls behind that of the first chick. Most breeders then prefer to remove both chicks, so that the parents will nest again more quickly and because hand-reared chicks are easier to sell as pets than those which have been parent-reared and thus take longer to tame.

THE EFFECTS OF ISOLATING CHICKS

The belief that hand-reared cockatoos will not breed is not correct *per se*. The fact is that most hand-reared cockatoos are kept alone as pets and, therefore, from an early age, are denied the opportunity to learn by example the behaviour of their own species. It is probably the effects of isolation during the early months which renders many hand-reared cockatoos unsuitable for breeding. Cockatoos are highly social creatures which have an even stronger need than most parrots to identify with another. In the absence of a cockatoo, they may become irreversibly imprinted on a human being.

Nest inspection

Minimum intrusion is essential when nests are inspected. Even so, there are often difficulties. Nervous birds may refuse to move, hissing and backing on to the eggs or chicks – which may be injured as a result. A nest box with a large base slightly minimizes the chance of this happening. Tame birds which have no fear of human beings may even attack an intruder. There is also the possibility of chicks being mutilated because inspection makes the parents nervous. One can usually predict how they will behave by knowing the individual birds. Both birds or only one might stay in the nest, or both might leave.

Fortunately, cockatoo chicks have such a loud food-swallowing vocalization (which sounds something like 'chip-chip-chip') that anyone frequently in the vicinity of the aviary will not need to inspect the nest to know whether a chick has hatched. Breeders from Cornwall, John and Pat King, use a baby alarm to monitor the nest of their Moluccan Cockatoos – an idea worth copying. On the intercom they can clearly hear a chick and when it is being fed.

If nest inspection can be carried out quickly and without upsetting the parents, inspection on a daily basis is recommended. It is not unusual for inexperienced parents to kill their first chick, probably accidentally when trying to feed it. On the other hand, one sometimes finds unfortunate newly hatched chicks – especially if they are the pair's first – bitten into many pieces, as though they were alien objects in the nest. In such cases they may have been killed, although as often happens after a parrot chick dies in the nest, the parents may have chewed at its feet or wings when cleaning the nest. It is usually impossible to determine whether injuries seen on a dead chick occurred before or after death. I have found that, because of the nervous temperament of cockatoos, there is a greater chance of losing newly hatched chicks in the nest than with most parrot species. Even the advocates of parent-rearing may like to give some thought to this following point.

MANAGEMENT OF YOUNG

It is important for the future of cockatoos in aviculture that the young hatched in captivity have a genetic base which is as broad as possible. The vast majority of imported parrots die without handing down their most precious possessions – their genes. For this reason I am in favour of removing the young in the very first nest hatched by a pair, for hand-rearing. After all, one of the parents might die, and then there would never be any more young from this pair. I make an exception in the case of the Palm Cockatoo, because this species is more difficult to rear from the egg than nearly all other parrots.

When chicks hatch there are two aspects of management that may need to be changed. One is keeping cleaning and disturbance to a minimum, at least until one knows the pair and how they react. Second, the diet will need to be altered by providing whatever they seem to need or like most. Pander to their every desire!

It may not be necessary to change the nest litter while chicks are being reared, but it is advisable to do so if there is any history of disease in young or adults, as the dry, dusty nest litter could be harbouring harmful organisms. In a damp warm climate, it should be changed if the young are not to contract the fungus disease, candidiasis.

In the white cockatoos, the female usually (but not always) plays the major or an equal role in feeding the young. As the young mature, the male generally takes a bigger part and may be solely responsible for feeding them after they leave the nest. I believe this is more often the case.

RICKETS

A hazard with parent-reared young is rickets, due to a diet deficient in calcium or one in which the calcium/phosphorus ratio is incorrect, or because of an unbalanced choice of food items by the parents. (I have never known this problem to occur in hand-reared parrots of any kind.) Rickets (metabolic bone disease) results in soft, easily broken bones. If there are no fractures, the legs, for example may be slightly bowed. If young appear weak on leaving the nest and spend much time on the floor, rickets should be suspected although, of course, there are other causes. If the bones are not broken, a series of calcium injections before or immediately after the young leave the nest may help or even completely rectify the problem. Injections of Calcium Sandoz 10 per cent are used by many veterinary surgeons.

What can be done to reduce the chance of rickets in parent-reared young? In my experience, calcium additives in the food are not effective as most cockatoos ignore foods thus treated. They will accept it in the water but not enough is passed on to the young. The most efficient method of giving calcium is to use a small syringe filled with a liquid calcium preparation (obtainable from veterinary surgeons). This can be given into the chick's mouth twice weekly after two weeks of age until they refuse it, or until they are feathered.

RINGING (BANDING)

Closed rings of the correct diameter are the only proof of captive breeding, except in Australia where the opportunity to remove young from wild nests exists. The age at which closed ringing can take place varies according to the rate of development; this often depends on

Closed rings of the correct size should be fitted to cockatoo chicks at about 3–4 weeks of age, depending on their state of development. This photograph shows a Triton Cockatoo (*Cacatua galerita triton*) which has been fitted with a 12 mm (½ in) ring.

whether chicks are parent-reared or hand-reared, and on the diet provided. However, ringing is usually carried out at between three and four weeks of age. Recommended ring sizes are given in Table 5 (see p. 79).

Is colony breeding possible?

Can cockatoos be bred on the colony system? The answer is that it is possible in a very large aviary, but not advisable. I know of two colony aviaries: one for Galahs (see p. 145) in which the young were hand-reared, and one for Moluccans which existed on exhibit at Loro Parque, Tenerife, until 1989. The latter measured approximately 12m (40ft) long, varied between 5m and 6m (16ft and 20ft) wide, with a height of 6m (20ft). Apparently, initially some birds died as a result of aggression. In both 1984 and 1985 a chick hatched and died but, thereafter, several young were hand-reared each year. In 1987, when there were 15 inhabitants, one youngster fledged into the colony on March 18, the only one ever to be parent-reared. At the end of April it was attacked. Immediate intervention resulted in it being removed from the aviary uninjured. This was the only occasion in two years in which I was aware of any disharmony in the aviary. All future chicks were removed either at pipping or at up to four days old.

One problem was an egg thief, which would remove an egg unbroken from a nest (trunks of palms and other trees), then turn it round in its foot until disturbed, when it would smash to the ground. Another problem was two females using one nest, resulting in three broken eggs. Finally, most of the young were produced by one easily identified female. I suspected that only three or four females ever laid, but the total number of females was unknown.

As a spectacle, however, the aviary was unrivalled in the park, except by the free-flying macaws. It was a joy to watch their behaviour in a flock. Often I saw a group of six or eight assemble on the ground and stand around as though deep in discussion. A sentinel was usually posted at the highest point and he would shout a warning at the appearance of my partner, whose task it was to check the nests (Low, 1988).

A large colony aviary for cockatoos, such as these Moluccans (*Cacatua moluccensis*), provides an opportunity to study their fascinating social behaviour.

Table 5
Recommended ring sizes for cockatoos.

Species	Ring sizes (internal diameter)
Gang Gang	11
Galah	10
Leadbeater's	10
Greater Sulphur-crested	14
Triton	12
Lesser Sulphur-crested	10 or 11
Moluccan	14
Umbrella	11
Eastern Long-billed Corella	12
Western Long-billed Corella	12
Bare-eyed	10
Goffin's	10
Red-vented	10
Black cockatoos, all species	14
Palm	11, 12
Palm, Goliath	14
Cockatiel	5.5

Hybridization

Many different cockatoo hybrids have been produced in captivity, especially between two *Cacatua* species or a *Cacatua* and a Galah. The Cockatiel is the only species which has not produced hybrids because the genetic distance between it and any other species is too great. Sometimes hybrids are produced accidentally – a mistake which should not be allowed to recur. Unfortunately, some aviculturists aim to produce hybrids in order to sell them with invented names. For example, there are crosses between Moluccan and Umbrella Cockatoos called 'Mol-brellas'. I totally condemn such irresponsible practices and call on all breeders fortunate enough to keep cockatoos – and especially the endangered Indonesian species – to use them only in a way which demonstrates the 'owner's' appreciation for the privilege of keeping them, i.e. they must never even consider keeping together two birds of the opposite sex of different species. Note that virtually the only barrier against hybridization when two *Cacatua* species are kept together is size difference. It would be very difficult for a Goffin's, for example, to fertilize a Moluccan.

Part of an eloquent plea against hybridization of parrot species is reproduced here, and is especially applicable to the Indonesian species.

There is considerable concern among wildlife specialists that, within the forseeable future, wild populations of a number of species may well be exterminated. In such an eventuality their sole chance of survival would depend upon captive breeding. For varying reasons zoological institutions and governmental programs alone would be unable to sustain this effort. Private aviculture, of necessity, would be the determining factor in a preservation effort. This would place tremendous responsibility upon the private sector, allowing no place for irresponsible or unethical practice.

The first responsibility of anyone involved in wildlife husbandry is to respect the best interest of the resource. This means the resource must be utilized only in a manner which ensures that the integrity of the species is preserved . . .

When birds of two different species are mated the reproductive potential of each individual is wasted. Far worse than the loss of breeding potential of the parent stock is the capacity for corruption of the gene pool by the mongrel progeny. In the hands of uninformed, or uncaring breeders, the potential for devastation is enormous . . .

Throughout the country are numerous groups, some of which have enormous influence, that are adamantly opposed to the keeping of any form of captive wildlife, especially birds. We need but examine some of the restrictions recently proposed to understand the determination of these groups. Nothing could give them a more powerful argument to use against us than the fact we are involved in irresponsible and unethical activities – specifically hybridization. Unless we move forward to control, and eventually eliminate the practice, we can be assured that legislation will be enacted that will restrict, or even deny, our privilege of keeping birds . . . . (Elgas, 1992)

Can aviculturists produce enough cockatoos?

As this book went to press, it seemed that the importation of wild-caught cockatoos into the USA and Europe (and probably elsewhere) would soon be ended. If this proves to be so, aviculturists alone will be able to supply the pet trade and other aviculturists with cockatoos. Can they meet the demand? At the present time, they cannot breed enough to equal the numbers of those imported during the 1980s – and probably never will. But at that time supply often exceeded demand. I believe that aviculturists can breed enough to supply those prepared to pay higher prices. Such prices will be inevitable after a couple of years with no cockatoos coming out of the quarantine stations. However, it is not the immediate future which will prove or disprove the efficiency of aviculturists. It is a decade or more hence, when there will be fewer pairs consisting of wild-caught birds. It is the first generation of captive-bred birds on which the future of cockatoos in aviculture will depend. If today's breeders cannot produce cockatoos which are capable of rearing young – or which are *permitted* to rear at least some of their young – then I believe that, outside Australia, cockatoos will die out in captivity. Because they are such long-lived birds, with a potential life-span equal to that of a human being, it might be many years before this sad fact becomes apparent. I remind all those fortunate enough to own pairs of these precious cockatoos that their future in aviculture – and for some species, perhaps, their very existence – lies in their hands.

8

Hand-rearing and weaning

Hand-rearing

I commenced hand-rearing parrot chicks in 1975 as a means of saving young, especially of rarely-bred species, which would have died in the nest. At that time little was known about hand-rearing and one had to learn as one went along. However, it is mainly a matter of common sense and careful observation plus, in the case of chicks reared from the egg, developing a diet which suits the species in question. However, there is one other, less easily defined factor. It is the ability to work with parrot chicks – an ability more likely to be present in a woman than in a man. One needs not only a sense of commitment, but unlimited patience, the tenderness to handle tiny creatures and, not least of all, the acceptance that one's social life will suffer unless someone else is available to assist.

For 17 years I have been engaged in this activity and, except for one period of five months, this has meant spending part of each day – often a very large part – wielding a spoon. During this period, a great change has occurred in avicultural practices. As with most things, this change started in the USA, spread to Europe and then began to make itself felt in Australia. The rearing of parrots, which was once a pleasurable hobby (and still is, for many) has gradually taken on another guise – that of a business from which handsome profits are made by a few. How true were the words of a friends who wrote to me:

> The fight for profit with mass-bred nestlings aimed at the pet trade is revolting. Bird-breeders are becoming avicultural slave traders. There's a lot of high technology and a lack of love.

Hand-rearing for the best motives – and this includes rearing young *lovingly* for pets – is giving way to hand-rearing for purely commercial purposes – to the detriment of the future of aviculture.

'What is wrong with mass-produced hand-reared birds?', some may ask, 'Especially if they reduce the trade in wild-caught parrots.' There is nothing wrong with mass-production of less 'sensitive' species, such as cockatiels, conures and lovebirds, because they are not so valuable that breeders are inclined to snatch every egg, as soon as it is laid, for artificial incubation. This is what happens to countless pairs of cockatoos, macaws and Amazons. Leaving one clutch with the parents every year, or even every other year, would be acceptable. But imagine how frustrating and disturbing it must be for a pair to have every egg or small chick removed. Breeders who remove every egg in this way are in danger of producing, after a few generations, birds which have lost the instinct to incubate.

Most cockatoo species are far more sensitive and, in some cases, nervous, than most other parrots. To produce young which are themselves capable of producing another generation requires a different approach from that currently being used by the 'mass-producers'. As I have already mentioned, hand-reared birds which are sold before they are weaned as pets usually become too imprinted on people to be suitable for breeding later in life. Often problems arise with cockatoos which mean that hand-rearing is essential if the young are to survive. However, if two or more young are reared together and not encouraged to become over-familiar with the feeder or feeders, by the time they are weaned they will be fearless but not clinging, friendly but not familiar. There are exceptions, especially with Moluccan Cockatoos, most of which seem to crave human attention, but even in this species the problem can be overcome (see p. 97). Young which have been hand-reared in the right way should be excellent birds for breeding, being less nervous and therefore less susceptible to stress than parent-reared young. The only problem is that their lack of fear can make them very aggressive towards people when they are nesting.

Unfortunately, some cockatoos kill or mutilate newly hatched chicks, so the eggs have to be removed. In this case I try to replace them with infertile eggs or eggs in which the embryos died early, so that the male and female (or the female only, in the case of black cockatoos) can incubate for the full period and destroy the eggs when hatching is overdue. No doubt many breeders would find this ridiculous. After all, their idea is to produce as many young as possible in the shortest time, and allowing birds to sit on eggs is counter-productive. Or is it? Allowing females to lay excessive numbers of eggs can be detrimental to their health, especially if the diet is inadequate. It also shortens their breeding span as, in their lifetime, they can produce only a certain number of eggs and, when these have all been laid, the ovary can produce no more.

Before embarking on hand-rearing, you must be totally committed to the task. You or a helper must be prepared to feed chicks from, say, 7 a.m. until 10 p.m. for several months, even up to eight or nine months in the case of some black cockatoos.

BASIC ITEMS REQUIRED FOR HAND-REARING

If you have rare or valuable birds in your collection, you should equip yourself with the basic items required for hand-rearing, even if you have no desire to carry this out. The day will come when you have an emergency on your hands and you will be pleased that you were prepared. Otherwise, unless you have good aviculturist friends close by, you will lose chicks which could so easily have been saved.

The most important item of equipment is the brooder. In an emergency a hospital cage or an incubator could be used for a few days, or you could convert an unused aquarium, making a cover containing a thermostat and a couple of red light bulbs. If you live in a warm climate, an aquarium and a small heat pad will suffice as a temporary measure.

There are now a number of commercially produced brooders available for parrot chicks. I prefer one which is easy to clean, allows easy viewing of the chicks without opening the brooder and which has the heat source at one end (not under the floor). This results in a couple of degrees difference in temperature at each end, which is useful if accurately recorded by two thermometers. A thermometer with a digital read-out is easier to read than the gradated type. (One brooder which fulfils these requirements is that produced by IBE, 10 Beaulieu Road, Alum Chine, Westbourne, Bournemouth, BH4 8EY, UK.)

Chicks should be placed inside the brooder in plastic tubs on a face cloth or a piece of towel. Some types of paper towel are unsuitable as

A good-quality brooder, with accurate temperature control, is essential for very young chicks.

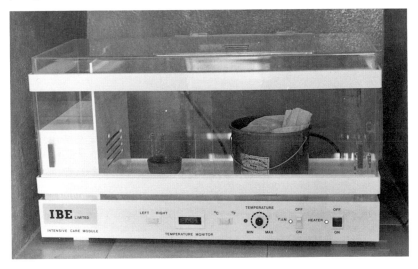

they contain chemicals which can cause severe bleeding of the tiny feet of chicks. After the age of about two weeks, the towel should be replaced by small welded mesh; the size of the mesh is important. If it is too large, toes could be trapped in it, resulting in injury or even a broken leg. The mesh should be raised off the base of the tub and newspaper placed underneath. This offers several advantages: the mesh enables chicks to grip from an early age and thus helps prevent foot deformities; where large numbers of chicks are being reared, replacing towels with newspaper saves much work in washing towels. Another essential item for a brooder containing young chicks is a small container of water, to prevent them becoming dehydrated.

When the chicks outgrow this brooder they should be moved to a larger one, without the tubs, and placed on a false floor of welded mesh. The newspaper placed below the floor should be changed once or twice daily. Heat should be gradually reduced and can usually be discontinued (depending on the temperature of the room) by the time the young are two-thirds feathered. Soon after, when they start to eat a little on their own, they should be moved to a small cage constructed of welded mesh. When they start to perch they can be moved to a slightly larger cage.

Always handle chicks with gentleness and sympathy. As they grow larger, it is best to pick up and support cockatoo chicks by the feet, not by the body.

An extremely useful – indeed essential – piece of equipment in my opinion is a set of scales with which to weigh chicks. They should weigh up to 1,000g (35¼oz), and should be graded to the nearest gram up to about 100g (3½oz). Suitable scales can be bought in most stores with a good range of kitchen equipment. I weigh all chicks which are being hand-reared before and immediately after the first feed of the day. This provides two useful pieces of information: how much weight the chick has gained (or lost) in 24 hours, and how much food it is consuming at one feed. I enter both these weights into a book immediately.

FEEDING

Spoon- or syringe-feeding
I prefer to feed with a spoon which has the sides bent inwards; it is safer, permits the natural head movement which occurs when chicks take food from their parents and, most importantly, allows them to refuse food when they have had enough, or if the food is too hot. Cases of severe crop burn in syringe-fed chicks are unfortunately common, due to negligence on the part of the feeder. Spoon-fed chicks are usually easier to wean and very rarely suffer from the beak deformities (crossed or crooked mandibles) often seen in syringe-fed chicks. The main disadvantage of spoon-feeding is that it is slow and therefore

impractical when feeding large numbers of chicks. Also, food is often spilt on the plumage, especially during the weaning period. It must be wiped off immediately after feeding; if the plumage becomes matted with dried food, its removal will cause stress to the young cockatoos. There are two different syringe-feeding techniques. In the first, the syringe has attached to it a length of rubber tube, which must be of the correct size for the species being fed. The tube is placed over the tongue, down the right side of the mouth, and then into the crop. In inexperienced hands this procedure is dangerous because the tube could enter the lungs and, if food enters the lungs, the chick will die. Alternatively, a 5ml syringe can be used (without a tube) and the food is merely placed in the chick's mouth. This is a safe and quick method, especially for small chicks.

The food used must be of a smooth consistency, without lumps, which will block the syringe. Chicks like to taste and chew particles in the food when they start to feed on their own but this is impossible with syringe-feeding.

REARING FOODS

In the USA most people feed diets based on monkey chow or on commercially formulated diets. New brands are continually appearing on the market. There has been correspondence in certain avicultural journals about the suitability of some of these but I cannot comment from personal experience. A brand which has been on the market longest, and which was formulated for Cockatiels (but is used for most species) is Roudybush (P.O. Box 908, Templeton, California 93465). Some breeders make up batches of their own formula and freeze it for future use. It should be pointed out, however, that freezing destroys certain vitamins.

Cockatoo chicks which have been parent-fed for one or two weeks and then removed for hand-rearing grow well on any reasonable diet if they are healthy. The needs of chicks hand-reared from the egg are far more critical. I mix my own food from a few basic items. It has proved suitable for rearing white cockatoos from the egg or any other stage. Contents are approximately two parts wheatgerm cereal (30 per cent protein and 10 per cent fat), two parts Milupa baby cereal, fruit or vegetable (about 13 per cent protein and 9 per cent fat), one part Nekton-Lori (powdered nectar mix for lories made by Nekton Produkte, Pforzheim, Germany), and one part home-made rearing food (hard-boiled egg, carrot, wholegrain bread and a small amount of non-fat cheese blended into a crumbly mixture). This is mixed in a blender with bottled water for small chicks or mixed by hand with bottled water for chicks aged more than about two weeks for which food with a slightly lumpy consistency is preferable. After heating, a little Nekton

MSA (a fine powder containing calcium, trace minerals and vital amino acids, and Vitamin D_3) is added.

This diet is low in fat which means that early growth is not rapid. However, I believe that this is preferable to diets which induce very rapid early growth, with the associated risk of liver problems and skeletal defects. If chicks appear a little thin, the fat content of the diet can easily be increased by adding peanut butter (about 50 per cent fat).

The growth of chicks hand-fed from the egg is often very slow for the first four or five days and feeding is very time consuming, because young chicks need to be fed between 7 a.m. and 10 p.m., as soon as the crop is empty. For the first couple of days very liquid food is necessary, which usually means feeding every hour or hour and a half. Then the food can be thickened slightly, but should still be very liquid, and should not stay in the crop longer than two hours. The crop should not be filled excessively.

The water content of food for chicks aged less than about four days should be quite high. For the first two or three feeds I may give only Ringers Lactate (a solution of salts, electrolytes, etc. which can be obtained from a veterinary surgeon and which has the appearance of water). At this stage the chick is still absorbing the contents of the yolk sac and fluid is equally as important as food. I am not concerned if weight gains are small during this stage.

If food is staying in the crop longer than two hours, it is too thick or too much has been given. Feeding thick food will not increase a chick's growth rate. Such food takes longer to digest, therefore fewer feeds can be given. Food remaining in the crop too long can result in bacterial infections.

Black cockatoos (*Calyptorhynchus*) chicks need a different diet. The diets supplied by four experienced breeders are described. Neville and Enid Connors (New South Wales) use equal parts of rice cereal, peanuts (or peanut butter) and sunflower kernels, with the juice of silver beet and carrot, mixed with water. They warn (Connors & Connors, 1991) against excessive protein during the first four or five days; losses of chicks at two to four weeks of age stopped when the protein level was reduced. Mark Schmidt (South Australia) uses semolina or digestive meal (340g/12oz), sieved soy-bean meal (185g/6½oz), sieved oatmeal (113g/4oz), meatmeal put through a fine sieve (71g/2½oz) and a little peanut butter. This is blended with water and the juice from silver beet. Mr and Mrs R. Rodda (South Australia) use Heinz Mixed Cereal (1.7g/¹/₁₆oz) protein per 15g/½oz) and wheatgerm cereal plus a little carrot and silver beet with the fibre removed. Sunflower kernels are added for the older chicks. In the USA, Bill Wegner reared White-tailed Blacks on a pre-boiled mixture of sunflower kernels, wheatgerm cereal and dried dogfood.

Note that the protein content of a food is significant only if it contains all the essential amino acics. These are found in some supplements made for birds, such as Nekton MSA. This product contains calcium and, once daily, I also add a liquid calcium supplement to the food after it has been heated. Cockatoo chicks have a greater need for calcium than those of small parrot species. Without calcium, and Vitamin D_3 (to enable the calcium to be absorbed), they will suffer from rickets (see p. 76).

Weight

It is normal for a young cockatoo to lose weight only as it approaches and enters the weaning stage. If its weight decreases before this period, the most likely reasons are as follows:

(1) It has recently been removed from the nest and has not yet adjusted to the new environment and food.
(2) The diet is incorrect.
(3) Insufficient food has been given.
(4) The temperature and/or humidity at which the chick is maintained is incorrect.
(5) The chick is sick.

It is not normal for hand-reared chicks to lose weight before they start to lose interest in being fed. Note, however, that parent-reared chicks usually reach their maximum weights well before they leave the nest; these weights remain constant for a considerable period and may decrease slightly just before fledging. In hand-reared birds the weight usually increases gradually until they start to sample food, usually about one month before they would have left the nest. It then decreases slightly. The weight gains in two Palm Cockatoos, one parent-reared at Palmitos Park, the other hand-reared in a private collection, demonstrates this difference well (Table 6). At day 33, for example the parent-reared chick was double the weight of the hand-reared chick.

Note that there can be considerable variation in weight of young of the same species, whether hand-reared or parent-reared, depending on sex, sub-species, food received and efficiency of parents or feeder. This is demonstrated in Table 7, which gives average weights and the highest and lowest weights of one species in two locations. If the weight of a chick appears low yet is continually increasing and the chick appears healthy, there may be no cause for concern.

Note that varying the foods and feeding methods can result in different rates of growth in different collections. All breeders should keep notes to establish the normal growth rate in their own collections. For example, the weights above are low compared with those recorded at the Aviculture Institute in California, no doubt because the food used was entirely different (see Table 8, p. 91).

Table 6
Weight gain in parent-reared and hand-reared
chicks of the Palm Cockatoo (*Probosciger
aterrimus*).

	Weight (g*)	
Age in days	Parent-reared	Hand-reared
19	288	76
26	430	160
33	545	c.260
40	598	c.380
47	610	482
54	610	c.520

* 1g = 0.0353oz.

Table 7
Weights of hand-reared Umbrella Cockatoos (*Cacatua alba*)
before and after the first feed of the day.

Day hatched	Weight (g*)			Number of chicks weighed
	Lowest	Highest	Average	
	13	18	15.6	5
1	15/16	18/20	17/18	6
2	16/17	22/23	19/20	6
3	17/18	25/27	21/22	6
4	18/19	28/30	22/25	6
5	19/21	31/33	25/27	6
6	20/22	36/38	28/30	6
7	23/25	43/45	33/35	7
8	25/27	47/51	35/38	7
9	27/30	52/56	38/40	7
10	29/32	55/60	42/45	7
11	31/35	59/66	46/50	7
12	32/36	64/69	51/55	7
13	33/38	68/74	55/61	7
14	36/38	76/84	62/66	7
15	38/42	84/92	68/73	7
16	39/43	96/104	74/80	7
17	45/49	114/124	84/90	7
18	49/53	120/132	90/99	7
19	50/57	132/144	99/109	7
20	53/61	148/160	109/118	7
21	59/67	163/176	115/125	6

Day hatched	Lowest	Weight (g*) Highest	Average	Number of chicks weighed
22	61/69	186/200	130/142	7
23	64/70	200/212	142/154	7
24	65/73	212/230	152/166	7
25	72/80	230/242	163/176	7
26	75/79	246/260	174/189	7
27	77/83	256/267	185/201	7
28	86/94	268/288	199/215	7
29	86/92	284/310	206/223	7
30	94/101	302/324	214/230	7
31	97/106	320/344	225/243	6
32	106/117	340/364	238/257	7
33	118/126	346/378	249/268	7
34	124/136	364/416	262/287	7
35	140/150	390/422	277/296	7
36	132/142	396/428	298/318	5
37	130/140	412/456	301/325	6
38	140/154	428/468	311/336	6
39	151/160	430/470	322/345	6
40	152/163	444/490	330/356	7
41	164/178	452/496	341/369	7
42	173/187	456/498	351/382	7
43	177/187	466/504	362/391	7
44	188/200	476/516	369/401	6
45	190/204	490/530	378/406	7
46	200/216	498/550	390/422	7
47	210/222	505/535	374/403	6
48	220/234	511/555	388/418	6
49	241/268	518/570	400/434	6
50	242/257	523/560	412/441	6
52	251/268	530/550	412/438	5
54	285/302	535/570	428/456	5
56	311/335	554/585	448/482	5
58	312/335	572/616	469/503	6
60	330/350	576/610	470/508	7
62	348/374	584/630	479/508	6
64	370/401	587/630	484/523	5
66	377/405	582/616	483/523	5
68	390/419	580/656	483/527	7
70	408/440	584/606	487/520	7
72	400/428	584/612	485/514	7
74	418/458	582/620	491/520	7
76	428/453	576/611	488/516	7
78	439/458	570/598	487/520	7
80	434/454	552/568	481/506	7

Day hatched	Weight (g*)			Number of chicks weighed
	Lowest	Highest	Average	
83	429/441	548/569	484/511	7
86	407/419	566/608	484/513	7
89	397/411	532/563	462/481	5
92	424/440	530/560	464/482	5
95	418/455	526/549	463/489	4
98	403/453	529/555	452/481	4
101	407/449	516/540	452/480	4
104	422/439	530/549	459/482	4
107	409/417	539/550	474/493	5
110	404/415	552/579	472/494	5
113	409/430	539/568	452/480	4
116	412/432	520/552	450/477	4

* 1g = 0.0353oz.

Table 8
Weights of hand-reared Umbrella
Cockatoos (*Cacatua alba*) at the
Aviculture Institute, California.

Day hatched	Average weight (g*)
	15.1
1	16.0
2	18.2
3	20.1
4	23.6
5	28.5
6	34.3
7	37.5
14	117.8
21	244
28	368
35	474
42	532

* 1g = 0.0353oz.
8–10 chicks were involved in the study.
No data was available beyond 42 days.
(After Joyner, Swanson & Hanson, 1990).

PROBLEMS ASSOCIATED WITH HAND-REARING

OVER- AND UNDER-HEATING

Retarded growth can be the result of maintaining a chick at too low a temperature. The energy in its food will then be used to maintain body temperature rather than to promote growth. If the temperature is too high and humidity within the brooder is low, a chick could become dehydrated and will start to lose weight. If a chick's toes appear thin and shrivelled, it is suffering from dehydration. Small, unfeathered chicks should be fed Ringer's Lactate or electrolytes at frequent intervals. Feathered chicks can be given this by subcutaneous injection (in the middle of the back).

It is difficult to suggest suitable temperatures for chicks being hand-reared; there are various factors to consider, such as environment, species and the needs of the individual. For newly hatched chicks the temperature should be the same as that at which the egg was incubated, with an extremely gradual reduction after a few days. In a brooder in which the heat source is two light bulbs overhead, I have noticed that chicks pant at a certain temperature, an indication that they are over-heated, whereas, at the same temperature in a brooder, where the heat from a dull emitter is circulated by a fan, the chicks appear quite comfortable.

Observation of the chick's behaviour gives a better indication of the correct temperature than does a thermometer! Over-heated chicks are restless, panting and widely separated from their companions. Chicks which are not warm enough are lethargic, huddled together and feel cool to the touch. Digestion may be slower than normal.

DISEASE

The first signs of disease are the crop taking longer than normal to empty and weight loss, or smaller weight gains. It might be possible to miss the fact that a certain chick's crop is slow to empty but if weight is measured daily, one has an exact record of each chick's development. If a chick's crop is nearly full when it should be empty, on no account give more food. Give only Ringer's Lactate, or molasses and water (some people give water in which rice has been boiled, but I have never tried this), and massage the crop. Repeat at normal feeding intervals until the crop is empty. If a chick is dying, these measures will not be effective. In the rare cases where there is no improvement, yet the chick is obviously not dying, the crop contents will have to be removed using a crop needle or syringe. If the hand-feeder does not feel confident enough to do this, he or she should take the chick immediately to a veterinary surgeon.

If chicks become ill their condition deteriorates quickly and, in many cases, one has little time to effect a cure. However, two of the most common causes, bacterial and fungal infections, can be confirmed or eliminated in a matter of seconds where the equipment and qualified staff are available. The breeder who works with a veterinary surgeon has a great advantage over those who work alone. It takes but a few minutes to prepare a Gram stain from faeces. With a microscope, one can see immediately if an excess of Gram-negative bacteria are present (indicating a bacterial infection) and whether the fungus *Candida albicans* is present or in excessive numbers. In the early stages, *Candida* infections usually respond well to treatment with Nystatin (Nystan) suspension (Squibb), which can be added to the food two or three times daily (three times initially).

The fungus *Candida* not only inhabits the mouth, where it can be seen as a soft whitish growth but may also grow in the crop. By the time this has occurred, and the chick is losing weight and vomiting, the infection will be very difficult to cure. However, infections will not reach this stage if weights are noted daily and weight loss acted upon.

These days parrot breeders have to be aware of the dangers of serious viral infections, such as papovavirus, which can reach epidemic proportions. If a virus condition is suspected, a veterinary surgeon must be enlisted to refer the case to a histologist, who may be able to isolate and identify the virus. Unfortunately, this is expensive and there is no cure for infected birds. But, if a virus is identified, appropriate action can be taken to prevent its spread. One step which can be taken is to use Virkon S (Antec Int., Chilton Industrial Estate, Sudbury, Suffolk CO10 6XD, UK), one of the few disinfectants which is effective against viruses. It can even be sprayed in the vicinity of small chicks. One very experienced breeder believed that it was responsible for stopping the spread of papovavirus among her chicks.

I have purposely emphasized some of the problems which can be encountered in rearing chicks, because every aviculturist should be aware of these before they start. They should try to make contact with an avian veterinary surgeon with some experience in paediatrics so that they waste no time searching for professional help in a crisis. They should also be in contact with an experienced aviculturist to whom they can turn for advice. However, when chicks are sick, they will need a veterinary surgeon for diagnosis and treatment.

Special attention must be paid to good hygiene. Everything with which chicks have contact – brooders, spoons, syringes and human hands – must be kept clean. Always wash your hands before picking up chicks, preferably in a solution of chlorhexidine (marketed under different names – e.g. Hibiscrub in the UK). If you syringe-feed, use a different syringe for each chick. If you spoon-feed, it is wise to either fill the spoon from a syringe or pour the food for each chick into a small container and discard what is left; this helps to prevent the spread of infection. Keep spoons and syringes in a solution of chlorhexidine and change this every day. Make up fresh food at least once, and preferably twice, daily and keep it in a refrigerator between feeds. Bacteria can grow on food very quickly.

Weaning

In my opinion, cockatoo chicks need the most careful attention during the weaning period. I have hand-reared nearly 100 species of parrots, including 11 species of cockatoos and, with the exception of Bare-eyed Cockatoos and Galahs, find them slower to wean than most other parrots. I believe it is wrong to hurry the weaning process because most cockatoos spend a long time with their parents in the wild. Galahs are easy to wean because of the short time they spend with their parents. At about 100 days they are deserted by their parents and form juvenile flocks (Rowley, 1990). On the other hand, black cockatoos (*Calyptorhynchus* species) have the most protracted weaning period of any parrot when hand-reared because they normally spend about one year with their parents. Those which are hand-reared take six to eight months to wean and most white cockatoos take about five months. Of course, many are independent before this age because the hand-rearer is simply not prepared to wean them slowly. However, some cockatoos, especially Moluccans, will allow themselves to be fed for weeks or even months beyond the age at which they are capable of existing without spoon- or syringe-feeding. One has to distinguish between those which genuinely need food from the spoon or syringe and those whch beg for food as a means of gaining attention.

Individuality is marked in cockatoos and becomes evident well before they are independent. The age at which young are weaned depends on factors such as whether it is reared alone or with other cockatoos, the sensitivity of the person or persons feeding it, and its sex. Males tend to become weaned earlier and be less 'clinging' than females. In commercial breeding establishments weaning has to be accomplished more quickly because of the numbers involved. At the Avicultural Breeding and Research Centre, Florida, the largest private parrot-breeding establishment in the USA, hundreds of cockatoos have been reared from the egg. There the weaning period commences at 45–50 days with two feeds per day. Weaning is completed at 85–95 days for the small species, 95–105 days for larger species (Umbrellas, Tritons and Long-billed Corellas, and Red-vented), 100–120 days for Greater Sulphur-crested and Moluccans, 120–130 days for Palms (nominate race), 130–140 days for Banksians and at 150–160 days for Goliath Palms (Schubot, Clubb & Clubb, 1992). However, it should be pointed out that, in many other collections, cockatoos are not weaned at such an early age.

Cockatoos differ from chicks of all other parrots known to aviculture in hatching with the ears open. This is clearly seen in this seven-day-old Umbrella Cockatoo (*Cacatua alba*).

FEEDING

Cockatoos usually start to pick up food when about two-thirds feathered. When seen testing items with the tongue, they can be given pieces of tender corn and wholegrain bread, for example. For a couple of weeks they will consume very little but the number of feeds should not be reduced. Soon they will be trying boiled maize and beans, peas, soaked sunflower and cracked walnuts. Orange and green items, such as raw carrot and leaves of spinach or cabbage seem to attract their attention. The initial food mixture can contain the above items plus chopped apple and orange and boiled peanut kernels. Spray millet is relished. Peanuts in the shell are crunched up for the pleasurable sensation and the nuts are dropped. (Note that boiling the kernels should kill any dangerous toxins they might contain.)

At this young age it is advisable to offer a very wide variety of foods because young birds are more inclined to experiment than adults. The items mentioned above are only suggestions. Countless others can be offered, e.g. peas in the pod, red and green peppers, zucchini, biscuits, muesli and other cereal, and cheese.

When young cockatoos start to eat on their own, the amount they consume is so small that hand-feeding should continue as normal. I do not reduce the number of feeds per day until they are eating significant amounts on their own. It is better to give slightly less food at each feeding, because the act of feeding seems to encourage them to eat on their own. When they are eating well, they may refuse food from spoon or syringe in the morning yet accept it eagerly in the afternoon and evening. Always ensure that the crop is filled at the last evening feed. Gradually reduce the number of feeds to three, then two, then one. If the young cockatoos seem excessively hungry, the number of feeds may have been reduced too soon and one feed will have to be reinstated. At the weaning stage, some cockatoos become very fussy about the consistency or the temperature of the food, so test an unwilling feeder with this fact in mind.

A problem sometimes encountered is that of a young cockatoo which is taking very little food from the spoon, yet is not eating sufficient on its own. Two tactics can be employed. First, try making the food more liquid than usual, as this is easier to give to an unwilling bird. Secondly, and this is probably the best ploy, introduce some competition. Instead of feeding the cockatoo on its own, take out another more willing feeder (of any species) and feed the other in front of it. Often it will reach for the spoon. Likewise, if a young cockatoo is slow to eat on its own, perhaps because it is the only cockatoo being reared, place it next to the cage of a young parrot which is eating well. Cockatoos are quick to learn by example. Many cockatoos tend to feel thinner at the weaning stage than most other parrots. This would be cause for concern only if a chick was very thin and not eating well, in which case it would need veterinary attention. In comparison with parrots of similar size, cockatoos tend to eat less. However, young ones need more food than adults and should have an unlimited amount until they are eight or nine months old.

CAGES FOR CHICKS

As soon as young cockatoos are old enough to perch, usually just after they start to eat a little, they can be moved from a brooder with a false wire-mesh floor to a cage. The cage should be made entirely of welded mesh, including the base, so that the young cockatoos are never in contact with their faeces. Newspaper can be placed beneath. If the birds come into direct contact with newspaper or a solid surface, it is very difficult to keep them clean. Large cages for cockatoos which are still being hand-fed are not recommended unless there is a door in each end; otherwise it can be difficult to reach inside and pick them up. Larger cages are not necessary until they are independent.

An experiment to minimize imprinting

In 1992 I hand-reared, from a few days old, two Moluccan Cockatoos hatched at Palmitos Park. For several reasons I was reluctant to leave them with their parents, although I have reservations about hand-rearing this species when it is required for breeding. My previous experiences with Moluccans related to young which were difficult to wean, cried pathetically for attention and continued to cry as long as a person was present. As they were kept in a small area where 60–70 other parrots were being reared simultaneously, it was difficult to ignore their cries but impossible to give them as much attention as they craved. Four years later, when the first Moluccans hatched at Palmitos Park, and where I alone fed them, I tried something quite different. From the start I tried to minimize contact with them. When they were 10 weeks old I moved them to an empty quarantine room. Next to their cage I placed an adult male Moluccan which had previously been on exhibit in the park, an untamed bird without a mate. For three weeks, until they started to flap their wings, I took them to the hand-rearing room four times, then three times daily, to feed them. For the rest of the day they saw only the adult Moluccan.

Their behaviour was totally different from that of those I had previously reared. They never cried for attention or swayed from side to side. Their vocalizations were the high-pitched whistling note and other sounds natural to the species. They were curious about me, as young cockatoos are curious about everything they come into contact with, but they never exhibited that disturbing 'clinging' behaviour which is unacceptable in birds destined for breeding.

Selling and buying unweaned young

Some breeders try to sell as many unweaned young as possible, because weaning is so time-consuming; indeed, there are some hand-rearers who have never weaned a parrot in their lives. They sell them to pet shops or to individuals who require a pet, persuading them that if the young bird is to become closely bonded to them they must complete its rearing. This is totally untrue. I abhor the sale of unweaned young. Too

Hand-rearing cockatoos in isolation, except for an adult member of their own species, helps to prevent them becoming imprinted on human beings. This is important if they are to be used for breeding purposes.

often they go to people who lack the experience to complete the task. Or they might go to a pet shop or dealer whose premises are not clean, pick up a virus and die. Of course this can happen to any cockatoo younger than about six months old, because its immune system does not function properly until this age.

Unweaned, feathered chicks are sometimes shipped by air and the stress of such a journey is likely to make them ill. If you do not have the time or the patience to wean chicks, and you cannot employ someone to do this for you, it is better to move them at any early age, perhaps at about the time the eyes open – although such a move should not involve a long journey. When they are nearly feathered, they are very sensitive to change. If you wish to acquire a young cockatoo as a pet, do not be persuaded by the breeder to complete the rearing of an unweaned chick. Do not learn on a cockatoo! If you wish to gain experience in this way, start with a couple of Cockatiels! (But do not try to rear them from the egg.)

Acquiring a hand-reared cockatoo

If you buy a recently weaned cockatoo which, you are told, is totally independent, ask if it was spoon-fed or syringe-fed and on what food. Because some species of cockatoo are so sensitive, they may not feed when moved to a new location. If an adult bird refuses food for 24 hours, no great harm is done, but lack of food and fluid can have a serious effect on a young bird. Be prepared! Be ready to hand-feed it for a few days. If it has been syringe-fed, but you do not wish to do this, be aware that most young parrots readily take warm food from a spoon if they are hungry.

A young hand-reared cockatoo is a sweet and trusting creature whose personality will be greatly affected by the way it is treated. If it is hit, teased or abused in any way, the damage done may take years to repair or could be totally irreparable. A household with young children or any other members who cannot be trusted to treat a cockatoo with respect, is no place for such a bird. The fact that you can sell it if it does not fit in with your household should not even enter your mind. You must be totally committed to keeping it as long as you or your family survive. Cockatoos and other parrots suffer terribly when they are discarded, sold and passed on like used toys. They are precious living creatures whose companionship will enrich the lives of those who treat them with love and respect.

9

Pets, personality and imprinting

Do you really want a cockatoo? Have you any concept of what you are taking on when you buy one – or a pair? Most first-time buyers of a cockatoo have no idea of the responsibility entailed in keeping it and, if they had, many would not have decided to purchase one. To a lesser degree this applies to all pets – but a cockatoo is possessed of greater intelligence than most. It is also a highly social creature which suffers acute boredom and loneliness. To keep one alone is to deprive it of what it needs most – the company of its own species. Some cockatoos accept a human companion as a substitute mate but so demanding do many become of the object of their affection that they will scream when their owner is absent. Or like many cockatoos which are not provided with a mate of their own species, they start to pluck themselves or, worse still, even mutilate their flesh.

In short, there are many reasons for not keeping cockatoos as pets. Their very destructiveness is reason enough for most people. They cannot be left unattended outside their cage in a room for two minutes because of the damage they can carry out. No one who is house-proud should even consider keeping a cockatoo as a pet because it is cruel to confine it permanently to a cage. Some cockatoo-owners are not prepared to adapt to the bird's needs, but neither will they admit that they have made a mistake. Instead, the unfortunate bird is relegated to some disused room or even outbuilding. This is the worst form of cruelty that anyone could inflict on a cockatoo, especially if it is also given metal rather than wooden perches (because they do not have to be constantly replaced). Deprived of any occupation for beak or mind, the poor bird will start to remove its feathers, or even to mutilate itself. I am constantly amazed at how little understanding many people have of the intelligence and psychological needs of the larger parrots. They treat them like overgrown Budgerigars and appear to believe they need nothing more than a cage, seed and water.

Wild-caught birds as pets

Cockatoos offered for sale fall into four main categories:

(1) Wild-caught birds which are not tame.

(2) Wild-caught birds which have been kept as pets and are tame.
(3) Hand-reared captive-bred birds which are usually extremely tame and affectionate.
(4) Parent-reared captive-bred birds, which may or may not be tame, depending on their history.

Wild-caught adult birds of nervous species such as Umbrella and Moluccan Cockatoos may never become tame. They suffer great stress from being closely confined and are suitable only for aviaries. Wild-caught birds which have spent many years in captivity sometimes make good pets. The personality of the individual bird, the way it has been treated, the sensitivity of the person caring for it and whether or not the bird likes that particular person are the relevant factors.

The effects of neglect

Unfortunately, one sees many cases of neglect in Australia where the native Greater Sulphur-crested Cockatoos – surely one of the most intelligent birds in existence – can be obtained for a few dollars. Because they are so cheap and plentiful, many end up in the hands of people who treat them in much the same way as they would an ornamental cockatoo made out of stone for a garden decoration. I have seen such birds, relegated to the garden, kept alone in a cage in which they can barely turn round, and thrown a handful of sunflower seeds when someone remembers. The owners may be quite unaware of the cruelty they are inflicting on a sensitive bird. I would implore Australians who are cockatoo-lovers to try, gently, to explain this to the owners of such birds, and to encourage them to give the birds to someone who has a single bird and a large cage. Nothing can transform the plight of such birds as quickly as a companion of their own species, even if the two are just kept side by side for company. On no account must one be placed immediately in the cage of the other as the newcomer is likely to be attacked.

Avicultural magazines are full of sad tales of cockatoos which have been rescued by sympathetic people; there are many more ill-treated cockatoos to whom fate is not so kind. The following is quite typical. A pair of cockatoos was advertized in a local paper. Out of curiosity a parrot-breeder went to see them.

In two small parrot cages were two Umbrella Cockatoos. The hen bird although fully feathered had bent all her tail and wing feathers, the cage being so small that she couldn't turn round without catching something on the cage bars or food dishes. The feather condition of the cock was awful, he had bitten every tail and wing feather in half, partially plucked his breast and legs although had not started on the down except in tiny patches. I questioned the young man; he had gone into a local pet shop 2½ years ago to "Buy a parrot" and had seen these two beautiful birds together in a cage. I quote: "They looked so nice" – so he bought them. The two birds remained in the same cage for the next two years until the cock bird started to pluck the hen bird: a separate cage was then purchased for the cock who then proceeded to pluck his own feathers . . . Entertainment was in the form of a rolled up newspaper stuffed through the bars of the cage; diet was sunflower, sunflower and more sunflower . . . (Paul, 1991)

The breeder fortified a spare aviary and returned two days later to buy them out of sheer pity. He wrote:

. . . one month later what a transformation; the hen looks quite presentable and I haven't seen the cock bird mutilate himself. The days are spent hollowing out an old tree stump, food of any description is eaten readily . . .

He added the footnote: 'My wife adores them.'

Relationships with people

Let me recount my experiences with a male Citron-crested Cockatoo. His history was known from the time he was received by a dealer; he was probably an unwanted pet bird. He was then purchased for breeding but no female could be found and he was sent on loan to a bird garden which possessed a female. The two birds were instantly compatible but, sadly, after a few months, the female died. No replacement could be found so, after a year or two, the male was returned to his owner. At weekends he came into my care – caged. I found he was highly nervous and hissed in fear when anyone approached. His dislike of men was very obvious. After several weeks I noticed that he would speak to me late at night when I was alone in the room for a short while. I would talk to him, from a distance of a metre or so, to gain his confidence.

After a few weeks he was in my care for seven days a week. He ceased to hiss when I replenished his food and water and called more often for me to talk to him, which I could do from a range of a few centimetres. He seemed to be inviting me to rub his head. However, nervous birds are often afraid of hands and are liable to bite out of fear rather than malice. As he accepted my face very close to him, with the bars of the cage between us, I moved my nose so that I could rub his head with it. From experience I know that parrots accept noses more readily than hands; obviously, one has to be very cautious at first. The Citron-crested enjoyed this attention so much that I was able to bring my hand up to my nose and rub his head with my finger after a few days. Never, at any time, did he try to bite me.

I knew that I had won his confidence but he then became extremely demanding: screaming loudly for me to rub his head, dancing up and down and erecting his crest to attract my attention. At times he was a little too demanding. The intention had never been to make a pet of him but to make his life a little happier until a female could be located. This took six months from the time he came into my care full time. As far as he was concerned, the relationship between us ended the second he set sight on the female. She was caged near him for a day but they were obviously so anxious to get together that I gave way to their wishes. His behaviour changed the instant he was placed with the female. It was as though I was a complete stranger to him. He hissed at my approach – as did the female – and no longer allowed me to rub his head. I was delighted that he rejected me so totally and wanted only the female's company. A month later the pair was placed in an outdoor aviary and the male no longer showed any sign that we had once been friends.

I wish I could say that they lived happily ever after, but with cockatoos there are too many stories which do not have fairy-tale endings. Six years later the male attacked the female. She died from her injuries. As is so often the case, they had always appeared compatible. Then came the problem that many cockatoo-breeders unfortunately have to face. What do you do with a male which has killed a female? Living on a small island, I could not obtain another female even if I had wanted one, and it was impossible to devote a breeding aviary to a single bird. The male therefore had to go into a cage in an area containing other single birds. He appeared unhappy and was continually throwing down his food and water pots. He remained extremely nervous.

Feeling sorry for him, I decided to bring him into my house. History repeated itself but the taming process was much more rapid. After several weeks I knew, again, that he wanted me to rub his head. From the moment he allowed me to do this – with my hand – he demanded more. I had to set aside a few minutes for him each evening or he would scream for attention. He was becoming very demanding when a tiny female Lesser Sulphur-crested arrived on the scene. She had been in a large aviary with other cockatoos for several years, then removed some of her flight feathers and was unable to fly. I housed the two side by side then, after a few days, placed them together in a 2m- (6½ft) long suspended cage without a nest box. I did not want to produce hybrid young but neither did I want either bird to be alone and bored. They live together amicably, but without the close bond that existed between the male and his previous female.

This story demonstrates several points. One is that the same cockatoo will behave differently towards people according to the circumstances, also that some cockatoos (in fact, many) will form a relationship only with a man, or only with a woman. Above all, it shows that some will give you their heart, but only until something better, i.e. a member of their own species, comes along.

Cockatoos behaving differently according to the circumstances is well illustrated by the example of a Goffin's which was given to someone who understood cockatoo behaviour very well. Its constant screaming, biting and feather-plucking led the owners to believe that it was unsuitable as a pet. In its new home, the Goffin's was kept in the living room for what was intended to be a temporary period. However, he behaved so well he became a permanent resident. From the start a schedule was adopted whereby he was not allowed out of his cage until 8 p.m., then:

> . . . when he would hear the clock strike eight, he would begin to strut about until given his freedom. He was an extremely loving bird, very obedient, a good talker, and an absolute clown. We could not have asked for a better bird in a home situation. (Atkinson, 1992)

Why had the bird's personality apparently changed? Simply because, in its previous home, it was competing for attention with two other birds and was kept in a separate room by the family's daughter. It naturally resented this isolation and lack of attention. As Julie Atkinson commented: '. . . one too many additions in the household can turn a loving, enjoyable pet bird into a biting, screaming monster!'

From the foregoing it should be clear that, in cockatoos, individuality is marked and their behaviour towards a particular person cannot be predicted. Many a man has bought himself a cockatoo, only to find it will have nothing to do with him but is totally devoted to his wife (or *vice versa*). If a cockatoo takes a dislike to someone, it is normally useless for this person to persevere with the idea of keeping it as a pet. Either a mate must be obtained for it, and the birds placed in an aviary, or it must be found a home with someone it does like. Much stress will be caused to a sensitive bird if it is forced to live in close proximity to someone it dislikes.

If a cockatoo has a good rapport with its 'owner', however, the joy it will show in the company of that person is unmistakable. A really tame bird will want nothing more than to sit on its owner's lap and have its head rubbed, or simply to snuggle up to his (or her) face and perhaps

Pet cockatoos, such as this Galah (*Eolophus roseicapillus*), often form a strong like or dislike towards members of their household. It is useless persevering with a cockatoo which dislikes you!

fall asleep. If permitted, some would stay in that position for hours on end. The tamest cockatoos are extraordinarily docile, lying down contentedly in a manner which is more cat-like than parrot-like. No other parrot behaves in quite the same manner except, I am told, the Kakapo (*Strigops habroptilus*).

Cockatoos in the house

The major problem with very tame cockatoos is that they scream to be let out of their cages, or for attention. The very strength of their voices means that they cannot be ignored at such times. A cockatoo has to be made to understand that it will be let out of the cage at the same time each day, perhaps for a couple of hours in the evening or whenever is convenient. Giving in to its demands at other times will result in an uncontrollable pet. Therefore, right from the start, one must develop a routine.

DISTRACTIONS

Some cockatoos may be persuaded to use a stand while out of the cage. This will help to distract their attention from the furniture. A stand can be made very easily by making a hole in the centre of an old coffee table and fitting a branch into it. Many happy hours will be spent gnawing the bark. When this has been removed, the branch can be replaced. Leather chews made for dogs will also provide amusement and beak exercise.

Do not provide any toys made of plastic as these would be quickly destroyed and the fragments could cause injury, especially if swallowed. Nuts which are difficult to crack are among the most suitable objects to occupy a cockatoo's attention. Offcuts of untreated wood are also good but usually last only a few minutes. However, a cockatoo *must* have something at which to gnaw; this is a normal behaviour which must not be denied.

FREEDOM WITHIN THE HOUSE

Cockatoos kept as pets (most of them in cages which are far too small) need a period of wing exercise every day, something they look forward to greatly. This is impossible unless the bird is hand-tame or stick-trained, as it must be possible to return it to the cage when desired. Even cockatoos which are not tame can, in most cases, be stick-trained without much difficulty. In many situations this is very important. Many purchasers of affectionate, gentle, hand-reared cockatoos which are as cuddly as kittens fail to realize that the day may come when their bird is adult and far from sweet-tempered. Some cockatoos remain easy to handle when mature; others, more especially males, are not.

STICK-TRAINING

Catching a cockatoo in a net or with a towel is quite safe if done properly but it does cause a certain amount of stress (certainly to the bird and often also to the catcher). If it can be moved or returned to its cage in a couple of seconds using only a stick, everyone benefits.

The shorter the stick, the less threatening it will appear to the cockatoo; it should be no more than 60cm (24in) long and the diameter should be similar to that of a normal perch. Leave the stick lying by the side of the cage for a couple of days before attempting any training. Cockatoos are very sensitive about unfamiliar objects, often displaying or screaming in fear at the most harmless things. (Remember this and never place things temporarily on top of, or next to, your bird's cage.)

It is easy to stick-train a hand-reared bird as it has less fear; it can be difficult or impossible to stick-train a wild-caught bird, which may associate sticks with ill-treatment experienced when it was trapped. If the cockatoos is wing-clipped but used to sitting on top of its cage, place the cage in a corner, let the cockatoo come out, then slowly approach with the stick. If it panics, do not proceed but repeat the process daily until it is used to the stick. Then, gently press the stick just above its legs. Try not to let it climb down the side of the cage. Be prepared for slow progress, repeating the lesson once or twice daily until it climbs on to the stick. Do not try to move the stick until the bird is quite confident about stepping on to it. Always talk quietly during the training period and afterwards reward the bird with a tit-bit. The next stage is to move the stick a small distance, always with slow movements and talking quietly. Continue the training until you can confidently carry the cockatoo on the stick for a short distance.

If the cockatoo is not wing-clipped but the cage is large, stick-training can be tried within the cage. If the cockatoo is tame, little training will be necessary. Start and end each session by scratching its head so that it associates the stick with pleasure. If you are hand-rearing a cockatoo for a pet, stick-train it as soon as it learns to perch. It is more comfortable for the handler to carry a bird in this way because the claws are sharp and young birds, especially the larger species, cling on tightly.

'TALKING' ABILITY

Generally speaking, cockatoos are not among the most talented 'talkers' within the parrot family. Many will learn to mimic a few words, especially when they are young. Those kept on their own have the greatest potential. Two young Goffin's which I hand-reared never learned a word, although they were kept indoors. Another hand-reared Goffin's from the same parents, which was kept on its own for several years, became a good 'talker'. Cockatoos mimic words because they are trying to communicate in our language. If kept with other cockatoos, most have no interest in this form of communication.

Initially a short, easy phrase should be repeated, such as 'Come on' or 'Hello'. When this has been mastered, another can be taught. If a cockatoo is capable of something more complicated, teach it your telephone number as proof of identity, should it be lost or stolen. The success of this will depend on the numbers involved; 'six' is a difficult word for a parrot to repeat. (As further proof of identification, ask a veterinary surgeon to implant a micro-chip in the bird.)

COCKATOO LANGUAGE

Someone who is not familiar with cockatoos will be unable to interpret some of their behaviour. Hissing and swaying, for example, which can be seen in all species except *Calyptorhynchus*, is indicative of fear, often induced by the close presence of a human being or other alien object. This behaviour is also exhibited by chicks in the nest well before they are feathered. To continue to disturb a cockatoo which is behaving in this way will cause it stress.

A common action by *Cacatua* species is to rapidly click the beak, moving the tongue at the same time. This means that the bird wants to make friends, although the action may be tinged with caution. If it is accompanied by a raised crest or other signs of excitement, exercise great care! Beak-clicking is probably normally used by females during courtship to have a calming affect on the excitable male. Do not confuse beak-clicking with the slower beak-clacking, which is a sign of alarm and fear. In the Moluccan, it is accompanied by foot stomping: clenching the foot and striking it on the perch. Such a bird is afraid and should be left alone. Most white cockatoos hiss and sway in fear, even chicks in the nest. Cockatoos have been described as dramatic birds, overflowing with theatrics and emotion. How true this is!

INTELLIGENCE AND AWARENESS

It is interesting to compare what we might describe as intelligence or awareness in different species. John Courtney, an Australian ornithologist who has also reared many native parrots, wrote to me in 1990:

> The young of some species being reared give the impression of being quite blank; others are quite 'aware' of what is going on around them – a few species enormously so. My impression of young Banksians was that they are not stupid, as are young Pink Cockatoos and Leadbeater's, but they were not all that bright. Glossys that were being reared and are quite big, seem to have an unnerving 'presence', or awareness of their environment. I have noticed that several very sensible people who lost big young Glossys that they were rearing, were somewhat distraught about it. Even years afterwards when offered another Glossy, some look at you with pain in their eyes and say 'Oh, no, I could never go through *that* again!'
>
> I think it is because Glossys *are* intelligent, and in addition are friendly and co-operative to people, so a very considerable rapport develops between the owner and their tame male (females are usually aloof). I do not know if 'awareness' or 'presence' is intelligence – perhaps just alertness. Young Yellow-tailed Black Cockatoos have little 'presence' yet, in the wild, adults are so intelligent that they *deliberately* create an artificial perch, on the side of a smooth vertical trunk, to stand on with the least fatigue while they take ten to 15 minutes to chop out a grub deep in the heart of a sapling!

Behavioural disorders

FEATHER-PLUCKING

Self-plucking (removing or biting the feathers) is common in parrot species of a nervous temperament, especially cockatoos. They usually start by removing the feathers of the breast, then the thighs; primaries and secondaries are bitten off in more serious cases. In extreme cases, they mutilate their flesh; if this occurs a collar must be fitted (but may not stay in place long) and the cause of the problem must be rapidly investigated. Plucking and mutilation are most often pyschological or stress-related and, much less often, due to pain or an infection.

Common causes are neglect, loss of the person to whom it was bonded, reaching sexual maturity without the opportunity to breed and, in females, fear of the male (even though they may appear compatible). The following are examples from birds in my care during the past two years. A Triton Cockatoo, an unwanted pet and probably wild-caught, was donated to the park. It was not possible to give it individual attention and so it started to pluck itself. After a year or more the decision was made to give it away to a lady who had no other pets and no children. She lavished attention on it, plucking ceased and it feathered perfectly. Case number two was a tame, wild-caught female Moluccan which had been kept alone and was badly plucked. She was obtained by the park and provided with a male with whom she appeared compatible. She quickly feathered up, except for a small area on the upper breast. The pair nested within a few months and produced a chick which died (probably killed) at four days. Since that time, three months ago, she has resumed plucking herself. Cases three and four were Tritons which had been reared in the park several years previously. Kept in a large aviary with other cockatoos, they both commenced to pluck themselves. Both were moved from the park to the breeding centre and placed in an area with various other birds in cages where there was fairly constant human activity. One ceased to pluck and feathered up well; the other become much worse. It was finally cured by placing it with a family.

Environmental enrichment
This process, i.e. providing the affected bird with more opportunities for activity and beak exercise, is to date a mainly neglected solution to feather-plucking, but one which will surely come to be recognized as the cure in many cases. The biologist at Rotterdam Zoo, Catherine King, devised a programme of environmental enrichment for the female of a pair of Blue-eyed Cockatoos which had been together for eight years. She was badly plucked, only the back, crest and tail feathers being in good condition. The pair was observed for three weeks

during the 'pre-enrichment' period then changes were made in the aviary based on these observations. Ropes were repositioned and smaller branches were added connecting larger perches, nest site and the inside shelter; the flightless female could thus more easily move about the enclosure, which measured 3m × 2m × 3m high (10ft × 6ft × 10ft high) with a small 90cm (3ft) cube shelter. A log was placed in a more central position. Two branch holders were filled with branches and corn stalks for gnawing and soft wooden blocks and rawhide dog toys were attached to ropes or chains close to perches.

Prior to the enrichment period, both birds had spent about 75 per cent of the observation time in the nest log or the inside shelter. During the enrichment period the female spent signficantly more time in object-orientated activities. This period of observation lasted only two weeks because the male began pushing the female off her perch; the relationship between the two birds did not improve and the male was removed to the adjoining enclosure six weeks later. A marked improvement in the female's plumage was observed about one month after environmental enrichment activities commenced and prior to separation of male and female. Her plumage continued to improve until the frequency of enrichment activities decreased; then she recommenced feather-plucking. The male was reintroduced in March 1992, copulation was observed on the second day and the female laid an infertile egg in mid-April. The female's plumage appearance started to deteriorate and the male was removed at the end of May (King, in press). My own interpretation of these events is that, while the enrichment activities had a beneficial effect on the psychological welfare of the female, the root of the problem was the stressful effect of the male's presence. I mentioned above the plucking female Moluccan which improved when placed with a male and hatched a chick. However, after they had been together for about a year, she started to mutilate the flesh under her wings. This behaviour continued when she was separated from the male.

IMPRINTING

Cacatua species
A cockatoo hand-reared in the absence of other cockatoos (but in the presence or absence of other parrots) usually becomes very imprinted on the person who has reared it. It is more difficult to wean and is constantly crying for food and/or attention. If, however, it is reared with a sibling, or even with another species of the same genus, from an early age, it will react with this cockatoo and show less interest in the person or persons rearing it. If it receives minimal human attention, a few months after independence it will be steady but not especially tame – perhaps tame enough to nibble one's fingers but not tame enough to

Self-pluckers, such as this Triton Cockatoo (*Cacatua galerita triton*), need to keep their beaks occupied. Pine cones – the larger the better – are excellent for this purpose.

permit being handled. Such birds are ideal for breeding purposes.

However, there is a difference in the way that hand-reared young of different species react. Generally speaking, the nervous, sensitive species, such as the Moluccan and the Umbrella, wean more slowly and imprint more easily, whereas the more independent species such as the Bare-eyed Cockatoo, and the Galah, wean more quickly and, unless they receive a great deal of human attention, are less likely to become imprinted. This may be connected with the breeding biology of the species. In those in which several young are reared in a nest, such as Galahs and Bare-eyed Cockatoos, the young have to be more forceful or 'pushy' to compete with each other. But in the species in which normally only one youngster would be reared, i.e. black cockatoos, Moluccans and probably Umbrellas, the single offspring is dependent on the parents for much longer and is more gentle in temperament.

Calyptorhynchus *species*

It seems that most imprinted white cockatoos are useless for breeding (proper research is needed into this subject), but this is not the case with the *Calyptorhynchus* species. It has been known for years that hand-reared male Banksian Cockatoos often remain imprinted on people yet, in some cases, this does not impair their ability to fertilize eggs. They can have a normal relationship with a female of their own species as well as close relationships with one or more human beings.

This is also true of the Glossy Cockatoo. I took part in what seemed an extraordinary incident when visiting Neville and Enid Connors in New South Wales. The Glossy is their favourite species and they have more than one breeding pair. One day I entered the aviary of their best breeding pair to obtain the photographs which appear in this book. Two days previously the female had laid an egg (which was in the incubator as she had shown no interest in it). As soon as I entered, the male, to whom I was an almost complete stranger, came and stood on my feet. I offered my hand and he at once allowed himself to be picked up. Then he displayed to me, bowing his head, spreading his striking tail and making the distinctive and unique double call. He would have kept this up for minutes on end to keep my attention.

Enid entered the aviary and picked up the female. To her surprise – as this had never happened before – the female started to 'copulate' with her hand. We could only surmise that, jealous of the attention the male was receiving, she was directing her attention to Enid. If this was a totally imprinted pair that were useless for breeding their behaviour would have been surprising, but in a pair regularly producing young, it seemed extraordinary. It is but one of the exceptional qualities owned by members of this genus.

10

Detecting, preventing and treating disease

Many aviary and pet birds die unnecessarily from disease: they could have been successfully treated if those caring for them had been quick enough to respond to the early signs of ill health. Cockatoo-owners must therefore learn to detect these signs. In order to do so, all aviary birds should be observed carefully twice daily, in the early morning and in the afternoon or evening, because the progress of some diseases is extremely rapid. Pet birds are generally under constant observation and therefore any change in behaviour should be quickly recognized as a possible indication of illness. In an aviary, however, accidents or injuries can be discovered too late to help the injured bird. For example a bird that has been trapped overnight by its ring or foot is likely to die from shock, whereas one which is quickly released will suffer little ill effect.

When making the twice-daily check, always investigate any sign of blood on the perches or floor. The most usual sources are injury to a toenail or toe or bleeding from a damaged blood feather (one which is still growing). Usually the bleeding stops quite soon and no action is necessary. If this is not the case, a broken nail, for example, must be cauterized and veterinary assistance sought.

Checking your birds

When checking your birds, there are three basic steps to take. First, carefully observe the bird itself, secondly look at its faeces and, thirdly, check the food.

APPEARANCE OF THE BIRD

An efficient observer can detect in a split second if there is something wrong with a bird with which he or she is familiar. Its eyes usually give an instant 'read-out'. If they are dull or slightly sunken, not shiny and bold, the cockatoo is sick. Except in a youngster, the same is usually true of a bird which has food adhering to the beak. Two signs of ill health which are almost too obvious to mention are:

(1) Ruffled plumage.
(2) Resting with the head tucked into the feathers of the back on *two feet* (quite often, very young birds do this, but healthy adults seldom do so).

More subtle warning signs may go undetected. For example, if one enters an aviary or passes close by it, and a bird takes longer than usual to fly away (assuming that it is not tame), look more closely. Some tame parrots seem to try to attract attention when they are ill, sometimes resorting to juvenile food-begging behaviour, moving the head up and down and making food-soliciting calls.

APPEARANCE OF THE FAECES

The second method of detecting illness is to look at the faeces. It is impossible to say what is normal for a species, as this depends on the diet. The observant keeper will know what the faeces normally look like in a particular bird – usually light or dark green or light brown with almost equal amounts of white (urine). Sometimes a change in the faeces is apparent before the bird itself shows any indication of ill health. Fresh blood in the faeces, or dark reddish-brown or reddish-black droppings, indicate that blood has been digested. This could be symptomatic of haemorrhagic enteritis, septicaemia or of poisoning. The advice of a veterinary surgeon should be sought at once; antibiotics will be necessary, usually given by injection, as they then act more quickly.

Do not try to treat a sick bird with any antibiotic for birds which you may already have. It may prove useless in the illness, or even harmful, and can prevent a veterinary surgeon or biologist from obtaining the correct result when an antibiogram is made using a culture of the faeces. An antibiogram indicates the most effective antibiotic to use. In cases of urgency, a veterinary surgeon will give a broad-spectrum antibiotic until the result of the antibiogram is known.

Sometimes a stressful act, such as the bird being caught from an aviary and placed in a cage, will cause a temporary alteration in the appearance of its faeces, which become white and very liquid. This is no cause for alarm if they soon return to normal. If nothing has stressed the bird, however, it is a sign of sickness. Very liquid droppings mean that the bird is passing a lot of urine and will soon become dehydrated, if it is not so already. It needs to be given fluid subcutaneously. Electrolytes such as Amynin (made by Rhone Merieux, also containing amino acids and Vitamin B complex) should be injected by a veterinary surgeon or nurse beneath the skin under the neck, or a little below this area. Electrolytes can be fed into the crop using a spoon or syringe, but will be absorbed more quickly by subcutaneous injection.

Examination of the faeces can also reveal that there is something wrong with the bird's digestive system. This is the case if they contain undigested food. The first step is to catch the bird and examine it. If it is very thin, yet appears to be eating well, it is seriously ill. The advice of a veterinarian must be sought as it could be suffering from proventriculus dilatation, a fatal disease which can spread through an entire collection of birds. It is one of the more recently discovered virus diseases which are responsible for the deaths of large numbers of parrots in collections, especially in the USA. Proventriculus dilatation is not the only diagnosis; there are a number of other causes of undigested food in the faeces. An avian veterinary surgeon may be able to establish the cause.

Affected birds must be offered food items which are easy to digest; however, they must be items which they willingly eat or they may stop feeding entirely. Severely underweight birds may have to be force-fed, using a syringe and plastic tube or a special crop needle. Do not attempt to do this without previous experience, or instruction from a veterinary surgeon or other qualified person.

Note that partly digested food on the aviary floor could have been vomited. Or it could be the result of courtship feeding in which partly digested food is regurgitated from the crop. However, unlike most other parrots, courtship feeding is rare in cockatoos.

If a sick bird has to be force-fed, a crop needle (above), or a syringe with a plastic tube attached, must be used to place food into the crop. Tame birds and chicks can be fed using a spoon with the sides bent inwards.

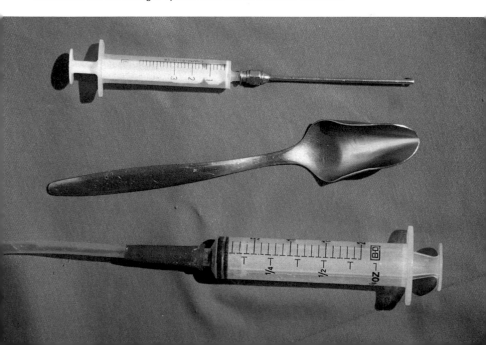

FOOD

The last item to be checked is the food. If you do not feed the birds yourself, ensure that the food dishes are present, in the correct position and containing the right food. If a food dish is, for some reason, placed on the floor instead of in an elevated position, some birds would starve to death rather than descend to floor level. During the second check of the day, note how much food has been eaten. In abnormal weather conditions, many birds will eat less than usual; otherwise, reduced food consumption could indicate that a bird is sick.

Other symptoms of disease are: discharge from the eyes or nostrils, prolonged sneezing and coughing, eye infections and lesions in the mouth. All these require the attention of a veterinary surgeon for proper diagnosis and treatment. For example, discharge from the eye could be a symptom of Chlamydia (psittacosis) or it could be as common and easily rectified a problem as Vitamin A deficiency. Many cage and aviary birds which are fed incorrectly, especially those which receive only seed, suffer from a deficiency of Vitamin A. There are a number of powdered supplements, made especially for birds, with a very high Vitamin A content. Sparingly sprinkled on food (most cockatoos will refuse food which has been liberally sprinkled with any powder), these supplements will correct the problem in most birds. Vitamin A can be injected but, because it is oil-based, it is a difficult and slow procedure. Fortunately, some foods which many cockatoos accept are high in Vitamin A (see Chapter 6).

Disease

PREVENTION

All parrot-owners should be aware of the fact that, in many instances, it is easier to prevent disease than it is to cure it. The five most important factors in prevention are as follows:

(1) Quarantining new birds for five weeks or more. The fact that they remain in good health during this period is no indication that they are not carrying disease; however, moving birds to a new environment is usually a stressful period in their lives, when disease is most likely to become apparent. Where an avian veterinary surgeon is available to undertake faecal and blood tests, take advantage of this important service which enables many serious diseases to be detected before the affected bird enters your collection, possibly endangering the life of every bird in it.

(2) A good diet, not deficient in the most important vitamins, minerals and amino acids.

(3) Reducing stress to a minimum. Common causes of stress are:
    (a) aggression or persecution by other birds; (b) extreme weather
    conditions, especially rapid changes of weather, for birds kept in
    outdoor aviaries; (c) change of accommodation, whether or not this
    involves travel; (d) in the case of pet birds, the absence of the
    person to whom they are emotionally attached and, in other birds,
    removal of the mate of a closely bonded pair; (e) in potential pet
    birds, excessive handling or disturbance of nervous birds.
(4) Good hygiene, especially in enclosed areas where dried faeces, dust
    from cockatoos' plumage, or mould growing on faeces or discarded
    food, can harbour harmful spores or viruses. Rodent and pest
    control also comes under this heading because of the diseases which
    can be spread by rats, mice, opossums, cockroaches, wild birds etc.
(5) A supply of clean water. Disease organisms, such as *Pseudomonas*,
    are commonly spread via the water supply. For a small collection,
    drinking water can be provided in the form of bottled water or
    water which has been boiled; in the latter case it will be necessary to
    add calcium. Where these measures are impractical, the water
    should be cultured on a regular basis in order to detect any bacteria
    present. This might seem extreme but it is a necessary precaution.

In abnormal weather conditions many birds eat less than usual;
otherwise reduced food consumption could indicate ill health. Most
cockatoos are active and noisy. Unless recently moved to a new location
or of a highly nervous temperament, those which are quiet and listless
are almost certainly sick. This book cannot cover all diseases and
parasites which can be found in cockatoos but at least one book devoted
to disease and treatment in parrots should be on the bookshelf of every
cockatoo owner. (See Further Reading, pp. 122–3, and References
Cited). One disease which unfortunately is encountered by many
cockatoo-owners is psittacine beak and feather (PBFD). Because of its
widespread incidence and fatal conclusion, it is accorded a separate
chapter (see Chapter 11). Other diseases with which cockatoo-owners
should be familiar are described below.

PACHECO'S DISEASE

Pacheco's disease is caused by a virus, undoubtedly one of the most
serious to affect parrots, because of the speed with which it can spread
through an entire collection. It is carried by many South American
parrots, especially conures, which may shed the virus under stress. In
the USA, where thousands of wild-caught conures enter pet shops
annually, pet stores are a common source of the disease. Unfortunately,
carriers show no symptoms and birds usually die four days after being
infected by the carrier. They may show no sign of ill health until an

hour before they die. Murphy (1991c) related the case of a Nanday Conure (*Nandayus nenday*) which was taken to a pet store to have its nails and wings clipped. Four days later three Umbrella Cockatoos and one Moluccan Cockatoo, plus a Blue and Yellow Macaw, died within hours of each other. The Nanday was a carrier of this disease. The disease is diagnosed by microscopic examination of tissue after an autopsy. Typical herpes inclusion bodies are present in the liver of a bird which has died from Pacheco's disease.

In the USA vaccines are available and it is recommended that birds which have been in contact with conures, or in breeding establishments which include conures, should be vaccinated. However, a veterinary surgeon reported (in the *Journal of the Association of Avian Veterinarians*) a severe reaction in Umbrella Cockatoos which had been vaccinated with Biomune Inc.'s Pacheco's Vaccine. Four were vaccinated and each one developed severe reactions under the skin. The lesions ulcerated at the site of the injection and spread down the body to the area of the vent. All required surgery on one or more occasions to remove the lesions. Further symptoms were vomiting, depression, listlessness and lack of appetite. In some, symptoms did not appear until up to two months after the second vaccination but, in one bird, abscesses formed within two weeks of the booster vaccination. One cockatoo had been vaccinated a year previously with an intramuscular vaccine (Pacheco's from Maine Biological) without reaction. It was reported that, in 200 birds vaccinated with Biomune, only Umbrella Cockatoos had suffered this reaction (Anon., 1991).

The reaction of one Umbrella was described by its owner, Cheryl Dawley. Three months after vaccination, he became very lethargic. A veterinary surgeon was unable to find anything wrong, except a reluctance by the cockatoo to use one foot. Gradually, however, his beak and nails began to grow long. Another veterinary surgeon was consulted, who took blood and faecal samples. The blood sample revealed that the cockatoo's white-cell count had reached astronomical proportions – more than 100,000 (a normal count ranges between 8,000 and 12,000). There was so much protein in the blood that it was difficult to prepare the serum. Examination of the bird revealed a small hard lump in the area of the vent and it was decided to operate two days later.

The cockatoo's owner waited at the surgery while the operation was performed and inadvertently discovered the origin of the problem, which, until then, was unknown. While waiting, she reached for the most recent copy of the *Journal of the Association of Avian Veterinarians*, which happened to be the one referred to above, and read the description of the reaction to the vaccine in Umbrella Cockatoos. The operation on the Umbrella revealed much 'soft, slippery' material which extended all the way up the bird's side. An incision nearly 10cm

(4in) in length was made to remove most of it. The operation was a success. Next day the cockatoo was screaming and displaying his crest for the first time in months. It was an early indication that a full recovery was to be made (Dawley, 1991).

SARCOSPORIDIOSIS

In areas of the USA where opossums occur, this has been described as a common cause of parrot fatalities in outdoor aviaries (Murphy, 1991a). The protozoal parasite *Sarcocystis falcatula* is excreted by opossums (see p. 44) and, when ingested by parrot, spreads to the organs from the intestines. Linings of blood vessels, especially those of the lungs, are affected, resulting in acute pulmonary haemorrhage. Normally there are no symptoms and death is sudden. Murphy reported:

> In the cockatoos, we often noticed that the mate would traumatize the dead bird. Unless an autopsy was performed, it would be easy to mistake the death for mate aggression. In more sub-acute forms of the disease, the birds appear to lose their balance (ataxia), and mentally appear dazed.

Affected birds may be suffering from dehydration because they cannot reach the water container. In the chronic form, they become emaciated and usually show neurological signs, such as loss of balance, trembling and stupor. Autopsy may reveal aspergillosis, a secondary disease probably due to immuno-suppression by the sarcosporidiosis. Murphy stated that diagnosis is very difficult; the parasite is barely visible, even when using a light microscope. Unless the pathologist is looking for sarcocysts, they are usually overlooked. There is no specific test in living birds.

ASPERGILLOSIS

One of the most serious fungal diseases to which parrots are susceptible is aspergillosis, which is usually due to infection by *Aspergillus fumigatus* and possibly other members of the same genus. It is most likely to affect the respiratory system but can occur in other parts of the body. It was (or is) often found in wild-caught birds which have been held in warm, damp, poorly ventilated buildings, especially in crowded conditions, prior to export, or even after export in quarantine. Some birds harbour *Aspergillus* spores without showing any signs of ill health but, when stressed by export, over-crowding etc., the disease breaks out. These days, the numerous commercial breeders who keep parrots in enclosed indoor areas, often at a high density, should be aware of the dangers of this disease. One effective method of diagnosis is laparascopy. When birds are sexed surgically, a competent veterinary surgeon will examine other organs, including the air sacs, where aspergillosis shows up as bluish-green areas. Another method is to make a swab from the trachea and culture it on special media. Treatment is unlikely to be successful in well developed cases, i.e. when the breathing is laboured and the bird has already lost weight. When diagnosed in the early stage as a result of laparoscopy, the prognosis is much better if the bird is nebulized. Nebulization is the inhalation of atomized fluid. Modern ultrasonic nebulizers produce a uniform drop size of only 0.1–0.5 microns, enabling the medicine to reach right into the lungs (Kaal, 1986a). The tank of the nebulizer is filled with distilled water, to which is added the appropriate medicine. The cage is covered so that the droplets do not escape and the bird is treated in this way for perhaps three periods of 20 minutes daily.

While in the Philippines, Dr Elisha Burr found that, in contrast to other species, the nests of Red-vented Cockatoos were often highly contaminated with *Aspergillus* spores (Alderton, 1989). David Alderton believed that the reason why wild-caught birds of this species have proved difficult to establish is due to aspergillosis contracted in the wild.

PARASITIC WORMS

Most cockatoos in aviaries obtain great enjoyment from walking about on the ground, digging and playing. This makes them vulnerable to parasitic worms, because worm eggs can remain viable for months in an aviary with an earth floor. In Europe few breeders use this type of floor surface and in the USA most cockatoos are (regrettably in all aspects except worm control) kept in suspended cages. In Australia, however, most cockatoos are kept on earth floors; thus *Ascaridia* and *Capillaria* worm infections are not uncommon. Melbourne veterinary surgeon Stacey Gelis described to me how he was called to attend a female Leadbeater's which could not fly.

> On examination the bird was so thin you could have shaved with its keel bone. A faecal smear revealed thousands of roundworm eggs. Judging by the bird's body weight, this was obviously a chronic problem. There was blood in the droppings, no doubt due to the high level of intestinal damage caused by the severe worm burden. Despite the poor outlook, and after one week's intensive hospitalization, the bird improved enough to be sent home.

In parrots, the most common parasite is the roundworm (*Ascaridia columbae*). Females are said to be capable of laying one million eggs per year; eggs can easily be seen if the faeces are examined under a microscope. The only other parasitic worm commonly found is *Capillaria*, usually *C. obsignata*. Both species usually inhabit the intestines. The third most common parasitic worm is the tapeworm, which grows in segments and can cause obstruction of the bowel. Newly imported parrots are the most likely to be affected with tapeworm, because the source of infection is consumption of an insect which has eaten droppings containing tapeworm eggs. Try to prevent worms from becoming a problem by taking the following measures.

(1) Ask a veterinarian or biologist to examine a faecal smear from any newly obtained birds. Note, however, that the result will not be conclusive as worm eggs may not be voided in all droppings.
(2) If a bird in the collection dies and an autopsy is performed, ask the pathologist to examine the intestines for worms. *Capillaria* worms can be overlooked as they are often difficult to observe.
(3) Avoid earth floors; if you have to use them, sterilize the surface with a blow lamp several times a year. Hose down concrete floors frequently and scrub them several times a year. Otherwise use a deep layer of large pebbles and hose it frequently, so that worm eggs will be washed downwards out of reach of the birds.
(4) If a bird is thin, has watery droppings and/or seems listless, seek veterinary help to rule out worms or to treat the problem.
(5) Do not place food dishes on the ground, as this encourages birds to spend more time there.

If *Ascaridia* or *Capillaria* worms are identified, the affected bird must be treated. Levamisole (Nilverm) is the most widely used drug against these species. Consult a veterinary surgeon for dosage (there are preparations of different strengths) and method. The most effective is to use a crop needle to place the preparation directly into the crop. As this medicine is bitter, it will rarely be taken if placed in the drinking water unless fruit, greenfood and water are withheld for about 12 hours or the drug is mixed with glucose or honey – and, in the case of birds in outdoor aviaries, it is not raining at the time.

Treatment for birds affected with tapeworms is Droncit, either as an injection or in the form of tablets which are not water soluble and must be crushed finely and disguised in a favourite item of food.

FILARIAL WORMS

Filaria, or threadworms, are parasites introduced into the blood by certain flies and mosquitoes. These worms, of the genus *Ornithofilaria*, can be diagnosed with the aid of laparoscopy. It may be possible to see the very thin filaria moving about in the abdominal air sacs (Kaal,

1986b). They can cause cutaneous swelling; swollen joints may be filled with fluid containing filarial worms, especially in Indonesian Cockatoos.

LEAD POISONING

Because of the inquisitive and destructive nature of cockatoos (and lack of thought by the keeper), birds have died as a result of swallowing foreign bodies. For example, a Moluccan swallowed a hair clip 5cm × 0.5cm (2in × 1/5in) which perforated the gizzard wall, causing severe peritonitis. The cockatoo had to be euthanized (Evans, 1992). Many items found in the house are potentially dangerous because they contain lead (e.g. foil bottle tops). Lead poisoning should be suspected if a cockatoo is lethargic and depressed, has convulsions or diarrhoea, or is regurgitating or head-twirling. An X-ray will confirm the presence of lead in the intestines. If radiography is not possible but the evidence points to this, treatment should commence at once; it can do no harm, even if the diagnosis is not correct.

Evans advises:

Treatment involves using a product Calcium EDTA which binds lead in the body and increases the rate of excretion. Antibiotic cover is also provided and fluids given to control dehydration due to decreased intake. Response to therapy is often dramatic, but if nervous signs were evident the prognosis is not good.

Two extremely experienced avian veterinarians commented that 'cockatoos tend to be the most resistant to psittacosis of all the large parrots', yet the most sensitive to disease in general, showing the least resistance to most psittacine diseases other than psittacosis (Rosskopf & Woerpel et al., 1990). This statement is interesting but does not concur with my own experience, which is mainly confined to keeping cockatoos in outdoor aviaries. They have proved very hardy with very few cases of disease, the main problems being feather-plucking and aggressive males. It may be that the writers' clients are primarily pet-owners and their cockatoos are kept indoors; under these conditions different problems arise.

Further reading

Arnall, L. & Keymer, I. F. (1975) *Bird Diseases* TFH, New Jersey, USA.
Doane, B. M. (1992) *The Parrot in Health and Illness* Macmillan, UK.
Gerstenfeld, S. (1981) *The Bird Care Book* Addison-Wesley, Wokingham, UK.
Low, R. (1991) *Hand-rearing Parrots* revised edition. Blandford, London, UK.

Low, R. (1992) *Parrots: Their Care and Breeding* 3rd revised edition. Blandford, London, UK.

Murphy, J. (1992) *Dr Murphy's Parrot Care* Avian Press.

Rowley, I. (1992) *Behavioural Ecology of the Galah* Surrey Beatty and Sons, Australia.

Schubot, R. M., Clubb, K. J. & Clubb, S. L. (1992) *Psittacine Aviculture* Avicultural Breeding and Research Centre, Florida, USA.

Sindel, S. & Lynn, R. (1989) *Australian Cockatoos* Singil Press, Australia.

11

Psittacine beak and feather disease (PBFD)

There is one disease, above all others, that can be described as the scourge of the cockatoo family: psittacine beak and feather disease (PBFD). It became recognized as a problem, then nameless, in the late 1960s. At that time I was answering queries on parrots submitted to the weekly magazine *Cage and Aviary Birds*. In 1972 I wrote in that journal:

> . . . there is one subject which recurs again and again. It never fails to fill me with despair because it is something to which I do not know the answer and, to the best of my knowledge, no one else does either. (Low, 1972)

It was years before a virus was identified as the cause of the problem.

At that time the Lesser Sulphur-crested was the most frequently imported and inexpensive of the cockatoos and the one most likely to be kept as a pet. I quote here from three letters received then.

> A few months ago I purchased a young Lesser Sulphur-crest in good feather but since it moulted out the new feathers are deformed and do not knit together. There are no flight feathers at all. This bird is lively and talks well.

> During the past year my Lesser Sulphur-crest has been constantly losing his feathers. He has only two flights left and no tail feathers; they grow until they are about 1in in length and then fall out.

> A few months ago I bought a Lesser Sulphur-crested Cockatoo. Its plumage was very dirty but it could fly. It has now lost rather than gained more feathers and is becoming bald on the head. It appears quite well in itself, eats a variety of seeds and is quite plump.

A fourth case involved a Lesser Sulphur-crested which died after about three years. For the first few months it was in perfect feather condition. Its feathers deteriorated and it became very thin and weak. After about two years the beak started to rot.

Since this period, 20 years ago, the disease has been named and recorded in every species of cockatoo. At first it was believed it might be peculiar to this family but over the years it has been found in 35 species of parrots, more rarely in neotropical species (Ritchie, 1990). It can affect them differently. For example, the disease is common in Vasa Parrots (*Coracopsis*), in which the first sign is the plumage becoming pied with white.

In cockatoos, the earliest symptoms may be seen in the beak or in the plumage. Affected feathers appear abnormal, break easily and usually have blood in the shaft. Sometimes there is a thickened sheath adhering to the feathers. The disease may be mistaken for feather-plucking but, often, the head and crest feathers are affected; as a single bird cannot reach these areas, clearly the cause is not self-plucking. Usually the plumage is affected before the beak, but the beak can be affected first. It grows quickly, develops fault lines, breaks or rots. Normally a cockatoo's beak does not have a shiny appearance (unless it has just had a bath) because the powder produced by the powder-down feathers makes it dull. If the beak is glossy it is due to the fact that the powder-down feathers have ceased to grow, another sign of the disease. A Palm Cockatoo with PFBD looks black, not dark grey. (The plumage of this species is actually black but is made dull by the powder down received during preening sessions.)

The gradual progression of the disease results in cockatoos becoming thin and listless. If the affected bird is a family pet and euthanasia is not acceptable (because the bird is not severely depressed), it must be kept warm and given unlimited food because, without feathers, it cannot adequately maintain its body temperature. Because PBFD damages the immune system, the affected bird is very susceptible to secondary infections. It should be isolated, not only to prevent further infection but also because it is continually shedding the virus. In an enclosed area, this virus, which is found in diseased and disintegrating feathers and in dried faeces, can be inhaled. Affected birds are therefore a source of danger to other young parrots. This is why the disease was so often found in imported young cockatoos at their first moult in captivity. When very young they were held in crowded and unhygienic conditions at the premises of an exporter; here they contracted the virus but this did not become evident until the next moult. There are reputed instances of cockatoos aged between 10 and 20 years showing the first signs of PBFD, but whether the disease was confirmed is not known.

According to David L. Graham, director of the Schubot Exotic Bird Health Center in Texas, the onset of clinical signs may occur as early as 3–12 weeks of age. In a series of 176 diagnostic submissions in which the ages of affected birds were known, 162 (92 per cent) were aged three years or less and 14 (8 per cent) were aged over three years. This indicates that susceptibility to the disease is strongly age-related.

Circumstantial evidence and anecdotal reports suggest that cockatoos maintained alone until one or two years of age are thereafter at much reduced risk of developing PBFD, even if placed in intimate contact with affected birds. It appears that nestlings and juveniles are most susceptible and older birds are resistant, if not totally unsusceptible to natural modes of infection. It was hypothesized that the bursa of Fabricius (functional only during early life and disappearing as a recognizable structure before sexual maturity) is a primary and requisite site of infection. The incubation period of PBFD appears to be variable, ranging from a few weeks in nestlings to two to three years or more in birds exposed as juveniles (Graham, 1990).

In Australia several species of parrots in the wild have been observed with signs of PBFD, in addition to cockatoos. Many young cockatoos collected from the wild and sold in pet shops are affected. Indeed, in 1992 it was stated that: 'Pet shops in Sydney have not dealt in Sulfur-crested Cockatoos over the past three years' because of the high incidence of the diesease (Marshall & Crowley, 1992). One man who examined stocks in various shops concluded that at one location 11 out of 12 birds were affected (Kerr, 1991). Possibly he was correct but, without a feather biopsy or blood test, it is impossible to make a correct diagnosis. Indeed, some aviculturists believed that the disease was identified in young cockatoos by dark feathers on the head and/or body. An interesting study in which 400 young cockatoos were taken from nests by a licensed and experienced trapper showed that 75 per cent of young carried dark feathers and that there was no correlation between this and PBFD (Marshall & Crowley, 1992).

The aim of the study was to determine a method of collecting wild young cockatoos, which were free of the disease, for the pet trade. It was felt that control of stress and exposure to the infection were the most important factors. Certain precautions were therefore taken, such as young, which had been pre-sold, being placed in darkened boxes on capture and immediately transported to Sydney, where they were placed with ther new owner by the following morning. Advice on hand-feeding, hygiene and cages, and instructions not to expose the young to other parrots until after the first moult, was given. Feather biopsies were taken from 50 of the 400 on capture, then each bird was clinically assessed every three months for one year after capture. Of the 50 examined, 38 showed no feather pathology at the time of capture but five of these developed clinical signs within one year. Of the 50, 11 had, or developed, PBFD. It was concluded that this number could be reduced significantly by leaving siblings of PBFD young in the nest; in future, no nestlings from infected nests will be taken.

Research on the development of a viral vaccine is concentrated at two locations: Murdoch University in Australia, led by Dr David Pass, and the College of Veterinary Medicine at the University of Georgia in the

USA. Dr Branson Ritchie, who leads the research team in the USA, has described the virus as:

> a 14–16nm diameter, icosahedral, non-enveloped virion. [The size of these particles is significantly smaller than reported for any previously described pathogenic virus isolated from animals (3–8nm smaller than parvovirus).] Based on the radical differences in virion dimension, polypeptide composition, and nucleic acid size and conformation, we suggest that the etiologic agent of Psittacine Beak and Feather Disease is a prototype for a new family of pathogenic animal viruses. (Ritchie, 1990)

In 1991, at the School of Veterinary Studies at Murdoch University in Western Australia, research was continuing to devise a reliable blood test to detect the presence of infection with the virus. The test is dependent upon producing antibodies against the purified proteins of the virus (there are three main proteins with a trace of a fourth). The proteins must be separated and antibodies produced against the separate proteins. Once this had been done, the blood test can be developed and the antibodies linked to fluorescent dyes to study the distribution of the virus in the body. The blood test will enable further work to be carried out on the disease in captive and wild populations. It is also an essential component of future research on vaccines (Pass, 1991).

This important research is being retarded by lack of funds. Such an important project deserves financial help from *everyone* who keeps parrots, partly because ultimately they will benefit when a vaccine is available. At the present time many aviculturists are suffering heavy financial losses as the result of the disease, to say nothing of the suffering of the birds involved. Breeders and clubs could do no better than follow the example of a lady called Sylvia Nolan, Northern Territory. She raised A$18,500 in 2½ years by holding raffles and street stalls and selling T-shirts.

As already stated, at the present time, there is no treatment for birds suffering from this disease. Dr Joel Murphy pointed out:

> Reports of birds responding to therapy are undoubtedly due to infections caused by polyoma virus which can mimic the clinical appearance of PBFD. Adult parrots with feather disorders caused by polyoma virus sometimes recover and occasionally respond to immunostimulating drugs. (Murphy, 1991b)

By late 1991 Dr Branson Ritchie and Dr Frank Niagro had developed a DNA probe test which is more accurate than a feather biopsy and which, predicted Dr Murphy 'will become the standard diagnostic test in the near future'.

PREVENTING THE SPREAD OF PBFD

Prevention is very difficult because parrots may shed the virus without showing any clinical signs of the disease. Therefore, before any cockatoo enters a breeding collection a feather biopsy should be carried out or, when available, a DNA probe test. A feather biopsy is done under anaesthesia. The sample is then examined by a pathologist for PBFD inclusion bodies. The experience of Dr Murphy over a period of four years was that only one out of 30 cockatoos which had negative results from a biopsy later contracted the disease.

Obviously, any bird which shows signs of the disease must be isolated, given away as a pet to a household with no other parrots, or euthanized. The risks of it being in contact with other birds have already been described.

One precaution which is taken by some commercial breeders in the USA is to remove eggs from all cockatoos for artificial incubation. The resulting chicks are reared in a separate, sterile environment. This has reduced the incidence of the disease in these collections. However, it is not totally effective. Dr Ritchie has shown that transmission via the egg is possible. In one case three chicks hatched from an infected Bare-eyed Cockatoo. They appeared normal until the age of 32 days when the oldest and the youngest were totally denuded by the virus. Even though viral DNA was detected in white blood cells of all three at only 20 days, the middle chick did not develop clinical signs until 80 days of age. Its body feathers were already mature so that the only growing, active, epithelial cell targets for the virus were the still-developing primary and secondary feathers (Ritchie, 1992a).

By 1991 Dr Ritchie's team had made important advances towards eliminating PBFD in captive birds and in ensuring it was correctly diagnosed. They had developed a specific test system in which infected feathers stain blue only when PBFD is present. Using this test, they discovered that many birds were being incorrectly diagnosed as positive for PBFD, and that some had been euthanized unnecessarily.

This technique also demonstrated that the virus circulates in the blood of an affected bird (in the white blood cells). This explains how a young bird's feathers can be destroyed in as little as five days. The virus actually lives in the cells which are responsible for defending the bird against disease. This may be why an infected bird does not develop protective antibodies.

Research into how the virus is transmitted has produced some significant results. The virus was isolated from 26 per cent of PBFD-positive birds sampled. PBFD virus particles could be demonstrated in crop washes from 21 per cent of birds tested. Finding virus in the crop suggests that adults can transmit the virus to chicks when feeding them. High concentrations of the virus were recovered from feather dust in a room containing infected birds. It was concluded that feather dust must be a major route for transmission and thus the environmental persistence of the virus is explained.

Ritchie's team discovered that it is not the age at which clinical signs first appear that determines the progress of the disease. The virus produces a different appearance in birds aged 35 days, 80 days and one year. There can be prolonged incubation periods, from three weeks up to many months. There are also asymptomatic birds (which carry the disease but show no symptoms). Unless such birds can be identified, PBFD will be impossible to control. Therefore a very sensitive, specific DNA probe was developed that can be used on a small amount of blood in order to diagnose all affected birds.

The research team produced evidence that a vaccine could be effective in preventing PBFD and produced an experimental vaccine, by taking virus from an infected Moluccan Cockatoo and mixing it with beta-propiolactone (to inactivate the virus); they then inoculated a group of parrot chicks aged 30–45 days and a group of adult birds, including Umbrella and Sulphur-crested Cockatoos. Local tissue reactions to the injections were minimal; a few Umbrella chicks developed a small area of reactive inflammation at the site of injections. It was found that all the birds would produce antibodies after these vaccinations. However, disease control will require vaccination of adults and chicks. It was found that chicks hatched from female Umbrella Cockatoos and Grey Parrots which had been vaccinated are temporarily resistant to PBFD virus exposure, suggesting that maternally transmitted immunity is important in protecting chicks from virus exposure. Maternal antibodies in chicks wane and then the chicks are susceptible to infection. The vaccine developed was a model whereby a commercially-feasible product could be evaluated. Its production would be a major advance in aviculture. However, it is unlikely that a cure for affected birds will ever be found (Ritchie, 1992b).

12

Phylogenetic studies of the cockatoos

by Simon K. Joshua and Prof. John S. Parker

All species of the Cacatuinae have the characteristic crest which can be raised as a sign of alarm or excitement. In addition, cockatoos have powder down, a gall bladder and feathers lacking the Dyck texture which gives many other parrots the green of their plumage. However the classification of this group of parrots has been revised many times using different features of the organism. Earlier studies of the cranial osteology (Thompson, 1900), tongue musculature (Mudge, 1902), and carotid arteries (Smith, 1975) have been enhanced by more recent biochemical and isozyme (enzyme protein) investigations (Adams et al., 1984) and DNA hybridization studies (Sibley & Ahlquist, 1990). These studies have been applied to a variety of species and none is complete. Van Dongen and de Boer (1984), and more recently Christidis, Shaw and Schodde (1991), have studied the chromosomes of five species and we have recently extended this chromosome data with studies of a further eight species (Joshua, 1992). Thus all seven genera and 16 of the 17 species have been studied by taxonomists, with four genera and 13 species (75 per cent of the total) having been studied chromosomally (Joshua, 1992). The Glossy Cockatoo (*Calyptorhynchus lathami*) remains to be studied either chromosomally or by any other techniques.

Morphology has been used as the basis of most phylogenies but is complicated or confused in some cases, due to a degree of convergent evolution of characteristics. Examples of convergence are shown by the crest of the cockatoos and Horned Parrakeet (*Eunymphicus cornutus*) and the brush tongue of the Loriidae and the Swift Parrakeet (*Lathamus discolor*). The chromosome complements (karyotypes) of the species of both these examples show that there is no close relationship between the species (Joshua, 1992). Divergent evolution can produce mis-interpretations of the relationships of taxonomic characters.

The subject of taxonomy is always one of considerable discussion and controversy. However the continuous discussion only serves to strengthen the arguments for and against the use of various characters as taxonomic evidence and enhances the resulting phylogenies and classifications of the group. We use here the taxonomy of Forshaw (1989) and make modifications using evidence from a variety of sources.

There are a number of features of the cranial osteology of the cockatoos which allow species within this group to be readily identified and defined as members of the Cacatuidae (Thompson, 1900). The cockatoos have a complete orbit and the suborbital bar is fused with the frontal and squamosal processes to form a bridge across the temporal fossa. The Cockatiel (*Nymphicus hollandicus*) also has features which are shared by the Cacatuidae, yet Thompson suggests, with reservations, that there are certain similarities to the Platycercines (rosellas). However the inclusion of the Horned Parrakeet (*E. cornutus*), as a species showing similarities to members of the Cacatuidae by referring to the presence of a crest, may have resulted in this somewhat erroneous statement. The crest of the Horned Parrakeet, however, is unlike that of any cockatoos in structure. Convergent evolution has resulted in the presence of a crest in both species but can perhaps also account for similarities in cranial osteology. Other studies (e.g. chromosomal, Joshua, 1992) do not reflect similarities between *Eunymphicus* and the Cacatuidae.

Mudge (1902) states that a number of muscles of the tongue are primitive in the cockatoos, suggesting the cockatoos are a primitve group within the Psittaciformes. A number of differences identify *Calyptorhynchus* species, *Cacatua* species, the Palm Cockatoo (*Probosciger aterrimus*) and Cockatiel (*N. hollandicus*), but also the Galah (*Eolophus roseicapillus*), as being distinct. The differences in tongue musculature between species often contradicts other taxonomic evidence, or shows convergence with other groups, and can serve to isolate the species in terms of their feeding methods and sources of food. However, they can also exhibit considerable convergence in development due to coincidental similarities in food, which confuses the phylogenetic relationships using these characteristics.

The phylogenetic positions of the species within the Cacatuidae can be suggested using a number of techniques in addition to the morphological data. The genetic and biochemical differences between species can give us an indication of their evolutionary relationships. The combination of a number of different and independent techniques which study different features of the organism reinforces these suggested relationships.

Adams *et al.* (1984) used biochemical characteristics to investigate the relationships between the cockatoos. A range of different isozymes were analysed by electrophoresis. The results were represented in terms of the extent of similarity (number of differences) in proteins between species – in simple terms, the greater the number of proteins that they have in common, the more closely related the species. The results of these studies demonstrate the genetic divergence and evolutionary relationships of the cockatoos, although the role of the proteins, with respect to evolutionary separation of species, involved in the analysis are unknown.

Twelve species were studied by protein electrophoresis and the Cockatiel (*N. hollandicus*) was shown to be more closely related to the cockatoos than to other parrots. Adams *et al.* suggest that the true cockatoos should form two groups – the white cockatoos (*Cacatua* species), the Galah (*Eolophus roseicapillus*), and the Gang Gang (*Callocephalon fimbriatum*) in one group, and the black cockatoos (*Calyptorhynchus* species) in the second group. The Palm Cockatoo (*Probosciger aterrimus*) was omitted from this study.

Sibley and Ahlquist (1990) studied the DNA similarity of Leadbeater's Cockatoo (*Cacatua leadbeateri*) with the DNA of the Galah (*E. roseicapillus*) and Cockatiel (*N. hollandicus*). DNA–DNA hybridization measures the overall similarity of the DNAs of different species, by allowing reannealing of DNA from two species at a time. This limited DNA data show *Cacatua leadbeateri* to be closer to *E. roseicapillus* than to *N. hollandicus*. The data also show *N. hollandicus* to be much closer to the other two cockatoo species, in terms of DNA hybridization, than to other species of parrots which were included in the study (*Trichoglossus haematodus*, *Barnardius zonarius*, *Brotogeris cyanoptera*, *Amazona ochrocephala* and *Poicephalus meyeri*).

The chromosomes of birds have a characteristic organization which is shared only by some reptiles. The autosomes (chromosomes which occur in identical pairs) can be grouped by size into macro-chromosomes (larger) or microchromosomes (smaller), although the distinction between these groups is often difficult to define and is a grouping mainly for convenience. The non-autosomal sex chromosomes are defined as the Z- and W-chromosomes. The male has two Z-chromosomes, the female one Z- and one W-chromosome. The Z-chromosome is a macrochromosome, usually the fourth largest, while the W-chromosome is usually a much smaller microchromosome. The total number of chromosomes in birds is relatively high in comparison to other animal orders, and averages 80 in the cockatoos.

The six species of *Cacatua* which have been studied chromosomally (*C. leadbeateri*, *C. sulphurea*, *C. galerita*, *C. alba*, *C. moluccensis*, *C. ophthalmica*) have identical karyotypes which consist of eight pairs of telocentric autosomal macrochromosomes showing a gradual decrease in size to the microchromosomes which are also telocentric. The chromosome number is $2n = 82$. The Z-chromosome is metacentric and the fourth largest chromosome, while the W-chromosome in female karyotypes is much smaller and usually acrocentric. The Moluccan Cockatoo (*C. moluccensis*) has been previously reported by Schmutz and

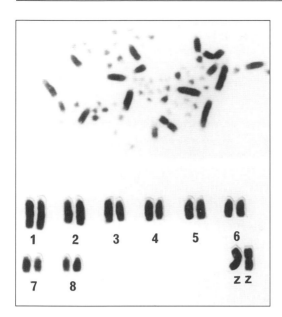

Metaphase cell and karyotype from a male Leadbeater's Cockatoo (*Cacatua leadbeateri*). The first eight pairs of macrochromosomes and the two Z-chromosomes are shown in the karyotype. There are 41 pairs of chromosomes in total.

Prus (1987) as possessing a single acrocentric pair (largest autosomal macrochromosomes); thus it would differ from the other species of *Cacatua* in this single characteristic. However, our own studies of over 20 different individuals of *C. moluccensis* have demonstrated a conventional, *Cacatua*, telocentric, autosomal karyotype. It is possible that the individual studied by Schmutz and Prus possessed a chromosomal polymorphism or an error has been made in the construction of the karyotype due to the low number of individuals and chromosome preparations studied. Goffin's Cockatoo (*C. goffini*) and the Long-billed Corellas (*C. pastinator* and *C. tenuirostris*) also lack acrocentric chromosomes although Adams *et al.* (1984) suggest a division of this group from the other species within this genus from isozyme data. Adams *et al.* (1984) have suggested that the Galah (*E. roseicapillus*) is most closely related to the corellas (*C. tenuirostris* and *C. pastinator*), although chromosomally it is more similar to the Cockatiel (*N. hollandicus*).

There is unfortunately no chromosome data from the Gang Gang (*Callocephalon fimbriatum*) and the relationship of this species to the other Cacatuidae remains unclear. Adams *et al.* (1984) suggest a link to the white cockatoos in isozyme analysis. Thompson (1900), however, suggests similarities in cranial osteology which link this species to the genus *Calyptorhynchus*, although *Callocephalon fimbriatum* has a number of characteristics which are not shared by any species of *Calyptorhynchus*.

The Banksian, or Red-tailed Black Cockatoo (*Calyptorhynchus banksii* formerly *C. magnificus*) has a similar karyotype to *Cacatua* species (Van Dongen & de Boer, 1984). The Z-chromosome is, however, submetacentric, unlike the metacentric Z of species in the genus *Cacatua*. There is also a reduction in chromosome number from 2n = 82 to 2n = 78. The karyotype of the Palm Cockatoo (*P. aterrimus*) differs greatly from that of the white cockatoos and *Calyptorhynchus* species. The four largest pairs of autosomes are acrocentric and there is a reduction in chromosome number from 2n = 82 in *Cacatua* species to 2n = 74. The number of differences in the karyotype would suggest that the phylogenetic similarity of *P. aterrimus* to *Cacatua* species is less than that of *Calyptorhynchus* species to *Cacatua* species. This relationship is not confirmed by the isozyme data (Adams *et al.*, 1984) although none is available from *P. aterrimus*. The cranial osteology (Thompson, 1900) and tongue musculature (Mudge, 1902) show *P. aterrimus* to be quite distinct from the other cockatoos but with some similarities to macaws.

The Galah (*E. roseicapillus*) exhibits fusions of telocentric macrochromosomes. Pairs 2 and 3 are acrocentric and there is a reduction in diploid number to 2n = 76 from 2n = 82 in *Cacatua*. It is therefore clearly distinct from *Cacatua* species as well as from *P. aterrimus* and *Calyptorhynchus* species, which all possess a telocentric karyotype considered by Christidis (1991) to be the ancestral arrangement. Adams *et al.* (1984) suggest a link between *E. roseicapillus* and the corellas (*Cacatua tenuirostris* and *C. pastinator*) but suggest an even closer relationship with the Gang Gang (*Callocephalon fimbriatum*).

The majority of evidence, whether from cranial osteology, tongue musculature, isozyme analysis or chromosome data, in addition to the feeding behaviour and morphology of the chicks, supports the inclusion of *N. hollandicus* within the cockatoo group which is otherwise divided into two main lineages – the predominantly white species and the predominantly black species. The tenuous evidence against the inclusion of *Nymphicus* with the other species of cockatoo includes the indirect head-scratching behaviour and the wing spots of the female and immatures. It is suggested that these characteristics link *N. hollandicus* most closely with the platycercine broadtails and polytelitine Australian parrakeets (Thompson, 1899). The studies of isozyme variation suggest that the closest link of *N. hollandicus* is with the black cockatoos (*Calyptorhynchus* species) (Adams *et al.*, 1984). Chromosome studies, however, have revealed considerable similarities between the Cockatiel (*N. hollandicus*) and Galah (*E. roseicapillus*) karyotypes and these are quite distinct from *Cacatua* and *Calyptorhynchus*.

The Z-chromosome of *N. hollandicus* is sub-metacentric (not metacentric as identified by Christidis *et al.*, 1991) and differs from that of *E. roseicapillus*, which is metacentric. Pair 2 is metacentric. This, coupled with the reduction by one pair of macrochromosomes from eight to seven, suggests a fusion of two pairs of macrochromosomes (pairs 7 and 8) to form the large metacentric pair 2. This suggests the separation, on the basis of karyotype, of *Nymphicus* from other genera within the Cacatuidae since it exhibits a unique chromosome arrangement. Adams *et al.* (1984) suggest a closer link to the black cockatoos on the isozyme data. It is thus clear that the lineage of the Cockatiel is quite distinct, its karyotype being unique. However, the link with the 'true' cockatoos is obviously a close one, demonstrated by the behaviour of the Cockatiel and the behaviour and appearance of the chicks. The main morphological differences are that the Cockatiel is the smallest member of this group and the only one to have a long tail.

The absence of chromosome data from the Gang Gang (*Callocephalon fimbriatum*) does not allow its genetic or evolutionary relationship with the other cockatoos, white or black, to be established.

The phylogeny of the cockatoos, based on the available evidence, shows a number of groups of species – *Cacatua* species, *Probosciger*, *Calyptorhynchus* species, and *Callocephalon fimbriatum*, *E. roseicapillus* and *N. hollandicus* being distinct. *Cactua* and *Calyptorhynchus* are more closely related than is *Probosciger* to *Cacatua*, with the remainder falling in between these groups.

Chromosome data, although incomplete at present, seems to offer some of the most consistent evidence for the taxonomy of this group.

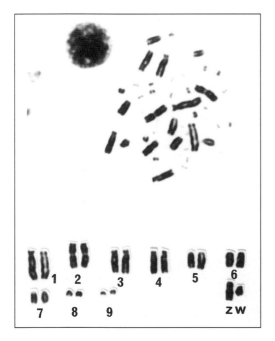

Metaphase cell and karyotype from a female Cockatiel (*Nymphicus hollandicus*). The first nine pairs of macro-chromosomes and the two Z-chromosomes are shown in the karotype.

Mutations in New Zealand parrots (skins of wild birds). From top to bottom, left to right: yellow Kea (*Nestor notabilis*); yellow Kakapo (*Strigops habroptilus*); white Kaka (*Nestor productus*) and red Kaka. What connection does this picture have with cockatoos? The author believes that these parrots were derived from the Western Long-billed Corella (*Cacatua tenuirostris*). The white mutation of the Kaka pictured here shows how the Kaka might have evolved from the Long-billed Corella. A few might have reached New Zealand and, by mutation, acquired the brown plumage, which would best protect them in their forest habitat.

Changes in karyotype are generally unaffected by the environment. However the evolution of new species can often be shown to be accompanied by changes in chromosome morphology. For example, differences in the chromosome structure can lead to reproductive isolation of individuals as different species. In combination with the other available evidence, it should be possible to build up an accurate picture of the phylogenetic relationships within this group. The chromosome evidence also suggests that the general cockatoo karyotype is quite distinct from that of other species of parrots and supports the separation of this group into a separate sub-family. The Australian rosellas and parrakeets, as well as all South American, African and Asian parrots represent the Psittacidae, while the other sub-family, the Loriidae, comprises the lories and lorikeets of Australasia, Indonesia and the Pacific islands.

Most chromosomal data have been collected from birds maintained in aviculture. Thus aviculture is playing an important role in the accumulation of scientific knowledge which would otherwise be impossible to obtain.

Part II
The Species

Gang Gang Cockatoo
Callocephalon fimbriatum

Crest Unique in being flimsy and less developed – almost like a disarrangement of feathers; red in the male, dark grey in the female.
Plumage Feathers grey, margined with greyish-white. Head red in the male, grey in the female. Outer webs of wing coverts tinged dull green. Feathers of female's underparts margined with orange and yellow.
Beak and eyes Beak horn-coloured; cere feathered. Iris dark brown.
Length 35 cm (14 in).
Weight About 280 g (10 oz).
Sexual dimorphism See Plumage.
Immature birds Can be sexed at about four weeks as males have a variable degree of red on forehead, crown and crest. Both sexes otherwise resemble the female except that the axillaries (wing feathers next to the back) and underside of the tail are barred with greyish-white. In most young the margins of the feathers of the underparts are a brighter yellow and more orange-red than in the female. Sindel and Lynn (1989) state that most of the male's immature plumage has been replaced by two years but full adult plumage is not acquired until at least three years.
Sub-species None recognized.
Captive status Uncommon but increasing within Australia; rare or very rare outside Australia.
Pet potential and personality Birds acquired young make attractive pets but should not be confined to a small cage. However, they are generally considered too valuable to be denied the opportunity to breed.
Aviculture and breeding As yet there are no chromosome data for this very attractive and highly distinctive cockatoo which would help to define its evolutionary relationship. I suspect that it is one of the most ancient. A particular problem associated with this species in captivity is feather-plucking. In the past an incorrect diet was usually blamed. Today, however, it is beginning to be recognized that the problem is stress and/or boredom. Gang Gangs need to be kept occupied, and different methods have been applied to solve this problem. One breeder found that supplying a live sparrow daily was the answer; it would be killed, plucked and eaten. Another provided ten fir cones daily and, when the supply ended, chicken bones and berries. A pair in my care at Loro Parque habitually plucked themselves until provided with an almost solid palm log with only a small indentation. They immediately started to excavate it and, within a few weeks, were fully feathered, except for the top of the male's head which was over-preened by the female. It took them months to excavate to a depth of 1 m (3 ft 3 in) and during this period they remained in perfect feather. (Subsequently the female laid for the first time; two young were hand-reared.)

Because of this need to keep their beaks occupied, no one should keep Gang Gang Cockatoos unless they can be given an endless supply of branches with leaves and, if possible, with berries, cones or nuts. Hawthorn bushes with berries are a particular favourite, both in the wild and in captivity. Branches of pine (especially the native *Callitris*), acacia, *Casuarina* and eucalyptus (especially stringy-bark – *Eucalyptus macrorhyncha*) are all relised. (If possible, the eucalyptus branches should be bearing ripe green seed capsules, not over-ripe brown ones.) Where these are not

Gang Gang Cockatoo (*Callocephalon fimbriatum*): male.

available, branches from fruit trees, such as apple, can be offered.

Gang Gangs are sexually mature at three years old and, in an aviary, generally start to breed at three or four years. An experienced breeder of this species in Australia, Gordon Dosser, provides a hollow log for nesting, approximately 60 cm (2 ft) long and 20–23 cm (8–9 in) in diameter, with an inspection hole in the side. The logs are hung at an angle or vertically; his birds have used logs in either position. Laying occurs from the end of October to mid-December. On at least one occasion three eggs were laid and three young reared. One problem encountered was that of chicks not being brooded after the age of 16 days, which resulted in their death if the weather was cold. This was overcome by placing a 25W light bulb under the log and switching it on at night until the chicks were feathered.

Courtship display This has been described by Sindel and Lynn (1989):

> The male will call excitedly to the female, often with his wings spread and his body stretched to its maximum height and his general appearance becomes particularly animated.

Clutch size 2 (clutches of 3 have been recorded, but rarely).

Incubation period Varying reports of from 25 days (Low, 1992a), 26 days (Dosser, 1989) to '28 days normally' but up to 30 days (Sindel & Lynn, 1989). Incubation (by male and female) usually commences when the second egg is laid.

This Gang Gang Cockatoo (*Callocephalon fimbriatum*), aged four weeks, can already be sexed as a male by the red feathers in the crest.

Newly hatched chicks Sparse creamy-yellow down; pink beak. Weight about 14 g (½ oz).

Young in nest Eight or nine weeks – or less; Dosser, an experienced breeder, states 'approximately 47 to 50 days'.

Origin Australia: south-east corner – eastern Victoria and south-eastern New South Wales are the stronghold of this cockatoo. It also occurs in extreme south-eastern South Australia. According to *The Atlas of Australian Birds*, the populations in the western part of the Gang Gang's range have become fragmented, leaving three populations virtually isolated: in the Otway Range, Grampian Range and the Portland district. It formerly occurred on King Island and is – or was – a rare visitor to Tasmania.

Natural history Gang Gangs inhabit temperate forests, mainly in the highlands in the northern part of the range. According to *The Atlas*, the reporting rate for the incidence of this species in the Snowy Mountains above 500 m (1,640 ft) dropped from 47 per cent in spring and summer to 20 per cent in autumn and winter, indicating that some birds leave the mountains to spend the winter at lower altitudes. Others which live in eucalyptus forests move in winter into woodland, parks and gardens.

From October to January, i.e. during the breeding season, Gang Gang Cockatoos occur in pairs or family groups. Out of the breeding season they gather in small flocks. Larger gatherings are seen where a favourite food source is available, such as the berries of hawthorn. Stan Sindel, for whom the Gang Gang is a favourite bird, wrote:

The presence of this cockatoo in an area is usually first determined by the sound of its unusual grating, clanging call which cannot be mistaken for any other bird in the Australian bush. Their flight is slow and laboured and has often been described as owl like. (Sindel & Lynn, 1989)

Forshaw (1969) describes how, on short flights, they swoop groundwards, then rise up before alighting. At the end of long, high flights they spiral down, twisting and turning in the same manner as Galahs.

They feed on seeds, berries, fruits and nuts, favoured food trees being eucalyptus, acacia, hawthorn (*Crataegus*) and pyracantha. As both hawthorn and pyracanthas often adorn gardens, it is easy for many keepers of this species to provide some of their favourite food items. They eat insects and also larvae, such as those of sawflies (*Perga* species) and moths. When feeding, even in city parks and gardens (in Canberra), they allow a very close approach. The nest site is invariably high up, often in a eucalyptus at more than 20 m (65 ft). Male and female prepare the nest site by chewing up decayed wood. This species is normally (or always) single-brooded in the wild.

Status and conservation The Gang Gang is described as common at the centre of its distribution, rare at the extremities of its range (Forshaw & Cooper, 1989). However, the findings of the compilers of *The Atlas of Australian Birds* pointed out how the western populations have become fragmented. This is surely a warning signal which should not be ignored, denoting the vulnerability of this species to habitat destruction, especially perhaps trees providing suitable nest sites.

Galah, Roseate or Rose-breasted Cockatoo
Eolophus (= *Cacatua*) *roseicapillus*

Crest Dense feathers of forehead and crown erectile; when relaxed the crest not apparent. Feathers white in the nominate race, tinged with pink at the base; feathers pale pink in *E. r. assimilis*.

Plumage Upperparts soft grey, paler on the rump and underwing coverts and around the vent and undertail coverts; tail darker grey, lower half of head, the nape, underparts and underwing coverts pink.

Beak and eyes Beak whitish, cere partly feathered. Iris dark brown to black in *most* males and pinkish-red, dark red or reddish-brown in *most* females. Naked skin around the eye greyish-white in *E. r. assimilis* and dull crimson in *E. r. roseicapillus*. Carunculations (small raised areas) on the skin larger in the male and more pronounced in birds from Western Australia.

Length 34 cm (13½ in). Males usually slightly larger.

Weight Wild birds about 330 g (11¾ oz). There is a wide variation. The weight range of a large number weighed in Western Australia was 275–430 g (10–15 oz) for males and 255–400 g (9–14¼ oz) for females (Rowley, 1990). Overweight captive birds may weigh 500 g (17⅝ oz) or more. Stacey Gelis (pers. comm., 1992) described an overweight Galah in Australia which was euthanized. At death it weighed 504 g (18 oz); after removal of all subcutaneous fat, it weighed 405 g (14¼ oz). There was also fat in the peritoneum and extensive fatty infiltrations in some organs, especially the liver.

Sexual dimorphism See Beak and eyes. However, note that in the opinion of Dr Friedrich Janeczek, a veterinary surgeon who laparoscoped a large number of birds, this species cannot be sexed with certainty by eye colour. He sexed seven males with reddish iris colour, and all were mature birds.

Immature birds Crown and breast strongly tinged with grey; plumage duller overall. Iris grey and adult eye colour not attained until about two years.

Mutations These are rare in cockatoos, with the exception of the Cockatiel and the Galah. At least eight mutations have been recorded in the Galah, according to Sindel and Lynn (1989). Among these are: albino (pure white where the normal bird is grey, with pink feet and red eyes); dilute (off-white where the normal bird is grey, with normal feet and eyes); cinnamon – three forms – (very pale fawn where the normal bird is grey, with darker flight feathers, pink feet and normal eyes); silver – possibly another form of cinnamon (very pale grey); off-white (lacks pink and grey); and grey and white (white where the normal bird is pink, with normal feet and eyes). Most of these mutations are not well established in Australian aviaries and are rare or non-existent outside Australia.

Sub-species *E. r. assimilis* has pale pink feathers on the crown and forehead and a fuller crest; its plumage is paler overall, and the skin surrounding the eye is greyish-white.

E. r. kuhli differs from *assimilis* in that the skin surrounding the eye is greyish-red. It is smaller, at least 6 cm (2⅜ in), according to Sindel and Lynn (1989), and the head is smaller in proportion to the body.

I suspect that many captive birds outside Australia are not pure but the result of crossing two sub-species; thus their description may not agree precisely with any of those above.

Captive status Extremely common and inexpensive in Australia; elsewhere it is not common and the price is high. It was once the most frequently exported species of cockatoo but, since Australia ceased to export its fauna in 1959, the price has risen steadily until the 1980s. Despite large fines for those apprehended, small numbers were being smuggled out until the late 1980s. Commencing in 1991, New Zealand permitted the export of captive-bred exotic species, and this included Galahs.

Pet potential and personality Birds acquired while young often make excellent pets and learn to mimic a few words. This species is commonly kept as a pet in Australia, more rarely elsewhere, although hand-reared young are popular in the USA. The Galah is much bolder and less nervous than, for example, the Indonesian cockatoo, and tends to be more independent and less affectionate. However, many do make affectionate and amusing pets.

Galah (*Eolophus roseicapillus*).

This hand-reared Galah (*Eolophus roseicapillus*) is typical of its species in developing more quickly than any other cockatoo – except the Cockatiel (*Nymphicus hollandicus*).

The Galah (*Eolophus roseicapillus*) is the species most likely to delight the visitor to Australia who does not have time to journey into the bush.

Aviculture and breeding Australian aviculturists do not bother with this species – except mutations – because of their low value. Elsewhere, good results are achieved in some collections, usually where low-fat diets are provided. This cockatoo is highly susceptible to fatty lipomas (growths), which are usually situated near the vent, resulting in infertility. Very careful attention must be paid to diet (see p. 69).

In captivity, this species is seen at its best in a large enclosure with plenty of branches (eucalyptus, where possible) for destruction. In a large aviary they can even be bred on the colony system. The best aviary I have ever seen for Galahs was at the Avicultural Breeding and Research Centre in Florida, in the collection of Richard Schubot. It was extremely large and I especially admired the idea of disguising the nesting sites. None of the nest boxes was immediately evident; they were reached through tunnels of wire mesh hidden behind vegetation. One of the 22 occupants, an inquisitive female, landed on my shoulder as I entered and seemed most reluctant to leave!

In Sweden, another successful breeder I visited used the conventional method of one pair per aviary, each enclosure measuring 4.5 m × 1.2 m × 1.8 m high (15 ft × 4ft × 6 ft high). Made of wood and not lined, the enclosures did not show any great degree of damage. While rearing young, Bengt Reinerfelt's four pairs consumed large quantities of greenfood. They were also offered a mixture of soaked seeds, eggfood and honey, and insectivorous food.

The temperament of this species is placid; it is rare for aggression to occur between male and female. However, it is unwise to generalize where birds are concerned. An Australian breeder related a sad incident to me. He witnessed the moment when his pair's first youngster left the nest. It was set about by the male, who was instantly attacked and killed by the female. Instinctively she protected her young above all else.

Courtship display There is no real display, only a moving of the head and a raising of the crest, while calling.

Clutch size 3–6, usually 4.

Incubation period 23 days for last egg (20 last eggs in wild clutches averaged 23.4 days, with a range of 22.2–25.9 days). However, the first egg in a clutch of eight hatched after 36 days (Rowley, 1990).

Newly hatched chicks Sparse pink down; beak pinkish. Weight 11 g (⅜ oz).

Young in nest About seven weeks. Weight on fledging about 300 g (10½ oz).

Origin Australia: almost the entire continent, including Tasmania. The range has expanded this century as a result of clearing for agriculture. Only 30 years ago it was unknown on the coastal plains of eastern Australia, for example. Rowley (1990) described it as: '. . . a vigorously expanding species thriving alongside humans as this continent continues to be developed'.

Natural history Galahs in the north of the continent apparently live a nomadic existence, especially in drought years. They may abandon large areas to travel in big flocks to wetter regions where they are found all year round. However, the results of observations for *The Atlas of Australian Birds* do not suggest a large-scale pattern of seasonal movement. The longest movement recorded is of an individual recovered 473 km (294 miles) from where it was banded. The exact ranges of the sub-species are unknown because one of the main distinguishing features, the colour of the skin surrounding the eye, is not discernible in museum skins. However, now that more field work is being carried out, it seems that the western deserts are the approximate dividing line between *E. r. assimilis* in the west and *E. r. roseicapillus* in the east. *E. r. kuhli* is believed to be found throughout the northern areas of the Northern Territory and Western Australia.

Flocks as large as 1,000 individuals are not uncommon. Favoured habitats are agricultural areas, eucalyptus woodland and water courses. Diet depends largely on location. Some Galahs feed almost exclusively on spilled grain; in southern Queensland grass seeds formed 80 per cent of the diet by volume of 34 birds collected, whereas, in Western Australia, only 40 per cent ate grass seed. Sindel and Lynn (1989) describe the diet of the Galah as comprising seeds, nuts, fruits, leaves and blossoms of various native and introduced grasses, plants, shrubs and trees, together with insects and their larvae.

The nest site is usually a hollow in a decaying or termite-ridden tree but, presumably due to a shortage of such sites, Galahs have been known to nest in crevices in rock faces, a tunnel in a cliff, even in vertical concrete pipes. Cockatoos seldom actually excavate a hollow; they take advantage of existing sites; however, there is a record of Galahs rearing young in holes which they excavated in palm trees in Melbourne parkland (Rowley, 1990). Nest trees, such as smooth-barked eucalyptus, can often be recognized by areas on the trunk where the Galahs have removed the bark. A habit unique to this cockatoo is the way in which it will continue to work on an area of trunk, in a ritualized manner, rubbing alternate sides of the beak against it 'as if stropping a razor'. Some birds wipe the side of their face on it, leaving a dusting of powder down.

Galahs appear to have a strong attachment to the nest; whereas most cockatoos leave the nesting area after the young fledge, a pair of Galahs returns every evening and roosts nearby, according to Rowley (1990). By wing-tagging many birds, he found that 60 pairs used the same hollow in successive years: in 19 cases the male reused the hollow with a different female; in 12 cases the male reused the hollow with an untagged female; in 6 cases the female reused the site with a new male, and in 12 cases the nest was occupied by the same female and an untagged male (untagged could have been the same bird or a different one to the previous year).

The Galah is the bird species most likely to delight and fascinate the observer, on a first visit to Australia, who does not have time to journey into the bush in search of rarer species. Flocks are so easy to observe, so unwary and so spectacular. Sindel and Lynn (1989) describe how:

A flock will suddenly appear, screeching, twisting, turning, zooming just above the ground, then soaring up among the treetops only to dive low again to buzz the motor vehicles speeding along a country road. The whole event is carried out with a wild abandonment and the birds themselves seem to ooze with the pleasure of living.

How true this is! The Galah has never been one of my favourite cockatoos in captivity, but when first I saw it in the wild, in the skies and the trees which are its true domain, it was like seeing a different species. Yet I did not feel this of, for example, the Greater Sulphur-crested or the Yellow-tailed Black Cockatoo. It is the *joie de vivre* of the Galah which indelibly prints on one's memory.

Status and conservation It might appear that no conservation measures are necessary for this widespread and abundant cockatoo. However, Rowley (1990) warned:

. . . there is no replacement of the large trees that were left when farms were cleared originally . . . we are faced with the prospect of a landscape bereft of hollows early in the next century.

[We] would be saddened to lose these or any other cockatoos, but that is the reality of what will happen unless trees capable of developing hollows when mature (and not all eucalypts do so) are established in reserves and shelter belts throughout the wheatbelt.

Leadbeater's or Major Mitchell's Cockatoo
Cacatua leadbeateri

Crest Strikingly beautiful when erected; white at the tip, then orange with a central band of yellow which, in many pairs, is broader in the female. See also Sub-species.
Plumage Upperparts and tail white; underparts and side of head salmon-pink; underside of flight and tail feathers suffused with salmon-pink.
Beak and eyes Beak whitish with a

tinge of grey; size relatively small, as befits a species which feeds mainly on small seeds. Iris dark brown to black in the male, reddish in the female.
Length 35 cm (14 in).
Weight Males 424 g (15 oz) (the average weight of 19 trapped in Western Australia, range 380–480 g (13½–17 oz)); females 392 g (14 oz) (the average weight of 23 trapped in Western Australia, range 360–455 g (12¾–16 oz)) (Rowley & Chapman, 1991).
Sexual dimorphism Pink of the underparts usually noticeably less extensive in the female in which the upper abdomen is usually white; in the male it is pink. See also Beak and eyes.
Immature birds Like adults but with the iris brownish.
Sub-species *C. l. mollis* from southern Western Australia (exact range has not been defined) is considered doubtfully distinct. Forshaw (1981) states that the crest is darker red, with little or no yellow in the male and with little yellow in the female. Rowley and Chapman (1991) dispute the validity of any sub-species suggested. Regarding the amount of yellow in the crest, they state: 'This was found to be a very individual character and not even reliably sexually dimorphic . . .'.
Captive status Fairly common in Australia (yet relatively expensive). Outside Australia it is uncommon and by far the highest priced of the white cockatoos. Although this species is breeding well in a number of collections, demand always exceeds supply.
Pet potential and personality Despite its beauty, Leadbeater's is seldom favoured as a pet, because it lacks the endearing qualities of most cockatoos and appears to be less

Leadbeater's Cockatoos (*Cacatua leadbeateri*) – part of a flock in Queensland, Australia.

intelligent. Also, its voice has an annoying grating tone which, to the author's ear, is more difficult to tolerate than the louder calls of the larger species.

Aviculture and breeding In Australia, it was deemed to be the most frequently bred native cockatoo in 1992 (Wilson, 1992) and is generally considered to be one of the easiest to breed there. Outside Australia the high price reflects not only the great demand but suggests that relatively small numbers are produced. In the *Register of Birds Bred in the UK Under Controlled Conditions for the Years 1987–1990* produced by the Foreign Bird Federation (which included the results from Parrot Society members), the breeding of 19 Leadbeater's was reported. Compare this with the breeding of 33 Lesser Sulphur-cresteds, 24 Citron-cresteds, 22 Goffins, 61 Umbrellas, 39 Moluccans and 2 Red-vented. Of course, total numbers reared in the UK are higher but not all breeders report their results.

This species will accept open-topped logs or boxes which need not be very deep. For example, a pair at Palmitos Park used a box measuring 30 cm (12 in) square and 40 cm (16 in) high. In Queensland, Australia, John Beardmore of Rosehill Aviaries bred this cockatoo in unusual circumstances. Eight immature birds were placed in an aviary measuring 6 m × 3 m × 3 m high (20 ft × 10 ft × 10 ft high). One pair nested and raised young for some years, until the female died at approximately 39 years old. Mr Beardmore believed that the group was compatible because they had been kept together since they were young (Beardmore, pers. comm., 1992).

Clutch size 2–5 but usually 3. Mean clutch size of nests studied by Rowley and Chapman (1991) from 1978 to 1982 varied annually but overall was 3.29. Half of the clutches contained three eggs, one-third contained four. Recognizable females tended to lay clutches of the same size each year.

Incubation period About 24 days; incubation may commence with the first or second egg.

Newly hatched chicks Almost naked with sparse, short whitish down, mainly on centre of back and nape. Weight 10–12 g (about ⅜ oz).

Young in nest Eight weeks.

Origin Australia: the arid and semi-arid interior, except the north and north-east, reaching the coast only in the mid-west and central south.

Natural history A specimen shot in February 1829 was said to be the first seen by a European. It was discovered later than other Australian cockatoos because it mainly inhabits the interior. Found in various types of timbered habitat, it favours mallee, callitris–eucalyptus woodland and casuarina–eucalyptus stands near rocky outcrops. It also occurs in sparsely timbered grasslands and trees bordering cereal paddocks and water courses. Usually seen in small groups, large flocks are indicative of dry conditions, when they invade new areas in search of food and water. In the St George district of Queensland, John Beardmore has recorded wintering flocks of up to 600 birds.

Leadbeater's Cockatoos prefer nest hollows with a depth of about 66 cm (26 in); this was the average depth of 28 nest hollows measured by Rowley and Chapman (1991). (Nest hollows of the Galah had an average depth of 1.18 m (nearly 4 ft) at one location and 1.07 m (3 ft 6 in) at another.) The nest entrance height of 20 Leadbeaters' hollows averaged 11.3 m (37 ft) above ground level, whereas Galahs' averaged 7.7 m (just over 25 ft) and 8.9 m (nearly 30 ft).

I count myself very fortunate to have seen Leadbeater's Cockatoos in the wild – in Queensland in March 1992. This could not have been achieved without the help of Peter Odekerken, who suggested that St George would be a good place to search for this often elusive cockatoo. We drove for nearly 12 hours to reach the area, arriving after nightfall. Next morning we set off at 6.15 a.m., knowing that we had little chance of finding any Leadbeater's after about 9 a.m., when they would be resting after feeding. By then the temperature was approaching 32°C/90°F. The area was an arid one with red earth, the vegetation being mallee and apparently narrow strips of callitris–eucalyptus woodland along the sides of the road – a favourite habitat of this species.

John Beardmore, a local aviculturist, has recorded that it first came to the area over 50 years previously. However, that day his family told us that they had seen no Leadbeater's on their large property for three years. We were only a few kilometres away, yet, at about 7.30 a.m., we had the enormous thrill of encountering a flock of about 40 birds not far from the road. They were partly hidden by the foliage of a large tree, but at all times some birds were readily observable: feeding, displaying to each other with raised crests and moving around in the tree. We could clearly hear one young bird giving the food-soliciting call. We watched them from about 15–20 m (50–65 ft) then, after half an hour or so, a group took off and flew across the road – and I was able to photograph them in flight. Lit by the sun, the underside of their wings appears to be on fire. It was an unforgettable sight, and a memory I shall always cherish.

The cockatoos landed in a tree,

then flew down and began to feed on the ground. We got into the car and drove slowly towards them, stopping about 15 m (50 ft) in front of them. As they fed they gradually moved towards us, until they were level with the car at a distance of less than 15 m. A vehicle is, of course, the perfect hide; without it, the birds would not have fed with apparent total disregard to our presence. They were busy picking up seed – we could hear seed cases being cracked – and ignored us. For half an hour we enjoyed this spectacle – and counted 26 birds. One bird (perhaps a sentinel) was perched on the top of a stick about a metre high, which was protruding from the ground. When they had finished feeding, the whole group took to the wing simultaneously and landed in the nearby trees. We were so exhilarated by this experience that we forgot to explore the ground where they had fed to discover the food source. It was then 8.30 a.m. and we set off on the long drive back knowing that whatever else we saw on the way could only be an anti-climax.

In their study of Leadbeater's Cockatoos on the margin of the Western Australian wheatbelt, Rowley and Chapman (1991) listed 28 plants on which the cockatoos had been seen to feed. Wheat (*Triticum aestivum*) and two exotic weeds, double-gee (*Emex australis*) and pie-melon (*Citrillus lanatus*) were the three main foods eaten at all times of the year in various stages of ripeness. Wheat was sown in autumn; seed spilt during sowing was eaten, and seed sown too shallowly was dug up and consumed after it had germinated. The cockatoos could not feed on the growing crop after it reached 20 cm (8 in) high, because it was then too dense. Of double-gee, they

fed on the spiny burr (as did the Banksian Cockatoos in the area), which carried two or three seeds, or seized the rosette of dark green leaves and walked around with it until it was effectively screwed out of the ground; it was then eaten. Timed feeds showed that adult Leadbeater's harvested 17 burrs per minute, whereas immatures averaged only 9.7 per minute.

Rowley and Chapman (1991) give some interesting facts about these cockatoos feeding on melons. The fruit was eaten green or after it had ripened, when the flesh had disintegrated and left a quantity of seeds – about 200 per 10 cm (4 in) melon. As melon vine becomes tangled in machinery, it is often raked aside into heaps where the melons provide a long-lasting food reserve. Other cockatoos were rarely seen to eat melons but Leadbeater's appeared to seek them out. However, this species did not show a preference for melon seed in captivity.

The strong beak of Leadbeater's Cockatoo is also used to open the stems of trees (various species of eucalyptus, acacia and *Codonocarpus*) to search for grubs, to open hard cases of fruits, such as those of *Hakea* and *Santalum acuminatum* and to prune and eat the growing points of sandalwood shrubs (*S. spicatum*). Large wood-boring grubs were eaten, especially from the native poplar (*Codonocarpus cotinifolius*).

The feeding and breeding habits of Leadbeater's Cockatoo in the St George district of Queensland were reported to me by John Beardmore (in pers. comm., 1992). He had been observing these birds for over 50 years. They were unknown in the area until about 1937 and were slow to build up numbers for the first 20 years. Their main sources of food there are the seeds of pie-melons and paddy melons, the hard seeds of Cypress pine cones (on which they feed their young), the seeds of pomegranate or wild orange, and the seeds of wattle trees and kurrajong trees. They feed on the ground on goathead seeds. In 1979 a flock of 600 Leadbeater's was feeding in a paddock, just to the south of Mr Beardmore's house, on the seeds of the large pie-melon. In the 24-hectare (60-acre) paddock, the melons were so thick (about 90 cm/3 ft apart) that it was impossible to plough it. In a few weeks the Leadbeater's had completely chewed up the melons and then scratched through old cow dung to obtain the seeds which had passed through the cows. He noted:

When the birds flock in the winter months, it is the available food that brings them together and I have proved that they congregate from at least a 15-mile radius and possibly 20 miles, or even further.

Regarding their nests he wrote:

Nearly all nests in the wild here are in dead trees, often at a con-siderable height, from 4.5 m (15 ft) to 24 m (80 ft) from the ground. I have only ever seen three nests in green trees and in each case the nest was in a dead limb or spout. They often nest in the top of a broken-off tree which is completely open to the elements and in some instances the young are drowned after a severe rainstorm. Most of the young are ready to leave the nest by the middle of November, but I have seen later nests in which the young did not leave until January.

According to Rowley and Chapman (1991): 'A characteristic and import-ant aspect of *C. leadbeateri* ecology is

that they do not nest near others of the same species.' This is certainly not the case in John Beardmore's area. He has seen eight nests in an area of 2.5 km^2 (1 sq. mile), the ones closest to each other were only 300 m (980 ft) apart. These eight nests produced young over a number of years.

Status and conservation This species is locally common but generally scarce. Unlike the Galah, it has not benefited from the growth of agri-culture, but its range has declined with the spread of wheat farming. Since the time of European settle-ment, it has declined in four of the six states where once it was wide-spread: Victoria, New South Wales, South Australia and Western Aus-tralia (Rowley & Chapman, 1991).

In the 1970s the authorities realized that these cockatoos no longer occured where once they had been common. Agriculture, resulting in the clearance of woodland, has been the main cause of its decline, but trapping and nest-robbing are also to blame. Removal of young from nests is now prohibited in all states. How-ever, it still occurs, despite heavy fines for those apprehended. In the late 1980s one man was prosecuted for taking about 70 young from nests in one locality. This must have represented nearly all the young hatched in that area. Formerly, young could be removed from nests if permits were granted. In 1957–58, 560 such permits to take wild Lead-beaters were issued in South Australia alone, and in the same state in the following year, 899 were issued. Undoubtedly, many Leadbeater's taken in the following three decades were destined to be smuggled over-seas; now that smugglers have turned their attention to eggs, and more Leadbeater's are being reared in

In this pair of Leadbeater's Cockatoos (*Cacatua leadbeateri*), and in many other pairs, the yellow band in the crest (the third band of colour from the top) is broader in the female.

Australian aviaries, it is to be hoped there is less pressure on the wild population. Also, as agriculture has perhaps penetrated as far into semi-arid areas as is economically profitable, further clearance of its habitat may not occur on a large scale.

Rowley and Chapman warn that care is needed in assessing the status of this vulnerable species:

A flock seen here today may be the same one as that reported 30 km away a week or so ago. If these movements are not appreciated, this may lead to the erroneous impression that the species is more common than it really is. In similar vein, a trapper who catches 50 birds may well have eliminated the population of 250 km² – perhaps an entire Shire. Likewise, a farmer attempting to rid himself of a cockatoo problem could eliminate a district's population of *C. lead-*

beateri by widespread poisoning directed at other species, though, hopefully, this is no longer legally permissible . . .

It is also important to recognise that a flock of 50, though appearing large and healthy, probably consists of only 10 pairs and 30 younger birds, progeny of the previous two or three seasons. *C. leadbeateri* are long-lived and have evolved life history strategies enabling them to reproduce slowly and to allow their young to spend several years learning how to cope with a capricious environment. They have learnt to exist in the deserts of central Australia, but unfortunately the ecological desert of the wheatbelt appears to be defeating them.

Rowley and Chapman's concern regarding the vulnerability of this species must be heeded if it is to survive.

Greater Sulphur-crested Cockatoo
Cacatua galerita galerita

Crest Yellow forward-curving feathers which lay flat on the head, except for the curved tip, and which, during display, are raised, each feather then being separated.
Plumage White; underside of flight and tail feathers suffused with yellow; bases of many feathers pale yellow.
Beak and eyes Beak black, cere not feathered. Iris dark brown, reddish-brown in some females; white skin around eye.
Length About 50 cm (20 in).
Weight Males about 880 g (31 oz). Females up to 100 g (3½ oz) less.
Sexual dimorphism None.
Immature birds Eye dark grey, soon changing to brown.
Sub-species *C. g. fitzroyi* has longer crest feathers. The beak is said to be broader and more depressed. Forshaw (1981) gives the weight of males as 610–720 g (21½–25⅜ oz) and the weight of females as 600–780 g (21⅛–27½ oz), i.e. about 200 g (7 oz) less than *C. g. galerita*. The skin around the eye is pale blue. *C. g. triton* and *C. g. eleonora* see Triton Cockatoos (p. 158).
Captive status *C. g. galerita* is extremely common in captivity (as pets, rather than as avicultural subjects) in Australia, uncommon and expensive elsewhere. The sub-species *C. g. triton* and *C. g. eleonora* see or unknown in aviculture.
Pet potential and personality Young birds make excellent pets for those who understand their demanding nature and are tolerant of their destructive and noisy behaviour. They can learn to mimic a few words, are exceptionally intelligent and full of character and curiosity.

Most captive birds are very confident – not nervous.
Aviculture and breeding In Australia the price of this species is so low that few aviculturists are interested in breeding it. Elsewhere the price is high but successes are not numerous, partly due to lack of pairs. Problems which can arise are finding a nest site which the birds will not destroy, and aggression on the part of the male. Nest boxes do not survive long, even if lined with welded mesh and metal.

There is a dearth of information on the captive breeding of this species. David Judd of Mildura, Victoria, Australia, kindly gave me information on two pairs. His own pair were housed in an aviary measuring 2.4 m × 0.9 m × 2.1 m high (8 ft × 3 ft × 7 ft high), which was half enclosed and half welded mesh. The pair were very attentive to one another, always only a short distance apart and often preening each other. Courtship feeding was occasionally observed. The female laid two eggs in a vertical box made from 25 mm (1 in) pine boards, about 1.5 m (5 ft) high. The pair demolished the top of this and lined the nest with the wood chips. It was completely open and the two eggs were laid only about 47 cm (19 in) from the top (so deep were the wood chips). Both birds were hand-reared and became very aggressive; nest inspection was impossible. One chick was reared by the parents; the other egg was infertile. The diet of this pair consisted of a seed mixture, apple and other fruit, silver beet, milk thistle and berries in season.

Ian and Rose Langdon, also of Mildura, housed their pair in an aviary 6 m × 1.2 m × 2.4 m high (20 ft × 4 ft × 8 ft high), half covered in galvanized corrugated iron and half in welded mesh. They were chosen from a group of 30 wild-caught young birds because they were obviously compatible, staying close together. They began to nest when they were six years old, but the first year their eggs were infertile. The next year, 1990, two eggs were laid, one of which was fertile. The chick left the nest in the last week in December. Unfortunately, about one week later it was killed by the male. Until then, the pair had been devoted parents. In 1991, the female laid two eggs during the first week in September. Both hatched and were removed for hand-rearing in mid-December, about two weeks before they would have left the nest.

The nest site is a natural log about 1.2 m (4 ft) long, with a nesting chamber about 25 cm (10 in) in diameter. It is hung at an angle of 45°. Nest litter consists of potting mixture and a very coarse red-gum sawdust mixture. However, most of this is thrown out; thus the nest is almost at the bottom of the log. Again, the birds are so protective that nest inspection is almost impossible. Food offered to these Sulphur-cresteds consists of a cockatoo mixture of seeds and grain, apple, pear, grapes and *Cotoneaster* berries when available.

Courtship display The male struts towards the female with raised crest and spread tail. He jerks his head up and down then swishes it from side to side in a figure-of-eight movement. During this display he makes a chattering sound.

Clutch size 2–3.

Incubation period 25–27 days.

Newly hatched chicks Fairly abundant yellow down; beak horn-coloured. One breeder in Australia, recorded weights of newly hatched chicks as 18 g, 18.5 g and 19 g, (about ⅝ oz).

Young in nest About 11 weeks; 9–12 weeks recorded.

Origin Australia: the nominate race occurs in the east and south-east and in Tasmania and has been introduced to Western Australia, the Perth region. Sindel and Lynn (1989) gives its range as:

. . . eastward from the southern-most section of the Gulf of Carpentaria and the Mount Isa–Cloncurry region of Queensland, where it appears to integrate with *C. g. fitzroyi* and then extends over the entirety of eastern Australia as far west approximately as the junction of the Thompson and Barcoo Rivers of central western Queensland down to the Menindee Lakes area of western New South Wales, and as far west as Spencers Gulf in South Australia, as well as Tasmania.

The range of *C. g. fitzroyi* extends from the Gulf of Carpentaria, Cloncurry and the Mount Isa regions of Queensland westward across the whole of northern Australia as far south as Tennant Creek in the Northern Territory to Broome and the Fitzroy River in Western Australia (Sindel and Lynn, 1989). This species has been introduced to New Zealand.

Natural history *C. g. galerita* is very common and may congregate in very large flocks. *C. g. fitzroyi* is more local and probably does not usually occur in large flocks. The nominate race has increased dramatically, especially as winter visitors, in major cities such as Sydney and Canberra (Forshaw, 1989). Sindel (in Sindel and Lynn, 1989) recounts how, in his childhood, this cockatoo was known to him, just south-west of Sydney, as a small nervous population. Now, 40 years later, in the same area:

They delight . . . in chopping huge pieces off my trees and shrubs, chewing at electric wires, television aerials and the timber on outbuildings and refusing to be driven away. What happened to this shy, wary species? Surely this change has happened too quickly to be classified as evolution. Perhaps it is just the unfortunate effect city dwelling has on all living things.

This cockatoo inhabits all types of habitats with trees. It usually feeds in open country and returns to the same stand of trees to rest during the day and to roost at night. The nest site is, of course, also normally in the limb of a tree; however, in South Australia, these cockatoos nest in the cliffs along the Murray River. The height above ground level ranges from about 15 m (50 ft) to about 45 m (150 ft) (D. Judd, pers. comm., 1992). There are hundreds of nests along these cliffs.

Status and conservation As already described, thousands of birds of the nominate race are trapped or killed annually without this having any effect on the population. However, see the warning regarding lack of nest sites (p. 148).

In South Australia, Greater Sulphur-crested Cockatoos (*Cacatua galerita galerita*) nest in cliffs along the Murray River.

Greater Sulphur-crested Cockatoo (*Cacatua galerita galerita*).

Triton Cockatoo
Cacatua galerita triton

Eleonora's or Medium Sulphur-crested Cockatoo
Cacatua galerita eleonora

Crest Feathers said to be broader and more rounded than in nominate race (Forshaw, 1989), but difference appears negligible.

Plumage Similar to that of *C. galerita galerita*.

Beak and eyes Beak appears proportionately larger in *C. g. triton* than in *C. g. galerita*. Forshaw (1989) infers that the smaller beak of *eleonora* is the principal distinguishing feature; it should be noted, however, that as males have larger beaks than females and as beak size may differ according to origin (as in *C. s. sulphurea*), in practice identification can be difficult. Bare skin around eye pale blue, larger in extent and more prominent.

Length About 45 cm (17½ in) in *triton*, slightly less in *eleonora*.

Weight Substantially less than the nominate race; about 550–600 g (19½–21 oz) in *C. g. triton*, slightly less in *C. g. eleonora*. Body less broad and massive in both these subspecies.

Sexual dimorphism Slight, little or no difference in eye colour in most pairs; iris brown in the female in others.

Immature birds Like adults, except for the grey iris.

Captive status Exported in large numbers during the 1970s and 1980s; formerly rare.

Pet potential and personality Hand-reared birds are extremely demanding and suitable only for those who can devote at least an hour a day to pet

birds. Many Tritons pluck themselves because they do not receive enough attention; others are persistent screamers. Their temperament is more nervous than that of *C. g. galerita* but they too are very intelligent and need to be kept occupied.

Aviculture and breeding Some pairs nest very readily and prove quite prolific. In the USA many are reared for the pet market; elsewhere numbers bred appear to be much lower.

Clutch size 2.

Incubation period About 27 days.

Newly hatched chicks Abundant bright yellow down on upperparts including head; beak pinkish. Weight of *C. g. triton* is about 20 g (¾ oz). At Palmitos Park, two weighed 20 g and 21 g (about ¾ oz) on hatching; one weighed 540 g (19 oz) at 6 months of age, 580 g (20½ oz) at 9 months (just weaned) and 595 g (21 oz) at 29 months. The average weight of nine chicks hatched at the Avicultural Institute in California was 17.8 g (⅝ oz); the range was 14.5–22.5 g (½–¾ oz) (Joyner, Swanson & Hanson, 1990).

Young in nest 11 to 12 weeks.

Origin *C. g. triton*: New Guinea: throughout except the central highlands, western Papuan Islands, islands in Geelvink Bay, D'Entrecasteaux and Louisiade archipelagos and islands in Trobriand and Woodlark groups. Indonesia: introduced to Ceramlaut and Goramlaut. Caroline Islands in the Pacific: introduced to the Palau Islands (Forshaw, 1989). *C. g. eleonora*: Indonesia: southern Moluccas – Aru Islands a group of five low islands (8,540 km²/3,297 sq. miles).

Natural history Scant field work has been carried out within the range of these two sub-species, thus information on their habits is scarce. *C. g.*

Pair of Triton Cockatoos (*Cacatua galerita triton*). This subspecies is smaller than the Greater Sulphur-crested Cockatoo (*Cacatua galerita galerita*) but larger than Eleonora's Cockatoo (*Cacatua galerita eleonora*).

eleonora was studied on the island of Warmar (a land mass of 6,000 km^2/ 2,300 sq. miles) from 28 August to 2 September 1985. During this period there were 11 observations of single birds, four observations of two birds and one observation each of five and six birds. (It is not known whether the species was breeding at the time.) Five of these sightings were made in parkland, 11 in forest and one in garden–plantation type habitat; however, less observation time was spent in the latter. The limited data suggested that this species showed a constant level of activity throughout the day with an increase after 5 p.m. (Milton & Marhadi, 1987).

Status and conservation Status assessments made prior to the 1980s can no longer be considered valid because of the intensive trapping of these cockatoos which has occurred. Milton and Marhadi found that, on Warmar, *C. g. eleonora* was unjustly considered

Triton (*Cacatua galerita triton*), on the right, and Leadbeater's Cockatoos (*Cacatua leadbeateri*).

This Triton Cockatoo (*Cacatua galerita triton*) weighed 20g (¾ oz) a few hours after hatching.

to be a crop pest, and that, in 1985, illegal trapping was still occurring. Depleted numbers due to over-trapping is almost certainly the norm throughout the range of *C. g. eleonora* and *C. g. triton*. Existing legislation to protect them must be implemented if they are to survive in the wild. On the Aru Islands, *C. g. eleonora* has been protected by ministerial decree since 1978, which means that it is forbidden to trap, trade or keep it. However, most of the wild-caught birds in captivity were exported after this date and, because this sub-species is found nowhere else, it is obvious that this decree is being ignored. Despite its legal protection, large numbers were exported every year, often via fishing vessels. Milton and Marhadi commented that illegal trade in *C. g. eleonora*, Palm Cockatoos and Eclectus Parrots, all protected species 'continues to under-mine the purpose of the ministerial decrees, and seriously jeopardize the species' population recovery'.

The Timor Cockatoo (*Cacatua sulphurea parvula*) is endangered due to deforestation of the Lesser Sunda Islands, Indonesia. These young were hand-reared in a Florida collection.

Lesser Sulphur-crested Cockatoo
Cacatua sulphurea sulphurea

Crest Consists of about five pairs of forward-curving pale yellow feathers, plus leading white feathers which cover half the crest when not erected.

Plumage Ear coverts yellow; underside of flight and tail feathers yellow; remainder of plumage white.

Beak and eyes Beak black. Iris black in the male and brown or red-brown in the female. Bare skin around the eye white tinged with blue.

Length About 33 cm (13 in).

Weight Males about 350 g (12 oz). Females about 300 g (10½ oz).

Sexual dimorphism See under 'Beak and eyes'.

Immature birds Beak pinkish marked with grey in very young birds, soon becoming entirely grey. Iris grey.

Sub-species Several have been described but only one, the Citron-crested (*C. s. citrinocristata*) is instantly recognizable. Because of this, and its importance in aviculture, it is described separately (see pp. 166–7). The other sub-species are very difficult to distinguish and, without knowledge of their origin (or DNA blood-testing when it becomes available), can seldom be identified with certainty. The following have been named: *C. s. djampeana* generally considered as synonymous with the nominate race, from which it supposedly differed only in its smaller beak; *C. s. abbotti* which has paler yellow ear coverts than the nominate race and less yellow at the bases of the feathers of the neck and underparts; *C. s. parvula* which differs from *abbotti* in being smaller; *C. s. occidentalis* which is generally considered as synonymous with *C. s. parvula*. In practice the above descrip-

tions are not definitive. I have seen wild-caught females as small as 28 cm (11 in), and almost every beak and body size up to 35 cm (14 in). Females are smaller than males. The problem is further confounded in captivity by the production of young from a male and female which differ substantially in size and originate from different islands. Schubot, Clubb and Clubb (1992) point out that distinguishing nominate *C. s. sulphurea* and *C. s. parvula* is very difficult at maturity but that chicks have different rates of beak pigmentation: the beak of *C. s. sulphurea* blackens between 19 and 44 days and that of *C. s. parvula* between 43 and 89 days.

Captive status Fairly common but unknown in Australia. In the 1990 TRAFFIC (USA) *Psittacine Captive Breeding Survey*, the Lesser Sulphur-crested was the nineteenth most common species; 133 respondents kept 410 specimens, of which 305 were wild-caught, 69 were captive-bred and the origins of 36 were unknown.

Pet potential and personality When acquired young, many Lesser Sulphur-cresteds make affectionate pets. Their potential depends largely on how much trauma they have experienced if wild-caught; mature adults do not become tame.

Aviculture and breeding Because of their nervous temperament, the problem of males attacking females is often encountered. Breeding results are not impressive. In the TRAFFIC survey referred to above, 151 pairs hatched 76 young during 1989, of which at least 69 survived.

In a letter to me of October 1991, Roland Wirth outlined what will surely be a major problem regarding the captive-breeding of this cockatoo:

As even the differences between the two main sub-species *sulphurea* and *parvula* may not be recognised by any except the most experienced cockatoo experts I am somewhat pessimistic that any pure populations of Lesser Sulphur-crested except *C. s. citrinocrista* can be preserved in captivity. Assuming that genetic research may provide us with an unmistakable marker gene for reliable identification of each sub-species (which is by no means certain), the only solution may be to start breeding programmes with closed populations of genetically-tested founders. While all this should, of course, not detract from our main responsibility to preserve remaining wild populations, I would be happy to have such an insurance of well managed pure populations of these endangered cockatoos, especially considering how slow are the efforts to conserve the species on Sumba, and nobody has even started on any of the other *sulphurea* islands.

Clutch size 2.

Incubation period About 27 days.

Newly hatched chicks Pale yellow down, not thick; beak pinkish. Weight about 15 g (½ oz) but varies with sub-species.

Young in nest About 10 weeks, but up to 12 weeks.

Origin Indonesia: Celebes (186,500 km²/72,000 sq. miles) and adjacent islands – Muna, Butung and Tukangbesi; islands in the Java Sea – Djampea (Tanahjampea) (*C. s. djampea*), Kalao, Kalaotoa, Madu, Kayuadi, Salembu Besar (*C. s. abbotti*); Lesser Sunda Islands (*C. s. parvula* except for Sunda Island) – Lombok (*C. s. occidentalis*; 4,660 km²/1,800 sq. miles), Rinco, Sumbawa (*C. s. occidentalis*; 14,760

km²/5,700 sq. miles), Flores (*C. s. occidentalis*; slightly larger in area), Noesa Penida (*C. s. parvula*), Semau, Timor (33,700 km²/13,000 sq. miles), Pantar and Alor.

Natural history This species is reported to prefer the forest edge to the interior, and also inhabits coconut palms and cultivated areas, up to 500 m (1,640 ft), sometimes higher. Until the 1970s it was common until trapping severely reduced its numbers. An ornithologist in central Sulawesi (Palu Valley and Lore Reserve regions) in 1981 described Lesser Sulphur-cresteds as 'relatively common and easily observed' but, on return visits in 1985 and 1986, intensive searches of the same areas failed to locate any cockatoos, although large areas of forest remained (Forshaw, 1989).

Status and conservation The draft of the International Council for Bird Preservation, *Parrots: An Action Plan for their Conservation and Management* (1992), states: 'This species is now considered rare to very rare throughout its range, and it is not known if, or where, viable populations survive'. It further states that there has been only one reported sighting on Sulawesi since 1982. US $20,000 was budgeted to survey the population there; existing reserves may not protect it. An investigation into its trade was also suggested – but trade should surely be halted without waiting for an investigation, by which time every survivor might have been trapped.

Population and habitat surveys projected for all the major islands of the Lesser Sundas would include the sub-species *C. s. parvula*. Within Indonesia these islands have been subjected to some of the highest levels of habitat destruction and degradation. It is not known whether

Lesser Sulphur-crested Cockatoo (*Cacatua sulphurea sulphurea*): immature.

Citron-crested Cockatoo (*Cacatua sulphurea citrinocristata*): male.

the sub-species *C. s. abbotti* still survives. According to Collar (1989), the tiny island where it was found was long ago cleared of forest and has seemingly remained unsurveyed for decades.

Citron-crested Cockatoo
Cacatua sulphurea citrinocristata

Crest Consists of five pairs of forward-curving orange feathers, plus the leading white feathers which cover half the crest when not erected.

Plumage Ear converts pale orange; underside of flight and tail feathers yellow; margins of some breast feathers yellow in some birds; remainder of plumage white.

Beak and eyes Beak black. Iris black in the male and reddish or reddish-brown in the female.

Length 32–34 cm (12½–13½ in). Males are larger.

Weight Males about 425 g (15 oz). Females 360 g (12⅝ oz).

Sexual dimorphism Females smaller, especially in beak and head; see also Beak and Eyes.

Immature birds Beak and iris grey.

Captive status Not uncommon; thousands were exported from Sumba during the 1980s.

Pet potential and personality See Lesser Sulphur-crested Cockatoo (p. 162).

Aviculture and breeding The Citron-crested has bred regularly in captivity, although not in large numbers, since the 1970s. As an example of relative numbers bred, I referred to the *Register of Birds Bred in the UK* (Foreign Bird Federation). In 1990, 24 Citron-cresteds were reared, compared with 33 Lesser Sulphur-cresteds, 22 Goffins, 61 Umbrellas, 19 Leadbeaters, 8 Tritons and 39 Moluccans. (Not all breeders report their results so the real totals were probably substantially higher.)

The major problem with the Citron-crested is the high incidence of males which attack females. Those who care for this species are urged to take every possible precaution to prevent this (see p. 66).

An attack could occur at any time. Note that, if it is necessary to remove the male due to aggressive behaviour, an uninjured female can rear young alone. In 1979 a pair at Brean Down Bird Garden, Somerset, UK, hatched their first chick. When it was 4 weeks old, the male had to be removed and the female reared the young one unaided (Low, 1980c).

Clutch size 2.

Incubation period About 27 days.

Newly hatched chicks Pale yellow down, not thick; beak pinkish. Weight about 13 g (½ oz).

Young in nest About 10 weeks but up to 12.

Origin Indonesia: Lesser Sundas – the island of Sumba (12,000 km²/4,600 sq. miles).

Natural history At the end of the nineteenth century the Citron-crested was so common on Sumba that the trees were 'white with cockatoos' (Zieren *et al.*, 1990). Large flocks were encountered until the 1970s. Its decline can be blamed on deforestation and trade. By 1990 only 16 per cent of the island was under 'forest cover', but this included plantations and secondary forest. These cockatoos are not popular with the inhabitants of Sumba due to their habit of attacking cultivated crops.

Status and conservation A survey was carried out in 1986 by *Balai Konservasi Sumber Daya Alam* (BKSDA), the Indonesian nature conservation authorities. Based on line-transect sample counts, the total population was estimated at approximately 12,000 specimens (a density of eight birds per km^2 in suitable habitat). Three years later a similar survey revealed a density of 1.8 birds per km^2 (247 acres) of suitable habitat, a decrease of nearly 80 per cent. This resulted in the recommendations that there should be *better control* of trapping activities and stricter regulations concerning illegal trade (BKSDA, 1989). It would surely have been more appropriate to have banned trade in any circumstances and to have imposed heavy fines for anyone caught in possession of these endangered cockatoos.

In 1990 members of a Manchester Polytechnic expedition to Sumba recorded the Citron-crested Cockatoo fairly frequently at both of their study sites. At Pengaduahahar, 97 per cent of the 34 sightings were of birds alighting from, or flying to, forest. At Tabundung, the figure was 86 per cent of 97 sightings, suggesting that this cockatoo is heavily dependent upon closed forest (Jones & Marsden, 1992). Further field work was planned for 1992, but initial observations suggested that the Citron-crested prefers primary forest – tall trees which branch above half their height – and also forest with dense cover at all levels. The conclusion was that *C. s. citrinocristata* was probably the rarest parrot on Sumba.

The cockatoo is rapidly declining and now rare. The Manchester Polytechnic population estimate was of 907 birds based on data from all observation stations, or the 'more realistic' 3,997 if based on estimates made in forested areas. This compared with an estimate (forested areas) of 485,138 Sumba Lorikeets (*Trichoglossus haematodus fortis*) and 15,665 Red-cheeked Parrots (*Geoffroyus geoffroyi*). In 1993, the most detailed survey to date estimated the Citron-crests' population as being between 1,150 and 1,850.

Until this cockatoo is efficiently protected from trapping and persecution by local people, it could surely decline to the point of extinction with extreme rapidity. An education programme and legislation with severe penalties for law-breakers are urgently needed. However, the major problem is that relatively intact forest survives only in the south of the island.

In 1990 (surely too late to save this cockatoo) a comprehensive conservation project was proposed for Sumba; its implementation would cost US $28,000 for the first three years.

Blue-eyed Cockatoo
Cacatua ophthalmica

Crest Consists of large backward-curving yellow feathers hidden, until raised, by similar broad white feathers.

Plumage White; bases of feathers of head and undersides of flight and tail feathers suffused with yellow.

Beak and eyes Beak black. Iris black in the male, reddish in the female. Bare skin around the eye blue – deeper blue than in any other cockatoo.

Length 50 cm (20 in).

Weight About 500–570 g (17½–20 oz).

Sexual dimorphism See Beak and eyes.

Immature birds Like adults but with the iris grey.

Sub-species None described but apparently some smaller birds exist. L. Saunders informed me of a cockatoo he bought while living in New Guinea; it was three-quarters the size of a normal *C. ophthalmica* and less stocky. Furthermore, the blue skin surrounding the eye was slightly less extensive and nearer cobalt than ultramarine. There is a possibility that it belongs to a population or sub-species which has yet to be described, perhaps even from Papua New Guinea. Griffiths (1965) also noted 'an appreciable difference in size' between two of his three birds and suggested they might be 'different subspecies'.

Captive status Rare; the rarest of the genus. At the time of writing, pairs were held in fewer than half a dozen collections known to the author.

Pet potential and personality This bird is too rare to be considered as a pet under normal circumstances. However, the single bird referred to above (see Sub-species) made an enchanting pet. Mr Saunders wrote to me:

. . . it turned out to be one of the most talented cockatoos I have ever kept. It can be handled by anyone and lifted up in any fashion (bodily, by a foot or on to the hand, even upside down!) and it positively enjoys lying on its back or wrestling with a toy. It laughs and chuckles, giggles and whistles. It delights in singing along to the radio, dances and plays with toys and balls. Last but not least, it is a fantastic mimic, copying our dog (as best it can), even whining as it

Blue-eyed Cockatoos (*Cacatua ophthalmica*): pair.

These young Blue-eyed Cockatoos (*Cacatua ophthalmica*) were described as gentle and sweet-tempered by their breeder in California.

does just to annoy it. Within a few weeks of being in my possession it learned to say a few words but, more to the point, it seems to be able to say the appropriate phrases at just the right time!

(When obtained, this bird apparently had reddish-brown eyes; within a few months the colour had changed to very dark brown, but not as dark as an adult male.)

Aviculture and breeding Because of the rarity of this cockatoo in aviculture, very few breeders have had the opportunity to breed it but there is no evidence to suggest that it is particularly difficult to breed. All the successes known to the author can be mentioned here. The first recorded is found in a brief note, without details '. . . Mr E. J. L. Hallstrom has bred the Blue-eyed Cockatoo (*K. ophthalmica*) of New Britain'. (Lendon, 1951)

The next breeder was Alan V. Griffiths of Wales in 1964 (Griffiths, 1965). Three (or more) were imported in 1963. In October the female laid; she became egg-bound on the second egg which was laid indoors. She spent the winter indoors and was not reunited with the male until April. In May she again became egg-bound but passed a soft-shelled egg. Two eggs were present in the nest on 19 July, one of which had hatched by 11 August. The chick was fully feathered at six weeks and left the nest on 10 November. It was handled from the time it perched and never attempted to bite.

In the following year the pair nested in the autumn and a single youngster left the nest on New Year's Eve. Believed to be a female, it had a much smaller head and beak than the first youngster (Griffiths, 1966).

In Europe, success in breeding

this species over a sustained period has been achieved only at Chester Zoo in the north of England. A pair was acquired in 1966 and a third bird was presented (in a plucked condition) in 1975. A male, it was paired with the first bird reared and this pair was still breeding in 1990. After the early success, this cockatoo was not bred again at Chester until 1979 when each pair produced a youngster – one male and one female. In 1981 each pair produced one male. In 1982 one chick was hand-reared (and subsequently stolen). In 1983 the young pair nested; two eggs were seen on 11 May. They resulted in two young being reared (Bloomfield, 1984).

Since then, another pair has bred: a female hatched at Chester in 1983 and a male bred by Mr and Mrs B. Higgs of the former Clee Hill Bird Gardens in Worcestershire, in 1979. Another was reared there in 1981

(Wilkinson, 1990). Of the three pairs breeding at Chester in 1990, one pair (a parent-reared male and donated female) first bred after being together for five years, and another pair, consisting of a wild-caught male and a parent-reared female, were together for six years before the female laid.

Dr Wilkinson informed me in 1992 that of young reared in recent years, females achieved maximum weight of 560 g (19¾ oz), decreasing to about 500 g (17⅝ oz) at five months old. A hand-reared male achieved a peak weight of 610 g (21½ oz) at 11 weeks; its weight then decreased to between 570 g (20⅛ oz) and 600 g (21⅛ oz) between 20 and 23 weeks of age.

In the USA the first breeders were probably Gloria Allen in 1984 and Sheldon Dingle, then both of California. In 1986 Sheldon Dingle informed me that the female of his pair was an egg-eater. Eggs were

Blue-eyed Cockatoo chick hatched at Chester Zoo.

placed in an incubator maintained at 37°C (98.6°F) and 55 per cent humidity. Under these conditions eggs pipped at 26 days and usually hatched at 28 days. Some eggs hatched after 29 or 30 days. In 1985 the female laid at intervals of 30 days after eggs were removed, and nine young were reared. They were fed on a mixture of cooked monkey chow, baby food from jars, peanut butter and sunflower meal. Weaned at five months old, they remained extremely gentle and sweet-tempered.

Courtship display Griffiths (1965) mentioned 'a mutual display screech which is repeated alternately by cock and hen in a staccato "barbet" fashion' in his pair. (Barbets are renowned for duetting.)

Clutch size 2.

Incubation period Usually 28 days in an incubator but up to 30 days; possibly slightly longer when incubated naturally.

Newly hatched chicks Three incubator-hatched at Chester Zoo: 15 g, 16 g and 16 g (about ½ oz) (Wilkinson, pers. comm., 1992).

Young in nest 12–13 weeks.

Origin Bismarck Archipelago: New Britain (36,260 km²/14,000 sq. miles) and New Ireland (8,500 km²/3,300 sq. miles), to the east of New Guinea.

Natural history Very little is known about this species. It was apparently common in the lowland primary forests and foothills of New Britain, up to about 1,000 m (3,280 ft), in 1970 (Forshaw, 1989). In early 1992 Jan R. van Oosten visited New Britain. He told me that he saw more than 50 kept as pets on plantations outside Rabaul in the eastern part of the island. Although the species is protected, he thought that some were shot on plantations. Occasionally one might be seen for sale in the local market. He thought its status

on New Ireland was quite good, based on what he was told. Forest survives, although fragmented, all along the central mountain massif. However, logging had commenced in the largest forested area in the southern tip.

Status and conservation No information exists on its status and no conservation measures are known, except that the species is protected in law.

Moluccan Cockatoo
Cacatua moluccensis

Crest Rounded orange feathers, each at least 15 cm (6 in) long, the backward-curving feathers are a magnificent sight when erected.

Plumage Head and underparts white or tinged with salmon pink; underparts vary in individuals from pink-tinged white to salmon pink; undersides of primaries and secondaries yellow and greater underwing coverts yellow-orange; underside of tail yellow and orange; bases of most body feathers salmon-pink; orange down at the bases of the feathers of the crest and nape.

Beak and eyes Beak black; iris black in male, dark brown in female, but perceptible only in good light. Bare skin around eye pale bluish.

Length About 50 cm (20 in).

Weight About 840 g (30 oz). (Four males weighed by the author from one collection ranged between 775 g (27⅜ oz) and 935 g (33 oz), an average of 852 g (30 oz), and the four females between 790 g (27¾ oz) and 890 g (31⅛ oz), an average of 831 g (29¼ oz).

Moluccan Cockatoos (*Cacatua moluccensis*): pair.

Sexual dimorphism Slight difference in overall size; head and beak usually slightly larger in the male.

Immature birds Like adults except for black iris of both sexes and slightly bluer skin around eye.

Sub-species None.

Captive status Fairly common since 1970s. Unknown in Australia.

Pet potential and personality Hand-reared birds are the most gentle and affectionate of all *Cacatua* species (some might say of *all parrots*) but they are also the most demanding and difficult to care for. They need more attention and affection than the average person – and certainly any working person – can provide. To some people, a Moluccan Cockatoo has become a substitute child; to others, who are unable to cope with the bird's demanding ways and high noise level, it is a source of despair.

Nervous and sensitive, the Moluccan can be extraordinarily gentle and affectionate.

Aviculture and breeding Generally speaking, this species nests quite readily in captivity. In the 1990 TRAFFIC (USA) *Psittacine captive breeding survey*, 183 species were kept by the 1,221 people or zoos who participated. Surprisingly, the Moluccan was the fourth most numerous species (indicating how large were the numbers which entered the USA); 820 birds were kept by 239 participants. Of these, 645 were known to be wild-caught and 93 were captive-bred; the origins of the rest were unknown. There were 317 pairs which hatched 158 young that year, at least 120 of which were reared. By contrast, in the UK, 1,401 members of the Parrot Society contributed to the 1991 *Register of Birds Bred in the UK under Controlled*

Moluccan Cockatoo (*Cacatua moluccensis*): chick hatching.

Conditions for the Years 1988–1991 (Foreign Bird Federation, 1991). Moluccan Cockatoos were bred by only seven of these members, and 23 young were produced.

At Palmitos Park, Gran Canaria, the females of four pairs put together in 1990 and 1991 all produced eggs within a few months (and three pairs produced young), even though conditions are not ideal in that the climate is very dry. One female had for years been a performing bird in a show. She was placed in the quarantine section of the breeding station in July 1991. A male which had been confiscated by CITES officials after spending months or years chained to a stand outside a restaurant, joined her in quarantine. At the end of August they were placed in a breeding aviary and the female laid the first of two eggs on 11 October; both were infertile. At the beginning of March 1992 she laid two more; the second hatched but the chick died at two days; it had food in its crop. Cause of death was unknown.

The first egg of the next clutch was laid by 4 May; there were two eggs in the nest on 7 May. The first hatched on 5 or 6 June and the second on 7 June. Both chicks were fed but I felt they were too valuable, genetically, to leave with the parents on this occasion, and removed them on 8 and 9 June. They were reared on the diet described on p. 86. For the first few days, papaya was included but they scarcely gained weight until this was omitted from the food on 13 June.

As described on p. 97 I carried out an experiment with these two cockatoos to minimize imprinting, which appeared to be totally successful. Because they never cried for attention or showed the abnormal 'clinging' behaviour of most hand-fed cockatoos, they were a joy to rear. By 5 August they were nibbling at fresh corn and fruit; on 9 August one screamed like an adult when alarmed. At this stage they were being fed four times daily. From 29 August, on which day the eldest perched for the first time, they were fed three times daily. By then they were eating a wide variety of items but not significant amounts. They liked cooked maize and beans, wholemeal bread, sunflower, pomegranates and raw carrot.

Clutch size Usually 2, rarely 1 or 3. Egg shape is a long oval (elliptical ovate).

Incubation period 28 or 29 days.

Newly hatched chicks Yellow down, fairly dense on the upperparts; most of this is lost after a few days. Weight about 20 g (¾ oz).

Young in nest About 14 weeks.

Origin Indonesia: central Moluccan islands – Seram (Ceram), the largest island of the Moluccas (18,410 km²/ 7,108 sq. miles). It was formerly present on Saparua and Haruku. It was introduced to Ambon (Amboina) (761 km²/294 sq. miles) but was believed to be extinct there by 1981 (Wirth, 1990).

Natural history Very little has been recorded about the wild life of this species. In 1987, however, two British ornithologists, John Bowler and J. B. Taylor, spent nine weeks in Seram as part of 'Operation Raleigh'. They studied the nine parrot species, including the Moluccan Cockatoo, between 20 July and 25 September in Manusela National Park in northern-central Seram. The park was founded in 1982 and then extended to cover 11 per cent of the total area of the island. Observations of the Moluccan Cockatoo were few. During 114 hours of observation at

Kineke (600–900 m/2,000–3,000 ft altitude), this cockatoo was seen on 17 occasions (0.1 per hour); at Solea (100 m/300 ft – lowland rainforest) it was seen on 11 occasions during 41 hours' observation. By contrast, the Red Lory (*Eos bornea*) was seen 422 times, the Pleasing Lorikeet (*Charmosyna placentis*) 72 times, the Red-cheeked Parrot (*Geoffroyus geoffroyi*) 186 times, Eclectus (*Eclectus roratus roratus*) 89 times and the Amboina King Parrakeet (*Alisterus amboinensis*) only three times. During 40 days of field work, the Moluccan Cockatoo was seen only 54 times; 20 of these observations were of single birds (Bowler, 1990). However, Taylor (1991) stated that young are in the nest during October, so perhaps the high incidence of single birds was due to the fact that the other bird was incubating.

In August 1990, J. B. Taylor returned to Seram. He then described Manusela National Park as covering 180,000 hectares (444,780 acres), 10 per cent of the total area of the island. He spent 23 days in the area where he had observed Moluccan Cockatoos in 1987 and saw cockatoos in the same place. There were 35 observations, mostly before 9 a.m. and after 5 p.m. The birds were very noisy and their calls carried one kilometre (over ½ mile). The observation rate was 0.2 birds per hour at Kineke and 0.5 birds per hour at Solea. Not surprisingly, they were shy and not easy to observe.

Their rarity was due to excessive trapping; until 1970 this species occurred in large numbers in western Seram and on Ambon. During the 1970s trapping for export on a massive scale commenced. Between 1981 and 1984 over 20,000 were exported legally (Milton & Marhadi, 1987); subsequently, it was believed that

4,000–9,000 Moluccans were being exported annually (Forshaw, 1989). In addition they were caught and sold for the domestic market.

It was quite obvious that trade on this scandalous scale could be sustained for a limited number of years. Wirth (1990) related the inevitable:

By 1985, the species had become extremely rare or even extinct in virtually all of its former habitats, with the exception of the virgin rain forests of the Manusela National Park, an area of 1,860 sq. km, which is now considered to be their last retreat.

Only two years later, in August/September 1987, British ornithologists John Bowler and John Taylor, discovered that even this population living in the far interior of this national park, had been ravaged by bird trappers.

During their forty day stay at Manusela, which gave them the opportunity to observe numerous birds of various species, the two scientists spotted Moluccan Cockatoos on only 54 occasions. Both are convinced that it was not 54 different animals that they saw but rather always the same ones, in all probability amounting to less than 20 individual birds.

In spite of this alarming news, the cockatoo trade continued in 1988 and 1989, with the blessing of the Indonesian authorities. At the end of 1989, far too late, a resolution was adopted to include Moluccan Cockatoos on Appendix I of CITES. However, in foresight of imminent conservation measures, in the very same year Indonesia's major exporters had mounted a final large-scale operation, depleting the few remaining stocks. Consequently, shortly before the new regulation came into force, hundreds of Moluccan Cockatoos were once again shipped from Jakarta to various overseas destinations. At present, nobody can tell how many survived the Seram holocaust on Ambon and in western Seram. Large areas of the island are still covered with dense forests, so there is a slight chance that possibly some viable cockatoo populations may have survived in some of the more inaccessible regions.

The foregoing is perhaps the most damning indictment of the trade in wild-caught parrots that I have ever read. Unlike some species which have been trapped in large numbers, much suitable habitat does survive – but it no longer rings with the joyous, quavering cries of this wonderful cockatoo. One cannot blame the trappers entirely: many people are responsible, from the Indonesian authorities to everyone who has ever bought a wild-caught Moluccan Cockatoo.

Status and conservation The Moluccan Cockatoo must now be considered critically endangered, perhaps the most endangered of all cockatoos. As Roland Wirth stated:

If conservation activists do not succeed in establishing a rescue programme for Moluccan Cockatoos similar to the one set up for the Imperial Amazon, the cockatoo in the wild might become extinct long before the Imperial Amazon . . . the essential action to take is to effectively protect the vast, and what is more, already existing Manusela National Park against bird trappers.

It is to be assumed that, due to the diminishing cockatoo populations left on Seram, the remaining

Note the shovel-shaped lower mandible of this 16-day-old hand-reared Moluccan Cockatoo (*Cacatua moluccensis*).

The same chick aged 38 days with its sibling which was one day older. This illustrates how cockatoos have lost nearly all their down yet, unlike other parrots, have not grown second down by the time the contour feathers are erupting.

The same chicks at 46 and 47 days.

The same chicks at 63 and 64 days old when only the tail feathers were not complete.

few will run the risk of genetic deprivation . . . The call of the hour is the creation of a co-ordinated captive breeding project to ensure the genetic viability of the founder population.*

Many parrot breeders have claimed conservation as one of their motives for producing parrots. They can justify this claim by producing Moluccan Cockatoos which are capable of breeding and which are maintained only for breeding purposes. If this species does become extinct in the wild, such birds could be used to re-stock the Manusela National Park. If re-stocking has to take place during the first or second decade of the twenty-first century, probably enough wild-caught birds will exist in captivity to re-condition for release. If it occurs after this time, captive-bred birds might have to be used. But if breeders continue to produce them only for the pet trade, no suitable birds for release would exist. The Moluccan Cockatoo would be effectively extinct, with no captive-bred birds available to take the place of their wild-caught ancestors which were producing all the young. I believe that the Moluccan Cockatoo is one of the most magnificent birds in existence. Its future will depend on the few genuine and far-sighted aviculturists who care more for the species than for their own bank balance.

ICBP's draft report, *Parrots: an action plan*, suggests that the most important remaining populations

---

* At the time of writing the estimated population of the Imperial Amazon in the wild was 80 birds, with only one in captivity on the island and a rumoured four illegal birds outside Dominica.

of this cockatoo may be outside Manusela National Park:

An assessment of the protection afforded to cockatoos by the park should be made, and if found insufficient, alternative areas should be proposed for protection. An awareness campaign among the villagers in the region should be initiated in an attempt to reduce trapping levels.

Umbrella Cockatoo
Cacatua alba

Crest Large rounded white feathers with pale yellow bases; the feathers of the back and side of the head open to make the head appear enormous.
Plumage White; underside of flight and tail feathers suffused with yellow.
Beak and eyes Beak black, usually larger in the male; cere grey (unfeathered). Eye dark brown to black in male, reddish-brown in female.
Length About 46 cm (18 in).
Weight About 550 g (19½ oz).
Sexual dimorphism See Beak and Eyes.
Immature birds Eye dark grey.
Sub-species None.
Captive status Common. Unknown in Australia. In the TRAFFIC (USA) *Psittacine captive breeding survey* of birds held in 1989 in the USA, the Umbrella was the most abundant of all cockatoos and the fourth most abundant parrot species. Of the 31,008 birds in the census, 798 were Umbrellas (239 owners). Of these 798, 604 were wild-caught and 136 were captive-bred; the origin of the others was unknown.
Pet potential and personality These birds are nervous but hand-reared

birds, obtained young, make enchanting and affectionate pets, quickly becoming demanding and, if not given sufficient attention, also noisy.

Aviculture and breeding This is the most free-breeding and often-bred of the Indonesian cockatoos, partly because it is readily available and easily sexed and also because it has a slightly less excitable temperament than most white cockatoos. In the survey referred to above, 318 pairs hatched 441 chicks of which at least 380 were reared. (The exact number is unknown because many American breeders sell young before they are weaned.) This is a far higher breeding success rate than for any other cockatoo, except the Cockatiel. Once they start to breed, most females lay two or more clutches each year, even if the chick from one clutch is parent-reared. Some are prolific; e.g. a female at Paradise Park, Cornwall, UK, produced about 40 young in the 14 years up to 1991.

A pair in my care in the breeding centre at Palmitos Park nested in July 1989; I do not know if the female had laid before. When the egg started to pip one of the parents removed the top of the egg, which then had to be placed in an incubator (made by Schumacher). It hatched on 16 August and the chick was returned to the nest (a substitute egg had been placed there) in the shell from which it had hatched. Unfortunately, it was killed within minutes. In 1990 the female again laid during the middle of July. The egg was transferred to the incubator. The first pip mark was seen at 4 p.m. on 6 August and the second at 8 p.m. The chick was unable to hatch unaided, perhaps because the incubator humidity was too low, and I removed it from the egg at 8 p.m. on 8

August. Next morning it weighed 15 g (½ oz). It was ringed on 29 August with a 10 mm (13/32 in) ring, when it weighed 82 g (3 oz) (very low weight). It left the hand-rearing room on 2 December, weighing 436 g (15⅜ oz), and was still being hand-fed twice daily. It was spoon-fed for a short while afterwards.

In December the female laid another egg (she laid single-egg clutches until July 1991) which proved to be infertile. In 1991 she laid between 12 and 15 February. On 11 March the egg had gone; there was a suspicion, but no evidence, that the chick had hatched and been killed. Towards the end of March she laid again; the egg was placed in the incubator on 1 April. The chick hatched at 11 a.m. on 20 April, weighing 18 g (⅝ oz). It was ringed at 18 days with a 10 mm ring. At 21 days this chick weighed 144 g (5⅛ oz). It was weaned by the middle of August when it weighed 530 g (18¾ oz). Easier to wean than the previous youngster, it was a male, whereas the first was a female.

On 29 July the female laid the first of two eggs. Both eggs were placed in an incubator on 24 August, and hatched on 26 and 31 August, giving an incubation period of 28 days for the first egg and a minimum of 27 days for the second. The first chick weighed 18 g (about ⅝ oz) on hatching and the second 16 g (about ½ oz). The difference in beak and head size was apparent by four weeks and on 1 October the second chick had overtaken the first in weight. Both had been ringed at the age of 19 days with 12 mm rings.

I was solely responsible for hand-feeding them. By this time it was known that *C. alba* was endangered; I therefore tried to minimize all interaction with them, in the hope that they would prove suitable for

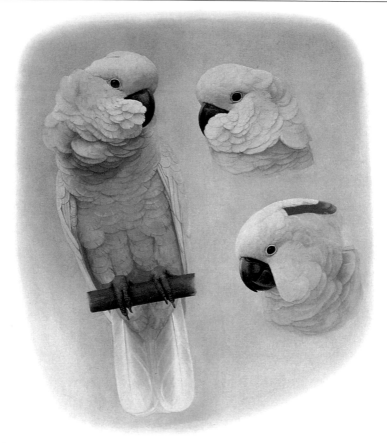

Moluccan Cockatoos (*Cacatua moluccensis*) portrayed by Elizabeth Butterworth. Cockatoos are popular in art and design.

breeding. They never showed the desire for human companionship which was characteristic of the first two young. At the time of writing they are 11 months old; the male is wary of human beings, the female less so – but she cannot be described as tame. Vocally and behaviourally their mannerisms are more mature than those of the young reared alone. They do not exhibit the juvenile food-begging posture and calls which may persist for months in tame,

hand-reared birds. At 10½ months their first complete moult commenced, by which time the lighter eye colour was the only clue to their immaturity.

In 1992, during the middle of March, the female laid two eggs which were left in the nest; however, the embryos died during the first half of the incubation period. On 30 May the female laid the first egg of the next clutch; it was damaged and removed on 3 June, by which day

Umbrella Cockatoos (*Cacatua alba*) aged 20 weeks.

there was a second egg in the nest. It hatched on 2 or 3 July. A parent-reared chick was my aim. Although nest inspection was simple (one had only to tap on the nest-box door for both birds to leave the nest), I decided not to inspect the nest because the pair was nervous and I feared that they might kill or bury the chick. On most days I heard it being fed. On 23 July I had to remove the chick from the nest quickly in order to ring it (11 mm ring). I felt that the most vulnerable stage had passed and henceforth weighed it on a few occasions and gave it liquid calcium. This was done very quickly. It did not seem to be growing quickly and had an empty crop on the few occasions when I handled it.

The weights are recorded in Table 9 and contrasted with the two chicks from the same pair which were hand-reared together.

Weights do not tell the whole story. By 50 days it was apparent that the parent-reared youngster was inferior in size, weight and appearance to those which had been hand-reared. I suspected it was because the chick was under-fed, also that, despite being offered a variety of items, the parents ate mainly fresh corn, sunflower seed and smaller quantities of walnuts, orange and ripe banana. The chick was plucked on the crown from about 50 days when its plumage looked dry, so I gave it an occasional light spray with water in the nest. However, it seemed in good condition but reached its peak weight later than the hand-reared young. Its death at 85 days, when it was still in the nest, was entirely unexpected. Autopsy showed that it had died as a result of ingesting a piece of a twig, 5 cm (2 in) long and 30 mm (1¼ in) at its widest point. This was lodged between the air sac and the kidneys.

Table 9
Comparison of weight gain in parent-reared and hand-reared Umbrella Cockatoos (*Cacatua alba*).

Age in days	Parent-reared	Weight (g*) Hand-reared	Hand-reared
25	261	170	230
30	292	228	302
32	301	258	340
34	320	302	364
36	316	322	396
37	332	342	412
41	402	388	453
44	406	415	476
50	432	470	515
54	432	475	535
68	–	–	530
70	444	495	–
80	512	470	500
82	520	460	495

* 1g = 0.0353oz.

Judging by the amount of scar tissue around it, the wood had been in position a minimum of two weeks, yet there was hardly any sign of infection, although the air sacs on one side were cloudy. A similar piece of wood, 3 cm (1¼ in) long, was found in the stomach.

Courtship display The crest feathers are raised and those of the sides of the head opened outwards, making the bird look enormous; in addition, the wings are held away from the body, adding to the impression of size. This display is also used for threat, to frighten an intruder. It is very effective, for the result is startling. In courtship this is accompanied by screaming and strutting in the male.

Clutch size 2; occasionally 1.
Incubation period 27–28 days.
Newly hatched chicks Bright yellow down, not dense, thickest on upperparts; beak pinkish. Weight normally between 16 g and 18 g (about ⅝ oz).
Young in nest About 14 weeks.
Origin Indonesia: northern Moluccan islands – Halmahera (18,000 km²/6,950 sq. miles), Bacan (5,700 km²/2,200 sq. miles). In the past, the range of this cockatoo was thought to include the island of Obi, and in the nineteenth century specimens were believed to have been collected from the small offshore island of Bisa. However, according to Frank Lambert (pers. comm., 1992), it is unlikely that they occurred naturally on either island. He spent four

At 43 days, this young hand-reared Umbrella Cockatoo (*Cacatua alba*) weighed 452 g (16⅛ oz).

Umbrella Cockatoo (*Cacatua alba*), parent-reared, aged 29 days; weight 295 g (10½ oz).

weeks in the field on Obi without seeing or hearing cockatoos and was told by people working in the forests throughout the island that the cockatoo did not occur there. Cockatoos from Bacan are sent to Ambon on boats which stop en route at Bisa and Obi, where some are bought as pets.

Natural history The Umbrella Cockatoo was locally common until the 1980s. During that decade it was trapped so intensively for export that, by the time it was the subject of a field study, more than two birds were rarely observed together, and then only in preparation for roosting (Milton & Marhadi, 1987). The local people stated that trapping was the cause of the decline. The cockatoos were not seen in roosting flocks of up to 50 individuals noted by Smiet (1985) in the interior of Halmahera.

Milton and Marhadi stated that they were found near the coast and inland, in primary and secondary forest, even forest being actively harvested and, on Bacan, in gardens and plantations.

Status and conservation Although not listed on Appendix I of CITES, by 1991 the Umbrella Cockatoo was considered to be endangered. Populations were not critically low at that time but would become so if trade were not controlled and suitable areas set aside to protect this species (Lambert, Wirth *et al.* 1992). In 1992 the Indonesian Government imposed a zero-capture quota for the Umbrella Cockatoo. There are several proposed reserves in the northern Moluccan islands but none, perhaps, if established, will provide adequate protection in the long term, because of altitude and topography. ICBP proposed that further surveys be carried out on Bacan to identify areas that would safeguard viable populations. Research needs to be carried out to assess the effects of current logging practices on breeding and food resources.

Eastern Long-billed Corella
Cacatua tenuirostris

Crest Short corella type, hardly visible when relaxed, like a small helmet when erected; feathers white, with orange bases.

Plumage Lores and forehead orange-scarlet; this colour also found at the bases of the feathers of head, nape, mantle and upper breast; undersides of flight and tail feathers tinged with pale yellow.

Beak and eyes Beak whitish; cere feathered. Iris dark brown. Bare skin around the eye blue-grey and more extensive under the eye.

Length 40 cm (16 in).

Weight About 600 g (21 oz). Males are usually heavier than females.

Sexual dimorphism None.

Immature birds Usually less orange-scarlet on the upper breast; upper mandible shorter.

Sub-species None.

Captive status A century or more ago this cockatoo was a fairly common and often highly cherished pet in Europe and in Australia. During the twentieth century it was not frequently exported and, by 1959, when Australia ceased to permit the export of its native fauna, it was rare and remains so, in aviculture. In Australia it was seldom seen as an aviary bird (being a popular pet) until about 1970. Aviculturists then started to

take an interest in it; however, in the early 1980s legal trapping was permitted because these corellas were damaging crops. Sindel and Lynn (1989) record what happened next:

> . . . the avicultural world was flooded with 10,000 wild-caught Long-bills. Aviary-bred specimens became difficult to dispose of thus making this cockatoo less desirable and the number of pairs held in aviaries for breeding purposes was drastically reduced.

Pet potential and personality Young birds make excellent pets. In Australia its popularity was due to its 'reputation of being the best talker of the Australian cockatoos', in addition to becoming 'remarkably tame and affectionate'. Lendon (1979) also

Eastern Long-billed Corella (*Cacatua tenuirostris*).

noted: 'The demand for young ones was so great that, until placed on the protected lists, the bird shops were crowded with them each season.'

Aviculture and breeding Although breeding successes in Australia must have been fairly numerous, little has been recorded on the subject. Shephard (1989) believes this cockatoo to be 'extremely hard to breed' and Sindel (Sindel & Lynn, 1989) has found it to be 'more difficult to please with nesting sites than any other cockatoo'. Because of its scarcity outside Australia, where its value is high, very few breedings have occurred.

The first proven success recorded occurred in San Diego Zoo in California in 1959. One was parent-reared – and this was repeated in the following year. Rearing foods included sunflower seed, whole corn, wheat, apple, carrot, sweet potatoes, bread, lettuce, fresh corn, pinenuts and peanuts. By 1980, only 15 individuals of this species were known in American zoos. These included a pair at Birmingham Zoo, Alabama, which hatched two chicks in April 1981, one of which was hand-reared and one parent-reared. At that time they were housed in an aviary measuring 2.7 m × 2.4 m × 2.4 m high (9 ft × 8 ft × 8 ft high). This was attached to an indoor cage where the food and water were placed. The cockatoos were provided with a nest box which measured 80 cm (32 in) high and 35 cm (14 in) square. It contained peat moss to a depth of 7.5 cm (3 in). The clutch size for 1981 was not stated. In 1982 the pair was moved to a larger aviary, 4.7 m (15½ ft) long. Two eggs were laid, one of which was fertile. The chick was being reared by the parents when the breeding was reported (Pfeifer, 1983).

In 1985 a third American zoo – San Antonio, in Texas – was successful in breeding this species. This success was repeated in 1986, in which year San Diego again bred this corella. During this period Auckland Zoo in New Zealand was consistently successful. A few zoos were able to obtain this species legally in exchange for other birds and animals – the only means of exporting it.

In Australia the first breeder was Alan Lendon in 1968. The male was timid and unable to fly due to a wing injury and the female was very tame with a strong tendency to human fixation. In August 1968 a hollow log was provided, measuring 1.5 m (5 ft) long with an internal diameter of about 15 cm (6 in). The first of three eggs was seen on 22 September. Incubation apparently started when the second egg was laid, the male performing this duty during most of the day, and the female during the early morning, later afternoon and at night. Two of the eggs were fertile and hatched on 16 and 17 October. One chick died at about 1 week old; the other left the nest on 10 December. The male fed the young cockatoo for several weeks after it fledged. He then started to pursue the female around the aviary but, being flightless, he was unable to harm her. The pair was then presented to Adelaide Zoo, where they reared two young in 1970 (Lendon, 1979).

After a pair had been in the aviaries of an aviculturist from Victoria for three years the male started to make 'a devilish noise with a peculiar call' at first light; this was continued for two to three hours. The male performed:

gymnastics by hanging upside-down doing somersaults until he got the female to follow suit. They would continue the same ritual for about four weeks, following which the female would edge her way slowly towards the male and then copulation would begin. ('Country Aviculturist', 1991)

Two eggs were laid and reportedly hatched 21–23 days later. The author emphasised that the down colour was grey, not white. One chick died and a second was found dying when the parents deserted the nest. The following season the diet was altered (see pp. 58 and 60) and the pair hatched and reared one youngster. During the first week of the chick's life the female was seen in the aviary only once daily. In the fifth week of its life, she left the nest four to six times daily to feed; the male also visited the log. This continued for 16–18 days; then one of the parents would sit on top of the log while the other fed the youngster, each making four to six visits to the nest daily. The young cockatoo left the nest at nine weeks when the orbital ring was still white.

Ian and Rose Langdon of Mildura, Victoria, own a pair which, in 1992, had been breeding for six years. For the first two years the pair hatched and reared a single chick; subsequently they reared two each year. They nest in a hollow log about 1.2 m (4 ft) long, hung almost vertically. The actual nest is only about 45 cm (18 in) from the entrance – a natural one near the top of the log. On one occasion they hatched and reared a Leadbeater's Cockatoo which left the nest one week before their own young. A very close bond exists in this pair, with much preening and mating before nesting occurs. Nest inspection is not difficult, thus development of the young can be closely monitored.

Outside Australia there are very few breeding pairs. In Germany, Dr R. Peters has bred this species since 1990 when two young were reared. He keeps two pairs, each in aviaries 4 m × 2 m × 2 m high (13 ft × 6 ft 8 in × 6 ft 8 in high), plus a small shelter. Because they are nervous, disturbance is kept to a minimum and they are tended only once daily. They have a choice of nest sites which, for each pair, includes a natural log about 1 m (3 ft) long, without a top, and fixed at an angle of 45°. One female laid three eggs in 1990, the second and third being laid on 6 and 9 April. The male incubates for part of the day. The first egg pipped after 23 days and hatched one day later. The three eggs hatched at intervals of three days. The smallest chick died at two days because it could not compete for food with its larger siblings. At 10 days the elder chick weighed 60 g (2⅛ oz) and the smaller was not growing so well. Both were therefore hand-reared and made delightful pets.

In 1991 the female laid the first of three eggs on 26 March. The first pipped after 24 days and hatched after 25 days but the chick died because the temperature fell to −5°C (23°F). A heating plate was then fixed on the bottom of the log. The second and third eggs hatched after an incubation period of 25 days. Dr Peters noted that the down colour of the chicks was orange.

The younger chick was not well fed, therefore the elder chick was removed and hand-fed. Dr Peters commented:

> The strongest one will fight his smaller brother and sister until he is overfull and can't take another mouthful.

When the elder chick was returned to the nest after two weeks, the size difference was greatly reduced. The young left the nest at the ages of 55 and 60 days. The following year the same technique of removing young from the nest for a period was used and three young were reared. At least half the rearing food consisted of oats which had been thrown on the aviary floor to germinate (Peters, pers. comm., 1992).

Dr Peters described the voice of this species as more melodious and less shrill than that of most other cockatoos. His gave loud trumpeting calls in the early morning and shortly before sunset.

Courtship display The male struts along the perch with crest erect, bobbing his head and calling loudly. The call has been described as 'an unusual gutteral yodelling sound, unlike the call of any other Australian cockatoo' (Sindel & Lynn, 1989).

Clutch size Usually 3; occasionally 2.

Incubation period 24 days.

Newly hatched chicks Variously described as having 'wispy off-white down' (Sindel & Lynn, 1989, yet the photograph shows the newly hatched chick with yellow down), grey down ('Country Aviculturist' 1991) and orange down (Peters, *in litt.*, 1992).

Young in nest Usually 55–60 days, but up to nine weeks has been recorded.

Origin Australia: its range is quite small, extending over south-eastern South Australia (from the Coorong region) as far east as Wagga Wagga in New South Wales and southwards to the Victoria coast (almost to Port Philip Bay) and northwards to the Mildura region. Several isolated populations have resulted from escaped or released birds on the outskirts of Perth, Sydney and Gosford.

Natural history This cockatoo occurs in the more open types of woodland and in trees near pastures and paddocks, usually near water. Once breeding is over, it is found in large noisy flocks, often feeding on the ground, sometimes with Greater Sulphur-cresteds or Galahs. During the breeding season, it is seen in small groups made up of pairs which do not move far from their nesting sites.

It feeds on the seeds of grasses and herbaceous plants, also roots, nuts, berries and fruits. Especially favoured are the corms of the introduced onion grass (*Romulea longifolia*) which it is adept at extracting with its long beak. Its habit of digging up newly sown crops and feeding on ripening cereal and sunflower crops has caused it to be persecuted by farmers. Forshaw (1981) stated:

Attacks on cereal crops were countered with poisoning campaigns and large numbers of cockatoos were destroyed.

Nests of this cockatoo are usually located in a living eucalyptus high up and near water. In the absence of suitable nesting trees, a hole in a cliff or bank may be used. Breeding occurs from July to November.

Status and conservation The decline of this cockatoo, which commenced in the nineteenth century, has affected its range and its numbers. At the time of European settlement its range in eastern Australia extended along the Darling and Murrumbidgee rivers, eastwards to the Mornington Peninsula (Blakers, Davies & Reilly, 1984). Forshaw (1981) believes that, at this period, it was already a relict species, having retreated from increasing aridity and the spread of drier conditions which were more favourable to the Western Long-billed Corella. It was once common in the Melbourne area but apparently

Parent-reared Eastern Long-billed Corellas (*Cacatua tenuirostris*) aged five weeks.

disappeared from there in the 1860s or 1870s. Its status now is generally rare but locally common. Its numbers have recovered from what was perhaps an all-time low in the late 1960s, which resulted from persecution, permission to trap birds on a large scale (see p. 32) and habitat (and nest site) destruction. Blakers, Davies & Riley (1984) stated that aerial and ground surveys indicated that the population in Victoria and South Australia exceeded 250,000 birds. Forshaw (1989) reported that:

> . . . a spectacular recovery has taken place, with numbers increasing to such an extent that serious depredations on crops are being experienced in parts of south-western Victoria and neighbouring south-eastern South Australia.

The apparent recovery should not give cause for complacency where this species is concerned. Further destruction of habitat and nest sites and renewed persecution would jeopardize the long-term survival of this distinctive cockatoo.

Western Long-billed Corella
Cacatua pastinator

Crest Typical corella type, hardly visible when relaxed, but like a small helmet (but longer than that in Goffin's, for example) when erected; feathers white, with orange-pink bases.

Plumage Lores orange-pink; rest of plumage white with bases of feathers of head, nape, mantle, breast and flanks orange-pink; underside of flight and tail feathers tinged with pale yellow.

Beak and eyes Beak whitish; cere feathered. Iris dark brown; bare skin around the eye blue-grey and more extensive under the eye.

Length About 42 cm (16½ in).

Weight About 600 g (21 oz). Males usually heavier than females.

Sexual dimorphism None.

Immature birds Pronounced orange-red feathers on forehead; skin around the eye bluer in shade; upper mandible shorter and less curved. By or before eight months, almost indistinguishable from adults.

Captive status Uncommon but increasing in Australian aviculture; very rare outside Australia.

Pet potential and personality For those Australians who can cater for a highly intelligent and mischievous bird that cannot be left unattended outside its cage, it has good potential. Outside Australia it is too rare to consider as a pet. Its personality is quite wonderful! For me, the appeal of this species is irresistible. It must be one of the most playful birds in existence and even appears to have a sense of humour! It is full of confidence, vitality and activity.

Aviculture and breeding Very little has been recorded about this species in captivity; no breeding was reported until the 1971–72 season when one was reared at Perth Zoo. This zoo subsequently recorded further successes. In 1985 Jim Gill of New South Wales reared one chick by hand from the age of 10 days. An egg from the same pair was placed in an incubator by Stan Sindel and the resulting chick was successfully hand-reared (Sindel & Lynn, 1989). In 1987, when I became curator at Loro Parque, Tenerife, the collection included a wonderful pair of *C.*

pastinator, the male of which (presumably the male as he was very excitable) unfortunately mutilated chicks. In 1988 seven eggs were laid during a period of 27 days; the eggs were removed to the safety of an incubator as soon as they were laid. Five of these hatched and all the chicks were reared. Thus started my affection for this marvellous cockatoo.

No parrot I have ever known had a stronger personality than the male of the pair; indeed, one admirer would come from Switzerland every year to look at him. On one occasion she was found in tears by the cockatoo aviaries. He was not there and she feared he was dead. I explained he was in a breeding aviary off-exhibit and his sons had taken his place to entertain the public. I am not sure who was the most amusing. The male could put on a wonderful performance, but only for one keeper whom he adored and who was permitted to pick him up and tuck him in his shirt. With this keeper he would play with the rake used to clean the floor, following it round and round until he fell over, dizzy. Or he would bound about, jumping up and down, both feet leaving the ground simultaneously. It was a hilarious performance which left visitors spellbound. However, if another keeper entered the aviary, that keeper had to keep his wits about him every instant to avoid being attacked.

Because there was a 'gang' of them, the young provided the most marvellous psittacine entertainment I have ever witnessed. They would play together on the floor for hours. Any object placed in the aviary became an item for investigation and fun. Early every morning I would take them a stale bread roll. This evoked a tug of war which usually left one or more lying on its back in the sand, with feet clenched. A couple of times I tried to photograph their antics but, on entering the aviary, I would immediately become the centre of investigation, my camera, hair, clothes and anatomy being thoroughly explored by mischievous beaks. The only sensible course of action was to beat a hasty retreat! Photography from outside the aviary was equally impossible as the cockatoos would come bounding up, often with Kea-like leaps, to look in the lens.

Development of these young from hatching to weaning was as follows: newly hatched (see p. 192); two weeks – eyes half open; three weeks – eyes open, sparse yellow down, wing feathers nearly erupting; four weeks – feathers of wings, body, head and crest in quills or starting to erupt; five weeks – head and crest feathers partly in quills, tail feathers starting to erupt, all other feathers erupted; seven weeks – tail not full length but otherwise fully feathered. They were weaned between 10 and 11 weeks of age.

Table 10
Average weights of five Western Long-billed Corellas
(*Cacatua pastinator*) hatched at Loro Parque, March/April 1988.

Day hatched	Weight before and after the first feed of the day (in g*)	Day hatched	Weight before and after the first feed of the day (in g*)
1	15/16	29	237/256
2	17/18	31	261/285
3	19/21	33	282/304
4	21/23	35	305/330
5	24/26	37	324/345
6	27/29	39	347/370
7	31/33	41	362/388
8	35/38	43	375/406
9	39/43	45	383/408
10	43/46	47	402/429
11	48/52	49	420/450
12	55/60	51	439/465
13	61/67	53	445/476
14	69/76	55	462/499
15	76/85	57	475/507
16	86/94	60	480/504
17	95/103	63	482/504
18	103/114	66	481/504
19	112/123	69	475/488
20	124/136	72	453/476
21	136/148	75	448/465
23	158/173	78 (one	
25	182/198	only, four	
27	209/226	weaned)	448/455

* 1g = 0.0353oz.

Western Long-billed Corellas (*Cacatua pastinator*).

Clutch size 2–4.

Incubation period 24 days; up to 26 days in an incubator.

Newly hatched chicks Down yellow and of medium profusion. Weight about 15 gm (½ oz). (Four of the five chicks which hatched in an incubator at Loro Parque in 1988 were weighed on hatching: 16.3 g, 14.1 g, 15.5 g and 14.1 g (½ oz).)

Young in nest About eight weeks.

Origin Australia: Western Australia – the south-western region. There are two isolated populations, separated at latitude 32°S, according to *The Atlas of Australian Birds*. The present range is that of relict populations; formerly this cockatoo was more widely distributed along the coastal plains and woodlands.

Natural history The Western Long-billed Cockatoo was formerly much more abundant; in the mid-1800s, large flocks were present along the Swan River, for example. At the beginning of the twentieth century it was widespread and abundant throughout the south-west but within a decade had disappeared from many areas (Forshaw, 1981) and its decline continued. Sindel and Lynn (1989) believe its numbers may have reached 'an all-time low' during the 1960s. Then, aided by legal protection, its numbers gradually increased. By the early 1980s the population was believed to consist of about 1,000 birds in the Lake Muir–Boyup Brook area and about 5,000 in the region bounded by Geraldton, Morawa, Mukinbudin, Northam and Jurien (CSIRO, 1982).

Much suitable habitat has been destroyed; this cockatoo prefers open forest, eucalyptus woodland, localities with trees along water courses, and farmlands with large trees. Small flocks occur in the isolated remnants of suitable habitat in the wheat belt. A study which commenced in 1977 at Burakin, 200 km (125 miles) north-east of Perth, showed that, during the breeding season, there were about 20 pairs of breeding birds and 50–150 immature birds. After fledging, all the *C. pastinators* in the breeding area congregate for two to three weeks, then move to the summer feeding area, perhaps 80–150 km (50–95 miles) distant.

A CSIRO report (CSIRO, 1982) states:

> The summer feeding area may draw all the corellas from an area of up to 6,000 km². During the summer the adults and their young stay together. These bonds are broken in the autumn when the birds start moving back to the breeding areas, and there the adult and immature birds form a single flock. As the breeding season approaches, the adults spend more and more time near their nest tree, and when egg laying is reached there is little or no contact between adults and immature birds.

The young cockatoos stay together in a flock until they commence to breed at 3–5 years. However, only 20–35 per cent survive to this age.

Status and conservation This cockatoo has adapted to existence in agricultural areas with large trees. Its future should be secure while its protected status is maintained and sufficient large trees survive with suitable nesting holes. However, it has already been demonstrated how rapidly it can decline under pressure.

Western Long-billed Corellas (*Cacatua pastinator*) aged 51, 54 and 55 days, hand-reared.

Bare-eyed Cockatoo or
Little Corella
Cacatua sanguinea

Crest Normally not evident; it lies flat on the head but erected forms an attractive helmet shape; white, the feathers being pinkish-red at the bases.

Plumage White; lores pink, also the bases of many body feathers; underside of wing and tail feathers washed with yellow.

Beak and eyes Beak greyish-white; cere feathered. Iris brown; a bare area of blue skin surrounds the eye, more extensive beneath it.

Length 38 cm (15 in).

Weight 430 g (15⅛ oz) to about 580 g (20½ oz); smaller sub-species approximately 350 g (12½ oz).

Sexual dimorphism None.

Immature birds Area of bare skin surrounding the eye paler, less prominent and less extensive. For a few weeks after leaving the nest, they bear a marked resemblance to *C. goffini*.

Sub-species *C. s. gymnopis* has a slightly darker blue area of bare skin surrounding the eye and more pronounced orange-red on the lores. It is slightly smaller than the nominate race.

C. s. normantoni differs from the nominate race in the slightly darker blue skin surrounding the eye (but not as dark as in *C. s. gymnopis*) and in its slightly smaller size.

C. s. transfreta differs from *C. s. normantoni* in the brownish-yellow suffusion to the underside of the flight and tail feathers (Forshaw, 1989).

Captive status Common in Australia, much less so elsewhere.

Pet potential and personality In Aus-

tralia many Bare-eyed Cockatoos are kept as pets, becoming cherished members of the family. If obtained young, they are generally affectionate, amusing and good mimics. Most of them are happy extroverts who constantly seek attention.

Aviculture and breeding Until the early 1980s, when some Bare-eyed Cockatoos were exported from Papua New Guinea (because its export from Australia ceased in 1959) this species was rare in aviculture. It was seen mainly in zoos which had been able to obtain birds from Australian zoos on an exchange basis. In Europe, for example, this cockatoo had reared young in zoos in Whipsnade and Penscynor in the UK and in Rotterdam and Wassenaar in the Netherlands. In private collections it was virtually unknown and remains uncommon. Few Australian aviculturists are interested in breeding it because it is so common and inexpensive. In the USA it is more popular and an increasing number are hand-reared for pets.

This cockatoo often nests readily and proves prolific. For example, a pair belonging to Ulf Rohlin in Sweden reared 12 young between January 1985 and November 1987, seven of these in the year from November 1986. Belonging to the sub-species *C. s. normantoni*, they were usually double-brooded and proved to be excellent parents. None of the young was reared by hand. Male and female fed the young, with the male doing most of the feeding after they left the nest. On two occasions the female laid a third clutch but the eggs were infertile, probably because the male was still feeding the young.

The Bare-eyed seems to be less sensitive to its surroundings than some cockatoos. It is perhaps more

Bare-eyed Cockatoos (*Cacatua sanguinea*) with their three young. Their offspring always leave the nest at 45 days.

suitable than other species for those who can provide only a suspended cage.

Courtship display The male spreads his wings, erects his crest and screams repeatedly. He bobs his head as he confronts the female, bows and spreads his tail.

Clutch size 2–4, usually 3.

Incubation period 24–26 days according to various breeders' reports. However, in the pair in my care at Loro Parque the incubation period was 23 days. In Ulf Rohlin's pair, the incubation period was 23 days on eight occasions and 24 on four occasions.

Newly hatched chicks Down yellow and of medium profusion; beak horn-coloured. Weight about 11 g (⅜ oz).

Young in nest About 7 weeks but reports vary between 6 and 8 weeks. Mr Rohlin told me that you can 'set the clock' by his young; they always leave the nest at 45 days.

Origin Australia: approximately two-thirds of the country – from the interior of eastern Australia, west to the central-western coast (*C. s. gymnopis*); northern Australia from the Kimberley division of Western Australia east to the south-western shores of the Gulf of Carpentaria (*C. s. sanguinea*); west of Cape York Peninsula (there have also been sightings on the east coast of Cape York), south to the south-eastern shores of the Gulf of Carpentaria (*C. s. normantoni*). Southern New Guinea: between Merauke or the Kumbe and lower Fly Rivers (*C. s. transfreta*).

Natural history The Bare-eyed Cockatoo is among the most widespread and numerous of Australian parrots; one flock in north-western Australia contained an estimated 60,000–70,000 birds (Serventy & Whittell, 1976). It has benefited from the spread of agriculture and continues to extend its range. In addition,

Bare-eyed Cockatoo (*Cacatua sanguinea*): flock at Fogg Dam, near Darwin, Northern Territory.

there are isolated breeding populations in the vicinity of some large cities, such as Sydney, Melbourne, Brisbane and Perth. They probably originated from released or escaped pet birds. Sindel and Lynn (1989) state that they are 'common around inland towns and their local garbage tips, where they forage for food scraps'. Their natural diet consists of seeds, berries, nuts, fruits, roots, corms, blossoms, insects and their larvae. In some areas they feed extensively on the weed-pest double-gee (*Emex australis*); in other areas they cause damage to crops, including rice, millet and sorghum. Almost any type of habitat near water is frequented.

Nest sites are eucalyptus trees, especially *Eucalyptus wandoo*, with entrances at heights varying between about 3 m (10 ft) and 10 m (33 ft). Mean clutch size of 15 nests in one study was 2.3. Thirteen of these were successful, producing 28 young. When food is plentiful, more than one nest may be produced in one year. In New Guinea, the Bare-eyed Cockatoo has been recorded in large flocks in Merauke, Morehead and Bensbach in the Trans-Fly region. Coates (1985) states that it is presumably a breeding resident subject to local movements. It is seen in twos, threes and flocks numbering from a few to 30 birds, or more. Hundreds have been seen in the rice fields at Kurik and as many as 200 were feeding on seed-bearing plants along the Kumbe River near Merauke.

Status and conservation The Bare-eyed Cockatoo is widespread and common in Australia and common in its limited Papua New Guinea range. No conservation measures, other than preserving trees suitable for nesting, are necessary.

Bare-eyed Cockatoos (*Cacatua sanguinea normantoni*): pair.

Goffin's Cockatoo
Cacatua goffini

Crest Normally not evident, lying flat on the head; erected to form an attractive helmet-shape; white, feathers pink at the base.

Plumage White, pink on lores; underside of flight and tail feathers suffused with pale yellow.

Beak and eyes Beak greyish-white; cere feathered. In good light, eye black in the male, brown in the female; in poor light, difficult to distinguish the iris colour.

Length 30–32 cm (about 12 in).

Weight About 300 g (10½ oz). Males slightly heavier than females.

Sexual dimorphism The head and the area of bare skin surrounding the eye usually noticeably larger in the male. See also Beak and eyes.

Immature birds Skin around the eye tinged with blue; eye dark grey. Coral-pink on lores and forehead usually more pronounced than in the adult.

Sub-species None.

Captive status Common (rare until early 1970s); unknown in Australia. In the TRAFFIC (USA) *Psittacine captive breeding survey* (of breeders and zoos) held in 1989, Goffin's Cockatoo was the second most abundant cockatoo and the ninth most common parrot species. Of the 31,008 birds in the census, 711 were Goffin's Cockatoos (215 owners). Of the Goffin's Cockatoos, 602 were known to be wild-caught and only 42 were known to be captive-bred. These figures are probably representative, percentage-wise, of the situation in other aviculturally-oriented countries.

Pet potential and personality Some hand-reared birds make good pets but others are too restless and destructive to adapt well to close confinement. Except when very young, they are quite independent and less likely to become an affectionate pet than an Umbrella, for example.

Aviculture and breeding Wild-caught birds are not among the easiest cockatoos to breed; many pairs seem very discriminating regarding choice of nest site or react adversely to something in their environment, and this deters them from breeding. In the USA most of the young hatched are hand-reared as pets. In most other countries, many breeders prefer to give their pairs a chance to rear their own young, which are less likely to be sold as pets. I made repeated pleas that aviculturists should heed the importance of captive-breeding for this cockatoos (e.g. Low, 1979b, 1980b) but not until 1991 was a breeding project set up for this species – in Germany. In October a group of breeders met and formed the *Erhaltungszuchtprojekt Goffin-Kakadu*. The aim of the project is to help the survival of this species in the wild and in captivity (Künne, 1992). [Further information can be obtained from Hans-Jürgen Künne, Natruper Strasse 235, W–4500 Osnabrück, Germany.]

Not a lot has been recorded about the rearing of young of this species by the parents. When I lived in London my pair nested for seven years in an aviary 2 m (6 ft) from my kitchen window. Their behaviour was a constant source of interest and amusement to me. They hatched their first chicks in 1979, after seven years in the aviary (see Low 1979a, 1979b, 1980b and 1992a). These two chicks were hand-reared from the age of three weeks. In 1980 the female laid about two weeks earlier than the previous year. A chick was heard on 11 May; an eggshell was thrown out of the log on 12 May. The second egg contained a fully-formed chick which had died before hatching. This time the female played a greater role in chick care; both birds spent most of the day in the log. As before, favoured rearing foods were spinach, sweet-corn kernels, sunflower seed and spray millet. After the chick was three weeks old, both parents roosted outside the log; fortunately (no feathers have erupted at this age), the weather was warm. At the beginning of July the young Goffin's was seen at the nest entrance; it would back away quickly if it saw anyone, open-beaked and swaying in alarm (the typical behaviour of young cockatoos.) A male, he left the nest at nine weeks old, was flying with confidence two days later and was seen eating corn the following day. The previous evening he had roosted in the log for the last time. He was seen soliciting food until the beginning of September, but only from the male. One day I was surprised to see the female also solicit food from the male, which is not normal behaviour; no doubt she resented the attention her young son was receiving. Within a couple of weeks of emerging from the nest he was almost indistinguishable from the adults, from whom he was separated on 20 September. It was noticeable that, at four months old, his voice was identical to that of an adult's whereas, at the same time, the voices of the hand-reared young from the previous year retained an immature quality (Low, 1980b).

In the survey referred to on p. 198, 297 pairs hatched 77 young, of which at least 68 were weaned (= 0.25 young hatched per pair, as against 1.4 hatched per pair in the Umbrella). While most cockatoos will enter almost any nest box, in my experience, this is not so of Goffin's Cockatoos. My own pair made no attempt to enter one of several nest

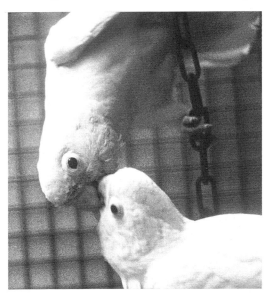

Male Goffin's Cockatoo (*Cacatua goffini*) feeding his young son.

boxes provided during a period of seven years. They would look inside and scream, apparently in suspicion. However, a horizontal log with a natural entrance placed on the ground immediately interested them. They accepted it and bred every year, until little remained of the original log which had been frequently repaired. The only pair currently in my care, at the breeding centre of Palmitos Park, did not enter a nest box in a period of three years. During this time they were kept in one suspended cage and three different aviaries. Not until the fourth move did they accept (almost immediately) a nest box. It had an additional entrance hole gnawed in the side by the previous occupants and this was the entrance they used.

It is unusual for an aviculturist to document the breeding performance of one particular pair of birds over an extended period, thus the account of the results from one pair of Goffin's Cockatoos during the period 1974–89 is of interest (Schulte, 1990). They had four different forms of accommodation: a small box cage indoors, outdoor aviary (1 year only), indoor aviary and a large box cage indoors. Schulte felt that a box cage was most suitable for his shy, imported birds, 'as shy birds feel more secure in a sheltered cage. However, compatibility of the pair is necessary, as the female cannot escape from an aggressive male.'

In only two years did the female nest twice. Of the 18 clutches, two failed to produce chicks, five produced one chick and 11 produced two. No young were reared from seven clutches, one was reared in three instances and two were reared on eight occasions. Results were erratic; young died at various stages

Hand-reared Goffin's Cockatoo (*Cacatua goffini*) aged about 28 days.

Goffin's Cockatoos (*Cacatua goffini*): male and youngster with female.

and three were saved by hand-rearing. The net result was 19 young reared in 17 years, or 1.1 fledged per year.

Courtship display The male erects the crest, gives a quavering cry, bows the head and sometimes jumps.

Clutch size 2, rarely 1 or 3. One breeder recorded the first 3-egg clutch after the female had been laying for 13 years (Day & Day, 1991). One female laid two clutches annually, of one egg and two eggs.

Incubation period 28 days. The average period for 13 eggs (latter two weeks in incubator) was 24.7 days (Schubot, Clubb & Clubb, 1992).

Newly hatched chicks Sparsely covered with white down. Weight 10–11 g (about ⅜ oz).

Young in nest About 10 weeks.

Origin Indonesia: Tanimbar Islands – the larger of the group, e.g. Jamdena, Foradate and Selaru (Künne, 1992); also on Tual in the Kai Islands.

Natural history Judging by the numbers exported, this must have been an extremely abundant species. According to ICBP's draft report *Parrots: an action plan* (1992), the cockatoo and the other Tanimbar endemic (*Eos reticulata*) have 'been traded in very large numbers during the last decade: in excess of 100,000 Tanimbar Corellas [Goffin's] have been recorded in trade'. Historically, nothing was known about it. In the first volume of *Parrots in Captivity*, published during the mid-1980s, W. T. Greene stated that, according to the *Catalogue of the London Zoological Society*, it came from Queensland, but Dr Karl Russ, the eminent German ornithologist, gave its origin as the Solomon Islands. Greene had accurately described the origin of other cockatoo species.

A century later Goffin's is endangered by over-trapping and still little is known about its wild life. When W. H. Timmis visited

Jamdena in 1962 it was heavily forested and he saw large numbers of Goffin's Cockatoos, on the coast and inland. At dusk they returned to their roosting trees, some of these along water courses, where they would settle on the outermost branches (Low, 1980a). In 1981, 10 years after mass export of this cockatoo commenced, F. Smiet found flocks of up to 35 birds on Jamdena. They were described as a serious pest of maize crops. It is believed that extensive deforestation has occurred, probably commencing when this species was first exported commercially in 1971.

Status and conservation The first move to conserve this species was taken in 1992 (a decade late) when it was placed on Appendix I of CITES. This came into effect in June of that year. However, at that time this cockatoo was not protected in Indonesia and officials contacted by the World Parrot Trust were unaware that it had been placed on Appendix I. At the same time ICBP developed a project proposal for Tanimbar which aimed to provide information on the status and ecology of this species and the Blue-streaked Lory (*Eos reticulata*). The primary objectives were to assess the status of both species, document the extent and organization of the bird trade on Tanimbar and the Kai Islands, produce an inventory of the bird fauna of proposed protected areas, survey them and identify future management needs. Finally, it was planned to investigate the habitat requirements and ecology of the islands' parrots and endemic bird species.

ICBP's project proposal, dated August 1992, noted:

The Indonesian Government has shown a considerable commitment to implement CITES, but its efforts have been hampered by the lack of resources, scientific data, and trained personnel. The difficulties faced are compounded by the very high external demand for CITES-listed species and the geography of the country with extensive coastlines and thousands of islands making control of trade extremely difficult.

Ducorp's Cockatoo
Cacatua ducorpsii

Crest A full helmet-type crest, much higher than in *C. goffini* or *C. haematuropygia*; feathers white, with pink at the base.

Plumage Entirely white except for salmon-coloured down below the feathers of the cheeks and upper breast. Dr R. Burkard noted (pers. comm., 1985): 'It has the finest plumage of all white cockatoos. The plumage takes on a rose-red glimmer in sunlight'.

Beak and eyes Beak white tinged with grey. Iris dark brown in males, reddish-brown in females; skin around the eye blue.

Length 30 cm (12 in). Males are slightly larger than females.

Weight 360 g (12¾ oz).

Sexual dimorphism See Beak and eyes.

Immature birds Like adults but iris dark grey. The female acquires adult eye coloration at about two years.

Sub-species None.

Captive status Rare; commercial export was not permitted until 1990. Previously a small number of birds were collected privately and went to collections in Switzerland and Tenerife.

Pet potential and personality Too rare to be kept as a pet, at the time of writing, but should this species become more widely available, birds obtained when young would make excellent pets due to their relatively small size and high degree of intelligence. A single male on exhibit at Loro Parque, Tenerife, during my period there, 'played to the house' in a manner equalled only by the male *C. pastinator* (of more than 1,000 parrots on show). There was often a crowd of admirers around his aviary. One keeper had even taught him to put out his tongue on command.

Aviculture and breeding Due to its rarity in aviaries, very few successes have been recorded. The first would appear to be that which occurred in 1982 in Hawaii, in the aviaries of Richard Hart and Hiroshi Tagami. (No details were published, to my knowledge.) Seven pairs collected in the early 1980s for Dr R. Burkard of Switzerland were kept in aviaries whose minimum size was 16 m (52 ft) square. Because of the highly aggressive behaviour of the males, their wings were clipped. One breeding attempt resulted in the loss of the female's life; the male killed her when the three chicks were between one and two weeks old. At Loro Parque, Tenerife, a female was also killed by a male. He was then paired to a female Bare-eyed Cockatoo who was better able to cope with his aggressiveness. She laid on 4 and 9 April 1984. The male incubated during the day (presumably the female incubated at night) and chicks hatched on 29 April and 2 May. The young were fed mainly by the male on bread and milk, fruit and vegetables, and left the nest on 30 June. When adult, it was difficult to dis-

tinguish them from true *C. ducorpsii* until they were closely examined.

Clutch size 2–3.

Incubation period About 26 days.

Newly hatched chicks No description known to author.

Young in nest About nine weeks (one record only).

Origin Solomon Islands (a volcanic archipelago in the south-west Pacific): Bougainville (the largest of the group, 10,600 km²/4,100 sq. miles) and eastwards to Malaita; it is said to be absent from the San Cristobal group.

Natural history All reports, including those of recent years, describe this cockatoo as common. On Bougainville, in 1964, it was seen by R. Schodde most frequently between sea level and 700 m (2,300 ft) in pairs or small flocks. It occurs in most lowland timbered areas, including the vicinity of village gardens, and even in stunted cloud forest at about 1,700 m (5,500 ft). In northern Guadalcanal in January 1979, it was reported as common in upland forests and in the lowlands (Forshaw, 1989). In September 1979, H. Leibfarth found them to be especially common on Guadalcanal and Malaita (Diefenbach, 1985). They have been described as noisy and conspicuous, but wary. They fly with shallow, jerky wing beats, interspersed with gliding. Food includes caterpillars and insects. They cause damage to villagers' crops, eating papaya and even digging up sweet potatoes.

Status and conservation This is the only island cockatoo which is still common, partly because trapping for commercial purposes has never occurred. Officials should heed the plight of several Indonesian island species which have been trapped almost to extinction, and ensure that, if export occurs, trade is strictly controlled and numbers are low.

Ducorp's Cockatoo (*Cacatua ducorpsii*): male.

Red-vented or Philippine Cockatoo
Cacatua haematuropygia

Crest Helmet type, white with bases of the feathers yellow and pink.

Plumage White with a slight yellow tinge; underside of tail and flight feathers yellow; undertail coverts red margined with white.

Beak and eyes Beak whitish with a tinge of grey. Iris dark brown in the male, reddish-brown in the female. Skin around the eye white.

Length 30 cm (12 in).

Weight About 300 g (10½ oz).

Sexual dimorphism See Beak and eyes.

Immature birds Like adults except for the greyish iris.

Sub-species None.

Captive status Rare. It was very rare until the 1970s and 1980s when commercial importation occurred. However, the numbers imported were never large (unlike those of Indonesian cockatoos) and this factor, combined with high mortality during the first few months in captivity, has resulted in the species remaining rare. Usual causes of mortality were psittacine beak and feather disease and aspergillosis – and females seemed more susceptible than males. The result was that the numbers of pairs kept has never been large (see p. 120).

One of the reasons why the Red-vented Cockatoo is not common in Europe is that, during the 1980s, this was one of the species banned by the European Commission from importation. It seems likely that, as a result, many birds entered Japan instead of Europe. There is very little information available about aviculture in Japan, and the status of this or any other parrot in captivity. There is no reason to believe that it has fared any better there. Its avicultural status must now be considered as rare and every possible step must be taken to locate pet birds, more than likely owned by people who cannot even identify the species. Aviculturists could help to direct any such birds they encounter into breeding situations by offering to exchange hand-reared young parrots of another species for Red-venteds which are not tame. Understandably, many people are reluctant to part with their pet birds but it is vitally important that as many wild-caught birds as possible are identified now, to strengthen the existing gene pool. None of these birds will have been recently imported and thus their long-term survival prospects should be good. If it is possible to pair up some of these genetically precious cockatoos, it goes without saying that they should be in the care of aviculturists or zoos who are interested in the preservation of the species. This means obtaining parent-reared young, if possible, or at least ensuring that the young remain with breeders and are not sold as pets.

Pet potential and personality It would be irresponsible to recommend this species as a pet, in view of its endangered status and the small numbers in aviculture. Its personality is closest to that of Goffin's.

Aviculture and breeding Worldwide there are few breeding pairs, but far more surplus males. The largest group is in the collection of Antonio de Dios in the Philippines: 20 pairs. In the USA it is now rare in private collections; by 1992 the only zoo breeding it was Fort Worth in Texas. Three hatched in April of that year, the second successful clutch from that pair. In France, Zoo Espace

Zoologique, St-Martin-la-Plaine, maintained two breeding pairs and one young pair in 1992, plus three young hatched that year. Also in France, Jardin aux Oiseaux, Upie, reared one youngster in 1992. A private breeder in the north had been breeding this species since 1990 (Boussekey, pers. comm., 1992).

In 1988 Antonio de Dios sent a pair of Red-vented Cockatoos to Loro Parque, Tenerife. They produced young a few weeks later. Another pair in the collection also produced chicks that year. Four were hatched, one died at four days and the other three were reared by

Red-vented Cockatoo
(*Cacatua haematuropygia*)
hand-reared from the egg.

hand. They were a great pleasure to rear. Their weights are shown in Table 11 and contrasted with one reared by John Heath of Cornwall in 1992. Chicks 2 and 3 were reared simultaneously. Peak weights were 333 g (11¾ oz) at 68 days (no. 1), 296 g (10½ oz) at 74 days (no. 2), 299 g (10½ oz) at 80 days (no. 3) and 308 g (10⅞ oz) at 51 days (no. 4) – which highlights the different rates of growth according to diet and other circumstances.

The parents of Mr Heath's pair were imported by Mrs S. Belford in 1981 and, in her care, produced fertile eggs. In 1984, when owned by Mrs Uebele, they became the first pair to breed in the UK. In 1988 they were obtained by Mr Heath and were the only pair known to be breeding in the UK in 1992. (At that time only eight birds were registered in the UK studbook.) In 1989 the three eggs laid by Mr Heath's pair were placed in an incubator, but failed to hatch. Eggs of the second clutch were laid on 1 and 4 June, left with the pair and hatched on 29 June and 1 July. One chick was hand-reared and the other remained with the pair and left the nest at the end of August. In 1990 the eggs laid on 4, 7 and 10 April were placed in an incubator but did not hatch. In 1991 the female laid on 22, 26 and 30 April and chicks hatched with the pair on 24, 25 and 28 May – which probably meant that incubation did not commence until 24 April. The chicks were removed on 24 and 31 May; they were independent by 24 August and 5 September when they weighed 344 g (12⅛ oz), 328 g (11⅝ oz) and 324 g (11⅜ oz). In 1992 eggs laid on 15 and 20 April were artificially incubated and these also failed to hatch. Eggs laid on 9 and 14 May hatched on 7 and 10 June; the first

Table 11
Weights of hand-reared Red-vented Cockatoos
(*Cacatua haematuropygia*).

Day hatched	Chick 1	Chick 2	Chick 3	Chick 4
	–	10.1	11.0	8.8
1	10.7	11.6	10.8	10.4
2	11.7	12.2	11.8	12.8
3	12.9	13.5	12.7	16.3
4	13.7	14.8	14.0	18.8
5	14.9	16.1	15.5	–
6	16.2	18.2	17.3	28.3
7	18.0	19.9	20.6	–
8	19.8	23.2	22.4	40
9	20.4	25.8	25.1	–
10	21.9	29.1	28.3	55
12	27	37	35	–
14	34	45	43	70
16	38	54	51	94
18	50	60	62	118
20	53	75	73	146
22	66	89	84	174
24	77	106	97	198
26	89	122	115	222
28	107	141	138	242
30	123	166	148	252
34	168	202	195	274
38	197	245	236	288
42	233	260	234	296
46	262	279	248	306
50	276	296	263	308
54	294	307	268	302
58	311	299	283	286
62	317	303	289	278
66	317	294	291	264
70	319	289	297	264
74	303	296	294	276
78	294	291	293	280
82	285	281	294	280
86	277	282	293	286
89	–	–	–	280

* 1g = 0.0353oz.
Chick 1, 2 and 3 reared at Loro Parque, Tenerife.
Chick 4 reared by John Heath, Cornwall, UK.

chick died at one day and the second was hand-reared.

Clutch size 2 or 3.

Incubation period 28 days in an incubator, sometimes slightly longer with the parents.

Newly hatched chicks Yellow down, not thick, on nape and upperparts; beak pink. Weight 10–11 g (⅜ oz).

Young in nest 9–10 weeks.

Origin Philippine Islands: formerly widespread throughout the islands, including the Palawan group and the Sulu Archipelago, it is now known to survive only on Palawan in the remoter coastal areas, on Mindanao and on Dinagat. By 1991 extensive ornithological surveys had failed to locate even a single bird on the four larger islands of Luzon, Mindanao, Panay and Negros (Tabaranza, 1991). However, surveys carried out in 1992 indicated that a few cockatoos did survive outside Palawan. They were found only in the following localities, all of which had populations estimated at about or fewer than 50 and up to 100 birds: Mindanao–Zamboanga del Sur, San Miguel and possibly also Linging; Siargao Island (north of Mindanao); Tawi-Tawi province and the small island of Masbate (Tabaranza, 1993).

Natural history This cockatoo was formerly common and widespread. In *Philippine Birds and Mammals*, published in 1977, it was described as 'widely distributed' but local, 'frequenting the well-forested areas in the interior so that it is not often encountered'. Flock size was described as 4–12 birds. Ripening corn and wild bananas (never cultivated ones) were favoured items of food. Several birds were seen in nest holes in tall dead trees in April and May in the interior of Negros. The trees were tall ones which had been left

standing in burned clearings that had been planted for rice for several seasons and then allowed to grow up with cogon grass. These clearings were interspersed with large patches of original dipterocarp forest in rolling country.

In 1985 Marc Boussekey searched various areas of eastern Cebu, western Leyte and southern Negros without locating any birds or obtaining local information on their presence. He was unable to find any on western Bohol but was told that there was a small population in the Bilar primary forest. It was inaccessible due to being a hiding place for the New People Army. In February and March 1987 he searched in vain for them in northern Luzon. Only on northern Palawan did he locate this cockatoo. On 28 February he found an active nest near Port Barton, in a tall dead tree in lightly degraded mountainous forest. The tree was standing alone in a clearing made by indigenous people, thus the pair was easy to observe. He made several more sightings on the western coast. A roosting group of 17 birds was observed in a large dead tree a few hundred metres from the coast. Many young and adult birds were seen in the Carty Mar market where they were sold as pets (Boussekey, pers. comm., 1992).

Four factors are involved in the decline of the Philippine cockatoo. First, deforestation in the Philippines has been extremely severe; one source stated that, by the early 1980s, 80 per cent of forests had been destroyed in the previous 50 years. These islands now have one of the highest percentages of endangered endemic birds of any nation in the world. Secondly, the cockatoo is, or was, considered a pest of corn and coconut crops and is, or was, shot and

Red-vented Cockatoo (*Cacatua haematuropygia*): male

persecuted, despite being protected by law. Thirdly, by the late 1980s, trapping had become the main threat to its survival. In 1991 the British ornithologist Frank Lambert completed a search for this species on Palawan on behalf of conservation organizations. Every single nest he located was guarded by a trapper who removed the nestlings when they were old enough. Worse, the cockatoos had become so scarce that trappers had started to remove one of the adults as well, by placing a sack in front of the entrance during the night. Those cockatoos remaining on Palawan are believed to be an ageing population with practically no recruitment because every known nest is emptied by trappers. Fourthly, introduced diseases have affected wild birds, and nest sites in some cases, are reported to be highly contaminated with the spores of the fungus *Aspergillus* (thus contributing to the high mortality rate of newly captured birds.)

Status and conservation The Red-vented Cockatoo is now considered to be critically endangered, with a rapidly declining population. In 1991 its numbers were estimated at between 1,000 and 4,000 birds, with between 800 and 1,000 on Palawan, its former stronghold. This is believed to represent a 60–90 per cent decline over the previous 10–15 years. Further research, including the surveying of numerous small islands, was to be completed during the early part of 1992. Implementation of the law protecting this species is vital if it is to survive. Illegal trapping, resulting in the cockatoos leaving the islands on freight and fishing boats bound for Japan and others being traded in Manila, must cease. Education of the local people is of paramount importance. The zoo at St-Martin-la-Plaine in France has funded the production of a poster promoting conservation of the *kalangay* (the native name for the Red-vented Cockatoo) in three languages – English, Tagalog and Cebuanão. It will be widely distributed in the provinces where the cockatoo survives. In 1992, Marc Boussekey, scientific advisor of the zoo, became the co-ordinator of a European Co-ordinated Breeding Programme (EEP) for this cockatoo. This and an international studbook will be vital for its survival within aviculture.

Glossy Cockatoo
Calyptorhynchus lathami

Crest The dense head feathers can be raised, but are not elongated and cannot be described as forming a true crest. (Many other parrots can raise their head feathers in display.)
Plumage Male – head, neck and underparts dark brown and upper parts black; the two central tail feathers black and the five on each side have a broad scarlet sub-terminal band. Female – a varying amount of bright yellow feathering on the head (or none, in rare cases); tail band red and yellow with horizontal black bars.
Beak and eyes Beak grey, usually slightly darker in the male; upper mandible bulbous and lower mandible exceptionally broad, an adaptation for breaking open *Casuarina* cones; cere not feathered. Iris dark brown.
Length 48 cm (19 in).
Weight About 430 g (15 oz).
Sexual dimorphism See Plumage.
Immature birds Feathers of the underparts widely margined with yellow.

A female Glossy Cockatoo (*Calyptorhynchus lathami*), one of a successful breeding pair, displaying to her owner.

Unlike adults, most of which completely lack spots, they are spotted to a greater or lesser degree in three areas: ear coverts, outer wing coverts and lesser underwing coverts (Courtney, 1986a). Tail similar to that of adult female but with more yellow in some birds. At 16–18 months half the tail feathers are moulted; the rest are lost at the next moult at 2½ years; however, one male still had five barred tail feathers at 3 years. Females lack yellow feathers on the head. One female acquired her first yellow head feather at 110 weeks and another at 123 weeks. Beak, in both sexes, greyish horn-coloured.

Sub-species None.

Captive status Rare but increasing in Australia; non-existent elsewhere.

Pet potential and personality Until this species is better established in aviculture it is not likely to be intentionally kept as a pet. However, I cannot think of any cockatoo – or, indeed, scarcely any other parrot – which is so endearing and affectionate. I make no apologies for repeating an opinion which perfectly describes this species:

. . . hand-reared males of the Glossy Black Cockatoo are the ultimate experience in bird ownership. They possess an extraordinary rapport with their human owners which is not possible to translate into words, other than to say that they are the 'dolphins of the bird world' . . . Perhaps rearing and owning a male Glossy may be the ultimate enlightenment for scientists who treat with disdain any suggestion of intelligence in birds. (Courtney, in Low, 1992a.)

It is not only with their 'owner' that Glossy Cockatoos are so remarkably affectionate. An encounter I had with a male belonging to Neville and Enid Connors will long remain in my memory. This male had briefly observed me on three or four occasions during the two days before I entered his aviary. The female was also present; she had laid an egg two days previously which she did not incubate. When I entered, the male instantly flew down to stand on my foot. I picked him up and he displayed, standing on my arm, spreading his tail to show the wide red band, depressing his back and making the distinctive double-call which Glossy Cockatoos use prior to copulation. He kept this up for some minutes. It was a wonderful feeling to be the recipient of this handsome bird's striking display. The Glossy may not be as large and imposing as the other *Calyptorhynchus* species but to me it is just as beautiful.

Aviculture and breeding There was a long-held myth that this species was unsuited to captivity because it could not survive without *Casuarina* seeds or cones. While most of those kept in Australia regularly or occasionally receive this food, not all do, and they have been bred in collections where *Casuarina* is not included in the diet. The Connors' Glossy Cockatoos receive a regular supply between February and September and a sporadic supply at other times. When young are in the nest about 30 cones per pair are given every other day. The basic diet consists of sunflower seed, almonds, peanuts, peas and silver beet.

A lengthy aviary is not essential for this species. The Connors keep their pairs in enclosures measuring 3 m × 1.7 m × 2.1 m high (10 ft × 6 ft × 7 ft high) and 4.5 m × 1.5 m × 2.4 m high (15 ft × 5 ft × 8 ft high).

The first breeding of this species occurred in the collection of Sir Edward Hallstrom in New South Wales in 1954. At that time few had even tried to maintain this cockatoo.

During the 1970s several breeding successes occurred but it was not until the 1980s that these increased significantly and a demand occurred which made this cockatoo one of the most highly-priced of native birds. Among the most consistent breeders at the time of writing are Neville and Enid Connors. They confidently predict that 'by the end of this century it should be the most frequently bred of all the Australian black cockatoos' (Connors & Connors, 1988).

Breeders invariably offer open-topped logs to this species. Breeding can commence as early as February but it is more usual for females to lay in April or May. It has been noted that some females will lay an egg which is neglected, then lay a second from a few days to up to one month later which will be incubated. Neville and Enid Connors recorded how one female left a one-day old chick unattended for 1¾ hours. They commented:

> With other parrot species such an absence would be of concern at that time of year, but young Glossys are covered with incredibly long fluffy yellow down. When looking down on the youngster you quite literally cannot tell which end is which until it moves!

Courtney (1986a) described the development of one parent-reared chick as follows:

> At one day old the chick moved about but did not hold up head. On 8th day was observed sitting upright some of time. At 20 days old was standing up, looking at observer, and still clad in dense yellow natal down, in size approximately a week old domestic fowl chick. At 21 days had acquired a dark appearance on head and

Glossy Cockatoo (*Calyptorhynchus lathami*): female.

back from tips of black pin feathers showing through down, this being a sudden noteworthy change, an 'age-mark'. At 27 days old, chick was size of a clenched fist, and a mass of short black feathers, tail estimated between 30–40 mm long, and uttered loud harsh grating alarm vocalizations when observed. At 70 days old, chick was observed to be completely feathered, but tail much too short for fledging. Although chick was first seen flying at 105 days old, it was observed that at slightest disturbance in vicinity, chick would quickly return to nest log, and sometimes even enter hollow, so fledging may have been some days before. Each night until fledging female stayed out of sight in log with chick. The male would roost away from nest until an hour after dark when he would quietly go to nest and camp, tail outwards, at entrance.

John Courtney noted that the juvenile food-begging call of this chick, in common with all others of this species which he had observed, was a brief repetitive, clear high-pitched squeak, very similar to chicks of the Banksian Cockatoo. As in the latter species, no food-swallowing vocalization is made.

In contrast to most cockatoos, males take little interest in their fledged young; some are aggressive towards them. If so they must be removed; otherwise they can stay four months with their parents (Sindel & Lynn, 1989).

Courtship display The male erects his 'crest' feathers, 'puffs out' all his head feathers, spreads his tail (to show the red band), bows and bobs his head. This is accompanied by a continuous double call-note – altogether a performance which is difficult to ignore.

Clutch size 1.

Incubation period 29 or 30 days, but up to 33 days has been recorded.

Newly hatched chicks Totally covered in long, dense yellow down (chicks hatch during winter and are sometimes unattended while the female feeds). Weight 15–18 g (½–⅝ oz), although one hatched in an incubator weighed 23 g (¾ oz) (Connors & Connors, 1991).

Young in nest About 90 days but 85–106 days have been recorded (Connors & Connors, 1988).

Origin Australia: eastern. According to *The Atlas of Australian Birds*, its distribution appears to reflect three distinct populations. The main one inhabits the Great Dividing Range and the eastern coast north to Shoalwater Bay and the Eungella district. There is a second population in the Murray–Darling region, in the Pilliga and Round Hill area. Kangaroo Island is the location of the third population, whose inhabitants move across to the adjoining mainland.

Natural history This species is associated with casuarina trees, on which it feeds almost exclusively. It extracts the seeds from the tiny cones. Cooper watched a female feeding for almost two hours, during which time she did not move more than a metre. Her feeding rate averaged one cone of *Casuarina littoralis* per minute and ranged between 20 and 90 seconds (Forshaw, 1981). Glossies have been observed eating the seeds of other trees, including acacia and eucalyptus, but these probably form a very small part of the diet.

They are rarely found far away from casuarina stands. They occur mainly in lowland temperate forest but in the north of their range, in central Queensland, they are more typically found in mountainous areas,

Female Glossy Cockatoo (*Calyptorhynchus lathami*) eating *Casuarina* cones.

Breeders invariably offer open-topped logs to Glossy Cockatoos
(*Calyptorhynchus lathami*).

including isolated massifs and plat-
eaus. *The Atlas of Australian Birds*
states that Glossy Cockatoos found
away from the main range may have
been forced to wander in search of
food during dry weather. Groups
seem to occupy an area permanently,
although individuals and sub-groups
may move around within this area.
Of 396 sightings of this species
recorded by *Atlas* observers, 84
per cent consisted of groups of
from two to nine birds. Group size
does not usually exceed 20 birds.
When feeding they can be closely
approached.

Glossy Cockatoos breed during
autumn and winter, eggs usually
being found from March to June.
The nesting site is the trunk of a
dead tree, usually a eucalyptus, or a
hollow limb. The single egg is incubated by the female. One person who
spent many hours watching this
species observed that during incubation, and for several days after
hatching occurred, females fed for
short periods on *Casuarina* trees
close to their nests, as well as being
fed by the male (Sindel & Lynn,
1989).

Neville Connors of northern New
South Wales has been observing this
species for many years. My single
glimpse of the Glossy Cockatoo in
the wild occurred when I was with
him. He pointed out to me two
nesting trees of this species. At one
of them he had witnessed a dramatic
sight. As the female returned to her
nest, a Wedge-tailed Eagle (*Aquila
andax*) appeared as if from nowhere

and pounced on her, just as she was entering. By some miracle, she escaped the eagle's clutches and lived to rear her chick.

Status and conservation Its status can be described as uncommon or locally common. There is no evidence of decline except perhaps on Kangaroo Island. Its population there was estimated in 1980 to consist of fewer than 60 breeding pairs. Obviously, the continued survival of this species depends entirely on the preservation of stands of *Casuarina*. This dependence makes it a vulnerable species.

Banksian or Red-tailed Black Cockatoo
Calyptorhynchus banksii
(formerly *C. magnificus*)

Crest Long black feathers which form a dense, wide backward-curving crest.

Plumage Male entirely black except for the tail in which all the long tail feathers have a broad scarlet band across the centre, except the central pair. Female brownish-black with small yellow spots on head, crest, neck and wings; underparts and underside of tail barred with yellow or orange-yellow or even with orange.

Beak and eyes Beak black in the male, whitish in the female; cere not feathered. Iris dark brown.

Length 60–65 cm (24–26 in).

Weight About 740 g (26 oz).

Sexual dimorphism See Plumage and Beak and eyes.

Immature birds Usually resemble the female but with fewer spots on the head. Rarely, young have a different appearance on leaving the nest, i.e. they have a red tail band, but it is not known with certainty whether these all prove to be males. Most young have greyish marks on the upper mandible; some believe that males can be distinguished by the darker upper mandible, but perhaps this is true only of certain populations. Sexing by plumage is uncertain before 3 years.

Banksian Cockatoo
(*Calyptorhynchus banksii*): male.

Sub-species According to *The Atlas of Australian Birds*, there are seven or eight populations whose sub-specific relationships have yet to be determined. Five are currently recognized. The nominate race is as described above. The females are relatively dull-coloured. *C. b. naso* is smaller with a larger beak. The females are more brightly coloured. *C. b. graptogyne* (the name means 'painted lady') is smaller with a smaller beak but the females are the most brilliantly coloured. *C. b. samueli* is also small with a small beak but the females are dull-coloured. The sub-species *C. b. macrorhynchus* (no longer accepted by some taxonomists) is so-called for its large beak. Females have no red in the tail, only buff-yellow and orange. Other notable differences are that *C. b. graptogyne* lacks a step in the cutting edge of the maxilla (Schodde, 1988) and that, in *C. b. naso*, the crest is shorter, rounder and smaller.

Captive status Uncommon in Australia, rare elsewhere – but the least rare of the genus.

Pet potential and personality Hand-reared birds remain friendly and affectionate and have endearing personalities. However, they are seldom kept as pets in Australia; elsewhere they are regarded as too scarce and valuable for breeding purposes to be sold as pets.

Aviculture and breeding Even in Australia, black cockatoos are very much a specialist interest and only since the 1980s has breeding this species ceased to be a rare event. More are reared than of any other black cockatoo and numbers increase yearly; nevertheless, the totals are still low. Some pairs are prolific, which shows that the potential for increased breeding is good. However, there seems to be a limit to the number of people prepared to house these large cockatoos in Australia. Elsewhere their breeding is thwarted by extremely high prices and low availability. Magnificent aviary birds, they are seen at their best in spacious enclosures. An absolute minimum size for a pair is 8 m × 2 m × 2 m high (26 ft 3 in × 6 ft 8 in × 6 ft 8 in high).

In Australia I have visited several successful breeders of this species and, during my two years at Loro Parque, one pair produced a chick which was hand-reared from the age of 11 days (when it weighed 55 g/2 oz). But this was the only breeding pair I have had in my care. Australian aviculturists have related to me some interesting happenings with this species. Colin McKecknie of the Gorge Wildlife Park, South Australia, showed me a trio on exhibit. The male had fertilized both females! Mark Schmidt, also of South Australia, owns what was, in 1989 when I visited him, the most comprehensive collection of Australian parrots (excluding all mutations) in existence. He was breeding three species of *Calyptorhychus*. He told me that because of the long weaning period, he had carried out a bold experiment with Banksians. When the hand-reared young started to eat on their own, he reunited them with the parents – who weaned them! However, one must issue a warning that this might not prove successful with other pairs! Mr and Mrs R. Rodda showed me a female who laid up to 11 eggs annually. Four of her young were being reared at the time. However, eggs laid towards the end of the season did not hatch; they were thin-shelled, underlining the importance of calcium supplementation for prolific females.

A characteristic of some male

Banksians is that they remain very tame, to the degree that breeding success seems unlikely. Yet they *do* breed. In 1988 Helen Grazier and Terry Spouse obtained a pair of Banksians, the male of which seemed 'more bonded to humans than to his own species'. The female was aloof. When released into an aviary, the male chased the female continuously. He had to be caged inside the aviary. Several weeks later some of his flight feathers were removed and he was released into the aviary. No more aggression occurred but the pair were never together, except at night. However, on 3 February 1990, an egg was found on the aviary floor. A log 1.2 m (4 ft) deep and 45 cm (18 in) in diameter, with an open top, was placed in the aviary. On February 26 an egg was laid in the log. Only the female incubated and she left the log for a few minutes about 4.30 p.m. daily to feed. However, the egg was infertile and was removed on 25 March. On 21 April the female laid again. On her daily outing from the nest she became very demanding for almond kernels and silver beet and spent some time foraging on the aviary floor, among the sprouting wheat. On 22 May there was a chick in the nest which could have hatched on the previous day. The female continued to come out daily at 4.30 p.m. The male would regurgitate food on to the perch and, if the female was near, she would pick it up. He was never seen to enter the log.

The night of 8 July was warm and the female did not brood the chick. The next night was cool and wet and she returned to the log. The climatic conditions dictated whether she brooded the chick at night. On 28 July the young Banksian was seen peering out of the top of the log. It emerged on 4 August at the age of 75 days and took its first flight two days later. It was aggressively protected by the female, who beat her wings, fanned her tail and shrieked at anyone who approached. The female was once seen to feed the young one but the male apparently took no interest (Grazier & Spouse, 1991). This is not typical, however. Sindel and Lynn (1989) record that both parents normally feed the youngster for 3–4 months after leaving the nest.

Courtship display The male erects the crest and spreads the cheek feathers to cover the bill. The tail is fanned to show the bright red area and a soft note is uttered while he struts along the perch, bowing to the female. A quite lengthy high-pitched 'song' is delivered.

Clutch size 1; rarely 2.

Incubation period Average 30 days, but 28–32 days recorded.

Newly hatched chicks Totally covered in long, dense yellow down; bill pinkish. Weight 15 g (½ oz).

Young in nest 11 weeks, but up to 96 days has been recorded.

Origin Australia: in the north and also in the western, central and eastern areas; eastern Australia from Cape York Peninsula to southern New South Wales (*C. b. banksii*) but, if one does not accept *C. b. macrorhynchus* as a valid sub-species, then its range extends continuously across the northern part of Australia; *c. b. samueli* is widely distributed from the coast of central Western Australia, through the central ranges of central Australia, to western New South Wales along the Darling river and much further east, into western Queensland (*C. b. samueli* – widely distributed); south-western Victoria and adjacent South Australia (*C. b. graptogyne* – a small range); south-western Australia (*C. b. naso* is restricted to south-western Australia).

Natural history In 1770 a draughtsman on Captain Cook's ship *Endeavour* sketched a female Banksian Cockatoo. This was the earliest known illustration of an Australian cockatoo and the first of any bird from eastern Australia. Noisy and conspicuous, especially when gathered in large flocks, it is not difficult to understand why this species should have attracted attention so long ago. In many parts of northern Australia this cockatoo is common; in the south its numbers are smaller and at least one population has been described as 'clearly endangered'.

Most immature Banksian Cockatoos (*Calyptorhynchus banksii*) have greyish marks on the upper mandible.

For the naturalist or bird-lover visiting northern Australia there can be few more memorable sights than a flock – often large – of Banksian Cockatoos. Feeding habits vary, according to the sub-species, and also to beak size. They occur in various habitat types but especially open woodland or trees bordering rivers. In the southern parts of their range they tend to be nomadic, no doubt in response to food availability, but, in the north, regular seasonal movements are observed. Like Yellow-tailed Black Cockatoos, they fly above the treetops, often at considerable heights; their wing beats are deep and accentuated, unlike the shallow wing beats of the Glossy Cockatoo.

Their diet is less specialized than that of other black cockatoos but, in most areas, eucalyptus seeds form the staple diet. In south-western Australia the seeds of the introduced weed-pest double-gee (*Emex australis*) are an important part of their diet, while in Victoria *C. b. graptogyne* feeds mainly on brown stringybark trees (*Eucalyptus baxteri*). These have very small seed capsules, thus the small beak must be an adaptation for eating this seed. Other foods eaten by this species include seed and nuts of *Hakea*, *Banksia*, casuarina and acacia, fruits, berries, blossoms and the larvae of insects.

In south-western Victoria, availability of the brown stringybark seeds is determined mainly by how recently the forest has been burnt. Forest with recent canopy burns do not contain enough seed, thus the cockatoos feed on bulloak (*Allocasuarina leumannii*), a tree which occurs mainly on roadsides in the agricultural land in the north of this sub-species' range (Emison,

Banksian Cockatoo (*Calyptorhynchus banksii*) aged 22 days, hand-reared.

A two-day-old Banksian Cockatoo (*Calyptorhynchus banksii*).

1991). It is available at about the time the young fledge.

The majority of the nest hollows found during a study of *C. b. graptogyne* funded by the World Parrot Trust in 1991, were in dead, usually ring-barked, river red gums (*Eucalyptus camaldulensis*). The rest were in live trees of the same species or in yellow gums (*Eucalyptus leucoxylon*). All these nests were on private agricultural land within 4 km (2½ miles) of Crown land supporting stringybark forest. During the seasons 1988–89 and 1989–90, 12 and 13 nests respectively were discovered (Joseph, Emison & Bren, 1991). These 25 nests were in 22 hollows in 21 trees. The nests were active between October and the beginning of April. It was believed that a large proportion of the total population nested in the area of Edenhope. Nine nests of Southern

Yellow-tailed Black Cockatoos were found during the study, thus the two species may compete for nest sites. However, there appears to be little competition for food with any other species.

Status and conservation This cockatoo is common or abundant throughout most of its range and will remain so where food sources and trees with suitable nesting hollows remain intact. However, the sub-species *C. b. graptogyne* has a population believed to number fewer than 1,000. It is considered endangered because its range is small and isolated and because breeding seems to involve only a small proportion of the population (about 10 per cent or less) and has only been recorded in the northern part of the range in an area of only about 3,500 km^2 (1,350 sq. miles). Its diet is specialized, its nest requirements relatively specific (deep hollows in dead river red gums) and its habitats are fragmented by past clearing. The dead standing river red gums are used for firewood; others are pushed over and burnt. The decline in available nest hollows may already be limiting the cockatoo's breeding ability.

In 1991 the Victorian National Parks and Wildlife Service embarked on a long-term management programme to ensure its survival. Funding will be supplied by the World Parrot Trust. Recommendations included: retaining as much as possible of the brown stringy-bark forests and bulloak stands, liaising with landholders to protect nest trees and potential nest trees, erecting nest-boxes to ascertain whether they would be used, searching for other nesting locations and encouraging the regeneration and replanting of river red gums and yellow gums. A network of individuals has been established to provide information on the distribution and abundance of *C. b. graptogyne*.

Northern Yellow-tailed Black or Funereal Cockatoo
*Calyptorhynchus funereus**

Crest The dense head feathers can be erected but crest poorly developed in comparison with most other cockatoos.

Plumage Brownish-black, browner below, with feathers faintly or heavily (neck and underparts) margined with yellow; ear coverts yellow, duller in the male; the two central tail feathers nearly black or blackish-brown, others yellow freckled with dark brown (more heavily freckled in the female) except for approximately one-fifth at the base and the tip, which are dark brown.

Beak and eyes Beak dark grey in the male, pale ivory in the female; large; the upper mandible elongated and pointed, enabling it to remove larvae from tree trunks and branches and seeds from hard nuts. Eyes dark brown, surrounded by naked pink skin in the male and dark brown skin in the female.

Length About 65 cm (26 in), of which the tail accounts for about 37 cm (14½ in).

Weight Wild-caught males – 749–760 g (26⅜–26¾ oz), females 840–900 g (29⅝–31¾ oz) Forshaw (1981). Three captive males weighed by the author were 775 g (27⅜ oz), 780 g (27½ oz) and 790 g (27⅞ oz) and one female was 695 g (24½ oz).

Sexual dimorphism See Plumage and Beak and eyes.

Immature birds Like the female except in having duller yellow ear coverts and lacking the faint yellow margins on the breast feathers. One male reared by Courtney (1986b) started to develop these yellow margins at the age of about 34 weeks and these were complete by 40 weeks. A second

---

* Current opinion is divided regarding the taxonomy of the four forms which make up the *C. funereus* superspecies: *C. baudinii*, *C. latirostris*, *C. xanthonotus* and *C. funereus*. As Courtney (1986b) stated:

> The interrelationships of the four components of the *funereus* superspecies comprising two white-tailed populations in the west and two yellow-tailed populations in the east, are somewhat confused.

I treat them as separate species because, at the present time there seems to be insufficient evidence to draw the correct conclusion. Also, from the avicultural viewpoint, it is important to emphasise their differences.

male had distinct yellow margins to the breast feathers at 35 weeks. Undertail coverts in very young birds are all black; the first male referred to had developed black and yellow undertail coverts by 60 weeks, and the second by 92½ weeks. However, at successive moults the colour of these feathers changed, being an unreliable indicator of age. Up to the age of 12½ weeks they had milky-white eye skin which was deep blackish-brown by about 16 weeks. At about 89 weeks the eye skin of the first bird became paler, with a pink tinge. At about 139 weeks, it was milky-white with a pink tinge. At about 140 weeks his eye skin was seen to flush deep pink during courtship display. In the second male, the eye skin started to turn pink-white at about 92 weeks but this male was four years old before he was recorded as having flesh-coloured eye skin. At 99 weeks the upper mandible of the first bird was completely dark, but the lower mandible was not completely dark until the bird was four years old. At 111 weeks the upper mandible of the second male was nearly all dark. One male had lost all the rectrices from his nestling plumage when just over one year old.

Captive status Uncommon but increasing in Australia; rare elsewhere.

Pet potential and personality Its comparatively aloof personality, its large size, which makes it unsuitable for close confinement, and its high price ensure that it is not considered in the pet category.

Aviculture and breeding Only the most committed aviculturists should consider keeping this species. It is expensive to purchase, expensive to house well, difficult to breed, takes 10–12 months to wean and is highly insectivorous when rearing young.

Although this species has been bred in smaller aviaries, I consider that 10 m (33 ft) is the minimum length suitable and that the height of the enclosure should be 3 m (10 ft) at least. A smaller enclosure seems more like a cage, for these birds have a huge wing span and are highly manoeuvrable in flight. Indeed, no matter how large the aviary, it could scarcely be large enough. They also enjoy aviaries which are planted with grasses or weeds, which they will destroy. A large water container for bathing should be provided as, unlike other black cockatoos, except the White-tailed Black, they will bathe in standing water.

This species is bred in only very small numbers in Australia, although successes are gradually increasing. I do not know of any breeding successes which have occurred outside Australia. However, as most Yellow-tailed Blacks have not been legally exported, successes may have occurred with breeders who did not wish to publicize their ownership of these cockatoos.

The first captive breeding occurred in the aviaries of R. T. Lynn of Sydney in 1965. The female laid two infertile eggs in 1964. Then the diet was altered by the addition of a dessertspoonful of raw minced meat twice a week. In 1965 she laid on 16 and 18 January and commenced to incubate on 19 January. The first egg hatched on 19 February after 31 days; the second egg did not hatch. The female brooded the chick closely for the first week, after which it was left unattended for long periods during the day. After 14 days the female roosted on top of the log at night. On 17 May the young cockatoo was perching just below the nest entrance. It left the nest on 17 May, weak and unable to fly. It never

Northern Yellow-tailed Black Cockatoo (*Calyptorhynchus funereus*) at Buderim, Queensland.

became strong and died at just over one year old. In 1966 the female laid her first egg on 14 January; it hatched on 14 February and the young bird left the nest at 90 days when it flew strongly. It was fed by both parents for the next three months, and then only by the male until the next breeding season. This pair continued to breed successfully for many years (Sindel & Lynn, 1989).

A successful breeder of Yellow-tailed Blacks, White-tailed Blacks and Banksian Cockatoos is Mark Schmidt of South Australia, whose aviaries I visited in 1989. He has found the Yellow-tailed Black to be highly insectivorous when breeding, consuming 100–200 mealworms daily when rearing young. In his experience this species is more sensitive to nest inspection and more difficult to rear than the Banksian Cockatoo.

This species usually lays two eggs but, even if the second does hatch, it is rarely fed. However, on one occasion, Mark Schmidt's pair hatched two chicks, both of which were successfully reared by the parents. The second chick was fed probably because the two eggs were laid only two days apart. The second chick can hatch up to one week after the first, in which case its chances of survival are practically nil.

Courtship display The male struts and bows with the crest raised and the tail slightly fanned, making a guttural clucking sound. The skin surrounding the eye becomes brighter red. John Courtney described the vocalizations of the male (in Low, 1992a) as a high-pitched squeaking, plus rapid, high-pitched twittering.

Clutch size 2.

Incubation period Usually 28 to 30 days.

Newly hatched chicks Long, dense bright yellow down. Connors &

Connors (1991) recorded the weights of two incubator-hatched chicks as 23.7 g (⅞ oz) and 18.8 g (⅝ oz).

Young in nest Approximately 90 days.

Origin Australia: Queensland, New South Wales and eastern Victoria, approximately north of Melbourne where its range meets that of *C. xanthanotus* (Sindel & Lynn, 1989).

Natural history This cockatoo occurs in forested habitats of all types, but especially wet coastal and mountain forests, and even plantations of introduced species of pine. It is found in family groups or small flocks and occasionally in large flocks of up to 200 or 300 birds. It is fairly common, though widespread, throughout much of its range. I find this one of the most exciting of Australian parrots to observe in the wild. In sustained flight (often very high) it looks magnificent with its huge wing span and leisurely almost ponderous flight. Seen in forested habitat its grace and manoeuvrability is remarkable for such a large bird. In my opinion, for sheer majesty no other south-eastern Australian bird can compete with the Yellow-tailed Black, not even the Wedge-tailed Eagle, although it is larger.

Field work carried out by members of the Royal Australian Ornithological Union (RAOU) indicated that most suitable localities have small resident populations whose movements are confined to areas approximately 200 km (124 miles) in extent. At times they form loose migratory flocks which follow established flight paths. Roosting sites are seldom used for more than a few consecutive nights.

The larvae of insects, particularly moths, are important in their diet. Their unique method of making a chopping platform to extract grubs is

The Northern Yellow-tailed Black Cockatoo (*Calyptorhynchus funereus*) is distinguished from the Southern species by its longer tail.

described by Forshaw (1981). In forested areas, the sound of Yellow-tailed Blacks gnawing wood is a good method of locating them. They also eat the seeds of a wide range of trees, especially *Pinus radiata* and other pines, eucalyptus, *Banksia*, *Hakea* and acacia, also shrubs and grasses, nuts and berries.

Breeding occurs during autumn and winter in the north of the range, during spring and early summer in the southern part. Eucalyptus are favoured nest trees, the entrance usually being 10 m (33 ft) to 30 m (100 ft) above ground. The internal diameter normally ranges between 30 cm (12 in) and 40 cm (16 in), and the depth from 60 cm (24 in) to 2 m (6 ft 6 in). M. J. Goddard and John Courtney examined one nest of a Yellow-tailed Black after the young cockatoo had fledged. The nesting material consisted of 640 chips and splinters, the longest being 203 mm × 16 mm (8 in × ⅝ in). (In contrast, there were several thousand tiny chips, 2,050 chips and some splinters in a nest of a Glossy Cockatoo (Courtney, in press). Normally only one egg is laid; if there are two and the second hatches the chick is not fed. Presumably normally there is sufficient food to rear only one chick. It stays with its parents until the start of the following season.

Status and conservation The Northern Yellow-tailed Black Cockatoo is fairly common in suitable habitat throughout its range. In some areas residents claim it is declining, due to loss of habitat. Sindel and Lynn (1989) however, believe that 'The versatile feeding habits of the Yellow-tail, together with the relatively high numbers throughout its often rugged range, suggests a bright future for this species'. The main concern must be that sufficient trees suitable for nesting remain within its habitat. As they point out, this is a very long-lived species and any decline in its populations might not be apparent until it was too late to rectify.

Southern Yellow-tailed Black Cockatoo
Calyptorhynchus xanthanotus

Plumage Similar to that of *C. funereus*.
Beak and eyes Similar to *C. funereus*.
Length About 58 cm (23 in). The tail is shorter in proportion to the body than in *C. funereus*.
Weight Males – 645–750 g (22¾–26½ oz); females 610–795 g (21½–28 oz) Forshaw (1981).
Sexual dimorphism As for *C. funereus*.
Immature birds Similar to those of *C. funereus* apart from the difference in size and tail length as described (see p. 222).
Sub-species *C. xanthanotus* is generally regarded as a sub-species of *C. funereus*. However, Courtney (1986) notes:

. . . although southern *xanthanotus* does seem intermediate geographically and physically between the very different *latirostris* and *funereus*, evidence is mounting that questions the view that *xanthanotus* and *funereus* are merely inter-grading geographical races. Indeed, *latirostris* and *xanthanotus* seem to have much in common including short tails, an apparently identical male epigamic display vocalisation, occurrence in more open habitat, a tendency to nest in loose colonies, and the formation of very large post-breeding flocks . . . the apparent overlap in distribution without an obvious merging of the breeding populations of *xanthanotus* and *funereus* seems significant.

. . . A possibility is emerging that *latirostris* may prove to be a subspecies of *xanthanotus* while the latter and *funereus* may be closely related sibling species, as are *baudinii* and *latirostris*.

Captive status Uncommon – fewer than *C. funereus*.

Pet potential and personality As for *C. funereus*.

Aviculture and breeding As for *C. funereus* except that the courtship vocalizations in the male differ.

Origin Australia: westwards of the Great Dividing Range in southern Victoria to south-eastern South Australia, Tasmania, Kangaroo Island and larger islands in the Bass Strait, such as King, Hunter, Flinders and Cape Barren. The ranges of *C. funereus* and *C. xanthanotus* meet and probably overlap north of Sydney.

Natural history This is basically similar to that of *C. funereus*. Some of the main differences are mentioned above.

Status and conservation As for *C. funereus*.

White-tailed Black or Carnaby's Cockatoo
Calyptorhynchus latirostris

Crest Dense black head feathers, not noticeably elongated, which can be erected to form a small crest.

Plumage Black, the feathers margined with greyish-white, more heavily on neck and underparts; the two central tail feathers grey-black, the rest being white, faintly spotted with grey-black except for approximately one-fifth at the base and the tip which are grey-black.

Beak and eyes Beak dark grey in the male, pale ivory in the female; shorter and broader than in *C. baudinii* – the main distinguishing feature. Eyes dark brown, surrounded by naked pink skin in the male and dark brown skin in the female.

Length 65 cm (26 in).

Weight Wild-caught males 540–760 g (19–26¾ oz); females 560–790 g (19¾–27⅞ oz (Forshaw, 1981). Saunders (1991) gives 650 g (23 oz) for both males and females.

Sexual dimorphism Ear coverts greyish-white in the male, pure white in the female.

Immature birds Like the female and usually cannot be sexed with certainty until three or even four years.

Captive status Rare in Australia, very rare elsewhere.

Pet potential and personality This species is unsuited to close confinement and is never, or virtually never, kept as a pet.

Aviculture and breeding The White-tailed Black Cockatoos, *C. latirostris* and *C. baudinii*, are the least popular of the black cockatoos as aviary birds in Australia. Partly because they lack the bright colours of the Banksian Cockatoo, they tend to be kept mainly by cockatoo specialists. Before about the 1960s White-tailed Blacks were very rare in aviculture and there was no distinction between *C. baudinii* and *C. latirostris*. There was no recorded breeding of either form until 1973 when R. T. Lynn of Sydney was successful. His pair occupied an aviary measuring 12 m × 3 m × 2.7 m high (40 ft × 10 ft × 9 ft high). They used a log which was at least 90 cm (3 ft) deep. Only one egg was laid, on 21 October 1973, and this hatched on 20 November.

Female White-tailed Black Cockatoo (*Calyptorhynchus latirostris*).

The youngster left the nest aged 87 days; it had rickets and had to be treated with a calcium supplement. This problem occurred in subsequent young but was solved by adding *Banksia* cones to the rearing diet. Previously a lot of *Hakea* nuts had been fed to the young, in addition to sunflower, corn, oats, safflower and greenfood.

In 1986 Bob Lynn achieved another 'first' with the rearing of two young in one nest. Incubation commenced with the laying of the first egg on 20 October; a second was laid on 27 October. The eggs hatched on 18 and 24 November. The young left the nest after 80 and 81 days and again, uniquely, could be sexed immediately by the colour of the ear coverts and beak. The young were left with their parents for almost 12 months. Ten days after their removal the female laid, but the egg was infertile. The second egg, laid on 30 November, hatched on 30 December and the young cockatoo left the nest at the age of 83 days (Sindel & Lynn, 1989).

The Division of Wildlife Research, CSIRO, bred *C. latirostris* in conjunction with its study on its biology and breeding behaviour. The pair had previously bred in the wild. In 1973, an egg laid on 24 October hatched but the chick died at six weeks old. In 1974, work carried out near their aviary prevented the pair from nesting. In 1975, the first of two eggs was laid on 20 October. Hatching occurred on about 18 November. For two weeks the chick was brooded continually; thereafter, the male assisted in feeding the chick. It left the nest on 8 February. Rearing food consisted of sunflower seed, mature nuts of marri (*Eucalyptus calophylla*), fruits of *Banksia grandis* and pine cones (Saunders, 1976).

I know of only one published report of the breeding of the White-tailed Black Cockatoo outside Australia. Judging by the photograph of one bird, they were *C. latirostris*. A pair which had been caged as pets for 11 years was obtained by Bill Wegner of New York in 1980. In 1982 eggs were laid on 24 and 30 June and incubated in a Marsh Roll-X incubator. The female laid again, the first egg on 21 July. Four chicks were reared; they were fully feathered at 11 weeks and weaned when just over eight months old (Wegner, 1984).

Clutch size 1 or 2. The CSIRO study of this species at Manmanning and Coomallo Creek from 1970 to 1976 showed a total of 31 nests with 1 egg and 63 with 2 eggs at Mannmanning, and 88 with 1 egg and 312 with 2 eggs at Coomallo Creek (Saunders, 1982). (At Manmanning food availability was poor compared with Coomallo Creek.) The average clutch size in 494 nests was 1.8 (Saunders, 1991).

Incubation period 28–30 days.

Newly hatched chicks Down can vary from off-white to yellow. Wegner (1984) describes it as bright yellow. Weight appears not to have been recorded.

Young in nest An average of 77 days in the wild (Saunders, 1991). In captive birds the few reports give lengths varying between 80 and 83 days, and 87 days for one with rickets.

Origin Australia: in the south-west, from the coast, south of the Murchison River, inland to Wongan Hills region, Kellerberrin, Norseman and Mississippi Bay, east of Esperance; also Rottnest Island, near Fremantle (Forshaw, 1989).

Natural history This cockatoo is an inhabitant of drier inland regions where the average annual rainfall is less than 750 mm (29½ in). Out of the breeding season it moves to areas of higher rainfall nearer the coast.

The White-tailed Black was the subject of intensive study from 1969 onwards. Its breeding success rate (the percentage of nests which fledged young) was 64.5 per cent (range 58–86 per cent) at Coomallo Creek (based on 529 nests) and only 35 per cent (range 24–66 per cent) at Manmanning, over 11 breeding seasons (based on 428 nests). In the early 1970s the breeding population at Coomallo Creek averaged 69 breeding attempts per season. Land clearance led to a reduction of the population and from 1977 to 1990 breeding attempts averaged 43 (range 38–52) per season (Saunders, 1991).

Many birds were individually marked and it was found that they returned to the same area to nest and, in many cases, to the same hollow or nearby. If their first breeding attempt failed, but had been early in the season, they were usually successful if they nested again. The success rate was higher in pairs which used the same hollow the following season – 90 per cent, whereas in females which used a different hollow the success rate was only 76 per cent (Saunders, 1982).

Their food consists of seeds and flowers of a wide range of proteaceous species, particularly *Grevillea*, *Hakea*, *Dryandra* and *Banksia*.

Status and conservation This cockatoo is declining due to destruction and fragmentation of its habitat. During the past 160 years 93 per cent of native vegetation in south-western Australia has been destroyed for cereal cropping and sheep farming. That which remains is scattered in small remnants across the landscape. Carnaby's Cockatoo has not been able to adapt to these changes and, between 1971 and 1991, has disappeared from over one-third of its range. In contrast the Banksian Cockatoo (*C. banksii samueli*) has expanded its range to invade part of that of Carnaby's Cockatoo. The latter is now absent from the central and eastern wheat belt. Saunders (1991) states:

The range of Carnaby's Cockatoo will continue to contract as it adjusts to the changes imposed on the landscape by humans. The final result may be as little as half its former range.

There was no shortage of nest sites. At Coomallo Creek the annual average occupancy of available sites by all species using the hollows was only 45 per cent (Saunders, 1979). The lower breeding success rate at Manmanning was almost certainly related to food availability. The birds had to forage further from their nests than those at Coomallo Creek and females had to leave their eggs to forage for food, whereas those at Coomallo Creek were fed by the males. The females at Manmanning had to cease brooding their nestlings during the day at an earlier stage and often did not return between dawn and dusk. Reduced number of feedings led to a slower growth rate of these young.

Only restoration of its habitat could improve the future outlook for this cockatoo and that is never likely to occur. Protection of the surviving habitat is the only means of ensuring the future of Carnaby's Cockatoo which, because of its limited range, is one of the most threatened and vulnerable of Australia's parrots.

Baudin's White-tailed Black Cockatoo
Calyptorhynchus baudinii

Plumage Similar to that of *C. latirostris*.
Beak and eyes Beak shorter and slightly broader than in *C. latirostris*; this is the main distinguishing feature. Eyes dark brown.

Length, Weight, Sexual dimorphism, Immature birds, Captive status, Pet potential and personality, Aviculture and breeding, Clutch size, Incubation period, Newly hatched chicks, Young in nest All as for *C. latirostris*.

Origin Australia: Western Australia – extreme south-western corner.

Natural history This cockatoo occurs only in heavily forested areas (with an annual rainfall in excess of 750 mm/29½ in). Out of the breeding season it moves further north and may encounter *C. latirostris*. The two breeding populations must have been isolated for some time as their contact calls and food preferences are distinct. *C. baudinii* nests have been found in forests of karri (*Eucalyptus diversicolor*), isolated by the coast and by the area of *E. calophylla* and *E. marginata* woodland (which contains few suitable nest sites), from the nesting localities of *C. latirostris*. Analysis of crop contents of *C. baudinii* and *C. latirostris* collected at the same location, Mundaring, east of Perth, show differences in food preferences; however, *C. baudinii* is a wandering visitor to the area. It fed mainly on the seeds of marri (*E. calophylla*) and larvae of wood-boring insects, whereas *C. latirostris* had consumed mainly seeds of *Dryanda*, *Hakea* and introduced species of pine (Saunders, in Forshaw, 1981).

Status and conservation This is a declining and vulnerable species, with a population estimated at fewer than 5,000 in 1992. The same source (ICBP's *Parrots: an action plan*) estimated the population of *C. latirostris* as fewer than 10,000. Preservation of feeding areas and of large *E. diversicolor* for nest sites are crucial for the survival of this cockatoo.

Palm Cockatoo
Probosciger aterrimus aterrimus

Crest Long, narrow backward-curving dark grey feathers which can be held erect or flat against the head.
Plumage Appears dark grey due to powder produced by powder down feathers but is actually black. Feet grey; bare skin on cheeks red or deep pink – whitish-pink in birds in poor health; colour may deepen when the bird is excited.
Beak and eyes Beak a unique shape among birds – the mandibles do not fit together and there is a gap in which one can see the red and black tongue. Among parrots, only the Hyacinthine Macaw (*Anodorhynchus hyacinthinus*) has a consistently larger beak but, in relation to body size, this cockatoo has the largest. The beak has two flat projecting areas of rhampotheca (horny covering) on the inside of the upper mandible, forming three step-like levels. The large innermost 'step' is used for small food items and the middle 'step' for larger ones. David Holyoak offered an assortment of seeds and nuts to one Palm. He noted that 20 hazelnuts of about 10 mm (⅜ in) diameter were all husked and crushed while being held in the middle 'step',

Baudin's White-tailed Black Cockatoo (*Calyptorhynchus baudinii*).

The beak shape of the Palm Cockatoo (*Probosciger aterrimus aterrimus*) is unique: the two mandibles do not fit together.

as were three walnuts of about 25 mm diameter. Sunflower seeds 2–3 mm (about ⅛ in) thick were husked on the innermost step, as were apple and orange pips. The outermost step is apparently used only for tearing at large fruits. He concluded that, without the steps, the bill would probably be inefficient when dealing with small seeds (Holyoak, 1972). Eyes dark brown.

Length About 57 cm (22 in) to 70 cm (28 in) according to sub-species; *P. a. goliath* is largest and those from the Aru Islands are said to be smallest.

Weight 500–1,100 g. Smith (1985) found that weights of eight captive birds ranged from 600 g (21⅛ oz) to 1,005 g (35½ oz) (average 774 g (27¼ oz)). Schubot (1990) gives range of males in his collection (nominate race *P. a. aterrimus* and *P. a. goliath*) as 545–1,092 g (19¼–38½ oz) (average 602 g (21¼ oz)) and females 503–950 g (17¾–33½ oz) (average 602 g (21¼ oz)). Range of 14 adults of nominate race weighed by author was 520–740 g in males (average 642 g (22⅝ oz)) and 540–735 g (19–26 oz) (average 642 g (22⅝ oz)) for females.

Sexual dimorphism The male is usually slightly larger and heavier. Smith (1985) noted that:

. . . the upper mandible of the male has a much greater length and is deeper at the base. Paradoxically, this gives the bill a narrower, less stocky, look. The curvature of the upper mandible of the female's bill therefore forms a more closed C.

Immature birds Plumage black because the powder down is apparently not produced at an early age; some young have very fine pale yellow barring on the breast or sides, also/or on the underwing coverts; skin surrounding the eye white (grey in adults); lower mandible whitish; upper mandible grey with culmen and edges white.

Sub-species *P. a. aterrimus* is described above. *P. a. goliath* is larger and heavier, males weighing 1,000 g (35¼ oz) or more whereas males of other sub-species rarely weigh more than 800 g (28¼ oz). *P. a. stenolophus* differs in its narrower crest feathers.

Captive status Rare until the mid-1970s; from this period until the late 1980s hundreds were exported via Singapore to various countries throughout the world, so that generally, in aviculture, this cockatoo remained uncommon and expensive. Despite being on Appendix I of CITES many Palm Cockatoos were illegally exported from Singapore until that country became a member of CITES in 1989. This had unfortunate consequences for hundreds of Palm Cockatoos then in dealers' premises in Singapore. Dealers were unable to sell the birds, even by substantially lowering prices, because without CITES papers they could not be imported legally. One correspondent with a special interest in the species informed me:

On a visit to Singapore in 1989 I did a survey on the live bird trade there and I was amazed to find over 1,000 Palms available for sale – various sub-species, mostly from West Irian – and the price per bird ranged in US$ from as low as $600 to 1,100.

In the USA several shipments of Palm Cockatoos were imported illegally with Malaysian documents in 1983. Two shipments were confiscated and the birds were sent to various zoos and private aviculturists

The Goliath sub-species of the Palm Cockatoo (*Probosciger aterrimus goliath*) is larger and heavier than the nominate race, males weighing 1,000 g (35¾ oz) or more.

on condition that they became part of the Species Survival Plan for this Cockatoo.

By 1992, the species was again rare in aviculture with, for example, perhaps in the region of 40–50 in the UK. In TRAFFIC (USA) 1990 *Psittacine captive breeding survey* (total of birds in census: 31,008), the total number of Palm Cockatoos recorded was 109 in 11 collections. Fifteen of these were known to be captive-bred. There were 42 pairs and these hatched 17 young and weaned 10.

By 1992 there were believed to be only five in Australia: a pair at Adelaide Zoo, two females at Taronga Zoo, Sydney, and a female at Pearl Coast Zoological Gardens in Broome.

Pet potential and personality It would be unethical to keep this rare species as a pet. The only justification for maintaining it in captivity is to breed from it. It is usually shy, nervous and wary. However, those kept in close proximity to people, such as in zoos where the public pass close by, become steady, but seldom tame like the *Cacatua* species.

Aviculture and breeding To date, relatively few collections have been successful with this species. Two secondhand reports mention early successes. The Marquess of Tavistock (1954) stated that a pair at liberty on an island in the Indian Ocean reared one youngster which they took home to feed. And David West of California related that, in 1949, D. Sheffler of Arizona had reared two, one of which was then in St Louis Zoo (Prestwich, 1951). The first documented breeding, however, is that by Robert T. Lynn of Sydney, Australia, in 1968. The pair had been collected in New Guinea about 30 years previously. They nested in a vertical log about 1.5 m (5 ft) high, with an internal diameter of 37–45

cm (15–18 in). The entrance was in the top of the log. On the first occasion the chick left the nest after 81 days. It was fed by both parents for 3–4 months after fledging and removed from the aviary at six months of age. It was a male. Subsequently two females left the nest on 16 February 1970 and 28 January 1972, both after 78 days. The male spent 81 days in the nest (Sindel & Lynn, 1989).

Young have been reared to independence in the following zoos: Leipzig, Germany, two in 1981 and one in 1982, 1983, 1984, 1985, 1988 and 1989; Birdland, Bourton-on-the-Water, England, one in 1984; Bronx, New York, five hatched and three reared in 1986, one reared in 1989; Greater Baton Rouge, Louisiana, three in 1988, one in 1989; Ragunan Zoo, Jakarta, Indonesia, one in 1988; Sea World, Orlando, Florida, one in 1989; Palmitos Park, Gran Canaria, one in 1991. In private collections the most success has been achieved at the Avicultural Breeding and Research Center (ABRC) in Florida; between 1987 and 1991, more than 20 had been hand-reared. Also in the USA, one was hand-reared in Denton, Texas (Sheppard & Turner, 1988). In Germany one was parent-reared by Dr R. Peters in 1988 (Peters, 1989). In the UK in 1984 one was reared by Mann/Smith (Smith, 1985). Also, Harry and Pat Sissen of Yorkshire had reared at least three young to independence by 1991.

In the USA, a studbook for the Palm Cockatoo has been maintained since 1985. It shows that, to date, there is unfortunately no firm trend to indicate steadily increasing hatching success. The information in Table 12 was provided by Mike Taylor, the North American Studbook keeper in 1992.

Palm Cockatoo (*Probosciger aterrimus aterrimus*): male.

Table 12
Breeding success in the Palm Cockatoo (*Probosciger aterrimus*) in the USA.

Year	Number of young hatched	Number which survived more than one year	Number of pairs producing	Collections with producing pairs
1985	1	0	1	1
1986	6	3	3	3
1987	7	1	4	4
1988	8	6	4	3
1989	22	16	9	6
1990	10	6	8	5
1991	20	17	7	4

Much remains to be learned about aviary breeding of this species, even, for example, incubation habits. Several breeders have recorded that incubation is shared by male and female. In the two pairs that have hatched chicks at Palmitos Park (in 1992 a second pair hatched a chick which died after a few hours), the male of the second pair was not seen to enter the nest during incubation except when the aviary was entered.

Brooding by a pair at Rotterdam Zoo was studied closely in 1991 when an egg was first seen on 11 August and hatched on 6 September. A total of 311 10-minute observation periods revealed that the male was in the nest barrel during 60.1 per cent of the observations and the female during 59.6 per cent (Rotterdam Zoo Research Report, 1991).

To date, the Palm Cockatoo has proved one of the most difficult of all parrots to breed in captivity. Hand-rearing, in particular, is beset by problems in most collections where it has been attempted. One problem almost invariably encountered is failure of the chick's crop to empty, i.e. poor digestion, apparently due to an incorrect diet. By far the greatest success with hand-rearing has been achieved at the Avicultural Breeding and Research Center (ABRC) in Florida. The diet used is as follows: 1 qt (1.2 litre) of dry monkey chow biscuits, 1 qt (1.2 litre) water, 2 tablespoonfuls of peanut butter and 112 g (4 oz) of a dry infant oatmeal cereal with banana. This is diluted with four parts of water (20 per cent solids). For the first few days the dilution is greater, 12 ml (2/5 fl oz) of liquid (water, Pedialyte [Ross Laboratories, Columbus] or Ringer's Lactate Solution) being added to 25 ml (4/5 fl oz) of the standard formula for the first day (6.5 parts of water, equals 15.5 per cent solids). For the next three days the dilution is 8 ml (¼ fl oz) of fluids to 25 ml (about 1 fl oz) of the standard formula. The first two feedings consist of Ringer's Lactate or Pedialyte. Each feeding is increased in volume by about 0.1 ml up to about 0.7 or 0.8 ml per feed by the end of the day. For the first few days chicks are fed whenever the crop is empty between 5 a.m. and 7.30 p.m.

Other problems have been due to chicks of this species being very susceptible to the fungus *Candida albicans* (see p. 93) and because initially the temperature in the brooder was not high enough (Sheppard & Turner, 1988).

Parent-rearing has not been problem-free either, with young spending as long as 100–110 days in the nest, one dying of a fall from the nest at 90 days and another not being able to fly until five months; all these tragedies could be attributable to a poor diet and rickets. Other young have suffered from candidiasis or chlamydiosis (psittacosis) (Muller, 1975). Or the parents have refused to incubate the eggs (Sheppard & Turner, 1988).

A good diet is vitally important. While rearing young, R. Lynn's pair consumed sunflower seed, peanuts, almonds, Brazil nuts shelled and cut up, *Hakea* nuts and silver beet. Dr Peters' pair consumed pine nuts, hazelnuts, walnuts, peanuts and sprouted sunflower; apple and carrot were eaten only when a chick was aged between 1 and 5 weeks. Berries of rowan, hawthorn and whitethorn were eagerly eaten.

In 1991, when the pair in the breeding centre at Palmitos Park reared a fine youngster, I was convinced that their consumption of one or two pomegranates daily was an important factor contributing to the success. The first chick of this pair hatched on 23 April 1991. At 8 p.m. the female left the nest which contained a dead chick with some bite marks on top of the head – but not the kind made by a parrot which deliberately kills a chick. In my opinion, she killed it accidentally when feeding it, or she had bitten it after it died. It then weighed 13 g (about ½ oz) and appeared to have a small amount of liquid food in the crop.

An observation camera was then mounted at the front of the aviary. Via the monitor, the pair was observed copulating on several occasions, either just after first light or just before dusk. Their second chick hatched on 3 September; thenceforth it was heard frequently. Unlimited fresh corn-on-the-cob was provided. The pair ate mainly soaked sunflower seed and walnuts, also carrot and orange. After a few days the oily, fibrous orange fruits of an *Arecastrum* palm were available and lasted until the chick was three weeks old. They ate two pomegranates daily while the chick was in the nest and one daily after it fledged. Their cheeks seemed to become redder after a few weeks of eating pomegranates.

The chick was quite vocal until it was about 1 month old, thus the nesting log was rarely checked. On 22 September a 12 mm (15/32 in) internal dimension closed ring was placed on its right foot. On that day, and every Sunday until 3 November, the chick was photographed and weighed. Usually its crop was half full and the following weights were recorded: 19 days – 288 g (10⅛ oz); 26 days – 430 g (15⅛ oz); 33 days – 542 g (19⅛ oz); 40 days – 598 (21⅛ oz); 47 days – 610 g (21½ oz); 54 days – 610 g (21½ oz); 61 days – the young cockatoo was too active to weigh.

While the chick was in the nest, small branches were occasionally provided to allow the male to add more splintered wood to the nest. This habit is said to be a precaution against flooding, as Palms prefer open-topped nest sites. It also ensures that the interior remains clean. By 20 October the nesting material was only 15 cm (6 in) from the top of the log. In case this caused the young one to leave the nest prematurely, some of this material was removed so that the level was 30 cm (12 in) below the top. Towards the end of October the young one started to look over the top and, on 5 November, was standing on the rim. On the morning of 18 November the young one was sitting on the aviary floor. It soon climbed on to a low perch and, three days later, to a high perch. To my surprise, it stamped its foot slowly in the manner typical of the species, when I spoke to it. I was as proud as the father of this beautiful young bird which, within a month, appeared as large as an adult. On the monitor, the male was seen to feed it on several occasions during the week after it left the nest. About one month later it was seen to feed itself, but probably did so before. At the beginning of February, I again observed the male feeding his offspring, as well as what appeared to be increasing animosity between it and the female. On 15 February she lunged at the young one and sent it flying. The next day the male was again feeding it and, unusually, the female was on the other side of the male. She approached him as though she wanted to be fed. She was undoubtedly jealous of the young one which was therefore moved to another aviary.

Courtship display The full display is more complex in this species than in any other cockatoo, and may even involve the use of a tool, a phenomenon which is almost certainly unique among parrots. Wood (1984) described the display of this species in the north-eastern part of the Cape York Peninsula between March and August 1983. Maximum display activity occurred early in the morning and late in the afternoon usually in June and July but also at other times. He observed the display on one occasion when one bird was:

. . . pirouetting around the top of the display tree trunk, wings outstretched, beating the trunk with an object in its left foot, as it turned. This display continued for a minute or more and was followed by head rolling and erection of the crest. During this performance the other member of the pair had been perched at a vantage point nearby. This bird then flew down to the trunk top and was stroked on the neck by the performer, using its head.

On another occasion he was able to approach within 5 m (16 ft) of the display trunk and to watch a bird drumming, using part of a branch about 12 cm (5 in) long. (See also Wood, 1988.)

I have often observed, via the observation monitor, the male of one captive pair displaying to the female. Perched next to her, he will turn his head sideways, briefly shake his head, open the wings and hold them open for a few seconds. He then whistles and calls *oow-whah*.

Clutch size 1.

Incubation period About 30 days but 28–34 days recorded; by male and female or mainly by female. Sindel and Lynn (1989) recorded 33, 33 and 34 days with the male incubating during the day and the female at night. Eight artificially incubated eggs at the Bronx Zoo usually hatched at '30 days, though one chick hatched at 32 days' (Sheppard & Turner, 1988). Schubot (1990), who has extensive experience with incubator-hatching, gives the incubation period for *P. a. aterrimus* as 28–30 days, initial egg weight as 23 g (1¾ oz) and average weight loss as 18.6 per cent during the incubation period, and for *P. a. goliath* as 30–31 days, and 19.23 per cent weight loss.

Palm Cockatoo (*Probosciger aterrimus aterrimus*): parent-reared youngster aged 80 days.

Parent-reared Palm Cockatoo (*Probosciger aterrimus*) at Palmitos Park.
At 19 days, the day it was ringed, weight 288 g (10¼ oz).

At 26 days, weight 430 g (15⅜ oz).

At 40 days, weight 598 g (21⅜ oz).

At 54 days; weight 610 g
(21¾ oz).

Drumming implements of wild Palm Cockatoos (*Prosbosciger aterrimus*) collected by G. A. Wood: three nuts of *Grevillea glauca* and two sticks.

Newly hatched chicks Completely naked with dark pink skin; as they develop they do *not* grow second down. On hatching the beak is almost normal cockatoo shape with no gap between the mandibles and a prominent white egg tooth contrasting with the pinkish-coloured beak. Weight 12–16 g, averaging 15 g (½ oz) for *P. a. aterrimus* and about 21 g (¾ oz) for *P. a. goliath*.
Young in nest About 80 days.
Origin *P. a. aterrimus*. New Guinea: southern area; western Papuan Islands – Misool; Irian Jaya. Indonesia: Aru Islands (also introduced to Kai Kecil Island, Kai Islands). Australia: Cape York Peninsula.
P. a. goliath. New Guinea: from the Vogelkop, Irian Jaya, eastwards through central regions to southeastern Papua New Guinea; western Papuan Islands – except Misool.

P. a stenolophus. New Guinea: north from the Mambero River; Irian Jaya eastwards to about Collingwood Bay (also Japen Island in Geelvink Bay); eastern Papua New Guinea (Forshaw, 1989).
Natural history Palm Cockatoos are mainly found in rainforest, forest edges, and locally in dense savannah, usually up to about 750 m (2,500 ft) but sometimes up to 1,300 m (4,250 ft). Forshaw (1981) states that in Australia, in the Cape York Peninsula, the southern limit of the range is roughly the southern boundary of the rainforest. He described them as confiding while feeding in rainforest, but timid in open country. However, according to *The Atlas of Australian Birds*, whose distribution maps are the result of observations of more than 10,000 birdwatchers during the period 1977–81, this species ranges much further south in

Cape York than Forshaw's distribution maps suggest, i.e. as far south as Princess Charlotte Bay in the east and Cape Keer-weer in the west. This distribution area was plotted as the result of 81 observations.

These cockatoos are observed as single birds, as pairs or in small groups. They roost singly in the topmost branches of dead or leafless trees, usually at the edge of rainforest (Forshaw, 1989). Well after sunrise, small groups depart to feed in open woodland or at forest margins. They feed on nuts, fruits, seeds, leaf buds and berries. Their liking for the fruits of the *Pandanus* is well known. These fruits (which look something like a large pale orange pine cone) contain many kernels within a hard fibrous exterior up to 10 cm (4 in) thick; kernel and fibre is eaten. They sometimes descend to the ground to feed on the old fruits, which are very hard.

Very little has been recorded about the behaviour of this cockatoo in New Guinea and Indonesia. In Australia, Peter Chapman recorded on video Palm Cockatoos feeding and displaying in one of the best film sequences of a parrot in its natural habitat which has ever been seen. (*Land of Parrots, Part 2, Black Cockatoos*). Chapman (1989) recorded the behaviour at one nest where the male arrived at 9 a.m., tapped on the nesting hollow and waited for the female to emerge. He then entered, presumably to brood or to feed the chick. One morning, at the Claudia River, five Palms were seen at a waterhole at a bend in the river, where it was overhung by the forest canopy. At this point a clear view of both sides of the bend would enable the birds to observe any approaching predators, such as the Red Goshawk (*Erythrotriorchis radiatus*).

Most information regarding nesting has been obtained from nests found in Australia; there, breeding usually occurs between August and January, depending on climatic conditions. An early study of nest sites (in tree trunks or hollow limbs) was carried out by McLennan (in Macgillivray 1914). Nest hollows were at an average height of 10 m (33 ft), with an average depth of 1.3 m (4 ft 4 in). The internal diameter varied between 25 cm (10 in) and 60 cm (24 in). The base of splintered twigs varied in depth between 10 cm (4 in) and 2–3 m (6 ft 8 in–10 ft). The unique display of the Palm Cockatoo within the vicinity of its nest site, must be one of the most remarkable sights in the world of parrots (see p. 240).

Status and conservation In Australia this species is protected; no trapping is allowed and its remote habitat enjoys protection from mining and agricultural use. In New Guinea it is not protected and has been heavily hunted for food and for export. It can no longer be found in the region of populated areas. This species was placed on Appendix I of CITES in 1987, which protected it from legal export, but many birds were exported from New Guinea and Indonesia until 1989, when Singapore became a signatory to CITES. Most Palms were exported via Singapore or Jakarta. Although this species is supposedly protected in Indonesia, because of the nature of the country, which is made up of hundreds of islands, it proved impossible to control illegal export. Many other species of parrots were trapped but the Palm Cockatoo was the prime target because of its high value. Although it is undoubtedly still possible to smuggle these birds out of Indonesia, these days very few people would be willing to risk buying them without the CITES documentation, which is now impossible to obtain for wild-caught birds. Will the native people continue to trap them – but for food – or will they leave them alone, with the chance that their numbers will increase on some of the islands where they declined due to trapping?

In 1991 Thomas Arndt (editor of the magazine *Papageien*) visited Salawati and afterwards wrote to me:

I found the Palm Cockatoo to be the most common species of parrot along the east coast (which is nearly undisturbed). On some parts along the beach I found a pair or three birds every 200 m in some special trees. When I couldn't see them I only had to throw a stone into such a tree and one to three birds flew off. Unfortunately, they were rather shy.

However, on the Indonesian islands, where deforestation was rapid and extensive during the 1980s, their survival will depend on the protection of forested areas. Protected reserves are planned throughout New Guinea and Indonesia; if these are large enough, some Palm Cockatoos will survive.

Cockatiel (Quarrion)
Nymphicus hollandicus

Crest Long feathers, usually carried nearly upright, decreasing in length from front to back; mainly yellow in male and mainly grey in female.
Plumage Mainly grey with bright orange cheek patches. Male – most of the head, except the cheeks, yellow; the underside of the tail

black. Female – head mainly grey, with some yellow around the eyes and lores; underside of the tail barred with yellow and grey.
Beak and eyes Beak grey. Eyes dark brown.
Length 31 cm (12¼ in).
Weight About 90 g (3¼ oz).
Sexual dimorphism See Plumage.
Immature birds Like the female but tail shorter.
Mutations Many colour mutations and combinations, too numerous to list here, have been established in captivity.
Sub-species None.
Captive status Extremely common. This and the Budgerigar are the only truly domesticated parrots in that they are bred in thousands and none has been exported from their native country for decades. In the 1991 *Breeding Register* of the Parrot Society, members reported breeding 6,785 Cockatiels, nearly twice as many as the next most prolific species, which was the Peach-faced Lovebird (3,482 bred).
Pet potential and personality The Cockatiel is the pet *par excellence*. Its voice is rather shrill but apart from that, birds obtained when young make perfect pets. They soon become tame, learn to 'talk' and are friendly and affectionate. They are very long lived (30 years recorded – and 20 years is common in well cared for birds). Their small size and less destructive habits, make them ideal pets for an apartment or aviary birds for those with limited space.
Aviculture and breeding Cockatiels are easy to breed in cage or aviary. Furthermore, they provide the perfect introduction to cockatoo breeding. Their behaviour is similar to that of their larger relatives, i.e. male and female incubate and feed the chicks, young hiss and sway in

Normal male Cockatiel (*Nymphicus hollandicus*) (upper bird) with two examples of the Pearl, one of the many mutations which are bred in large numbers.

the nest in a similar manner when alarmed, and courtship feeding does not normally occur.

Cockatiels can be bred in a colony aviary but better results are invariably achieved with one pair per enclosure. However, for those who enjoy keeping birds in a colony and observing their behaviour, a flock of Cockatiels will provide much enjoyment. The aviary should be as large as possible and not overcrowded. Nest boxes should measure about 25 cm (10 in) square and 35 cm (14 in) deep.

Clutch size Usually 4–6, but up to 8 or even more.

Incubation period About 20 days.

Newly hatched chicks Abundant yellow down; pinkish beaks. Weight 5 g (1/6 oz).

Young in nest Five weeks.

Origin Australia: except some coastal areas, Cape York and Tasmania.

Natural history This species is mainly nomadic, in response to food availability, but resident populations occur in the southern part of Australia. Favoured habitats are in the vicinity of water, and maybe grasslands with scattered trees and open forest. They feed on grasses, small seeds and grains, fruits and berries.

One of my own most exciting field experiences was finding myself in the midst of an enormous flock of Cockatiels. In was in April 1989; I was staying in New South Wales with a good friend and excellent ornithologist John Courtney. One day we drove for two or three hours towards the Queensland border to Goondiwondi and beyond. For two hours we drove through what seemed

Cockatiels (*Nymphicus hollandicus*): adult, left, and immature male.

Typical Cockatiel habitat; there were hundreds of Cockatiels perched on one tree, on the edge of this field of sorghum in Australia.

Cockatiels display their preference for perching on bare branches.

to be an ornithological desert; even the most common birds were conspicuous by their absence. A distant lake turned out to be a mirage in the shimmering heat haze – and then our luck changed. We saw a few Cockatiels quite close to the roadside. We stopped and made our way towards the birds we had seen in flight. There were more, many more. Suddenly I took in the sheer numbers. It was not only a breathtaking sight but an experience whose impact relied very much on sound. The noise and the activity was almost overwhelming. There were hundreds of Cockatiels perched in one tree on the edge of a field of sorghum. Some fed in the field, others wheeled about the tree looking for a perching space. Hundreds and hundreds more sat in the tree, calling their shrill call, the volume like an enormous aviary, amplified a dozen times. It was awe-inspiring.

At first I took out my cameras and clicked and clicked, fearing they would go away, but I soon realized that they were ignoring our presence. I did not know then that Cockatiels are not easily disturbed; if they are, they generally fly to the nearest tree and soon resume feeding. They seemed to prefer to perch on the bare branches, row after row, every other inch of perching space covered. The sky above was filled with Cockatiels milling around, and there was a continuous flow of Cockatiels between tree and field. At that time I did not realize how fortunate I was to see such large numbers. John told me afterwards that it was by far the largest flock he had ever observed, and estimated that we had seen at least 2,000 birds. I felt privileged to have had a brief insight into a species with which I had been familiar for 30 years (I bred it as a teenager). Yet I had no true understanding of it until the day I saw it in the wild.

Status and conservation Common, especially in the north. No conservation measures are necessary.

Appendices

Appendix I
CITES listing of cockatoos as at July 1992

CITES (Convention on International Trade in Endangered Species of Wild Flora and Fauna) regulates trade, classifying fauna into three appendices:

Appendix I

Species threatened with extinction which are, or may be, affected by trade. There is presumption against all trade in species on this Appendix. (The year in which the species was placed on Appendix I appears in parenthesis):

Moluccan Cockatoo (1989)
Goffin's Cockatoo (1992)
Red-vented (Philippine) Cockatoo (1992)
Palm Cockatoo (1987)

Appendix II

Species which, although not necessarily now threatened with extinction, may become so unless their trade is strictly regulated (by licensing) to prevent over-exploitation and to facilitate monitoring. Also contains species which, by virtue of their visual similarity, may be confused with those listed on Appendix I:

Gang Gang Cockatoo
Galah (Roseate or Rose-breasted Cockatoo)
Leadbeater's (Major Mitchell's) Cockatoo
Greater Sulphur-crested Cockatoo
Lesser Sulphur-crested Cockatoo
Blue-eyed Cockatoo
Umbrella Cockatoo
Eastern Long-billed Corella
Western Long-billed Corella
Bare-eyed Cockatoo (Little Corella)
Ducorp's Cockatoo
Glossy Cockatoo

Banksian (Red-tailed Black) Cockatoo
Northern Yellow-tailed Black Cockatoo
Southern Yellow-tailed Black Cockatoo
White-tailed Black (Carnaby's) Cockatoo
Baudin's White-tailed Black Cockatoo

Appendix II
Studbooks for cockatoos

At the time of going to press the following studbooks were operating:

Species	Studbook keeper	Address
Blue-eyed Cockatoo*	Dr Roger Wilkinson	North of England Zoological Society, Caughall Road, Upton-by-Chester CH2 1LH, UK
Moluccan Cockatoo*	David Field	Penscynor Wildlife Park, Cilfrew, Neath, Glamorgan, South Wales, UK
Goffin's Cockatoo*	David Woolcock	Paradise Park, Hayle, Cornwall TR27 4HY, UK
Red-vented (Philippine) Cockatoo*	The Parrot Society	108b Fenlake Road, Bedford MK42 0EU, UK
Red-vented (Philippine) Cockatoo**	Marc Boussekey	Espace Zoologique, St-Martin-la-Plaine, 42800 Rive-de-Gier, France
Palm Cockatoo**	Dr Roger Wilkinson	See above
Palm Cockatoo (North America)	Mike Taylor	White Oaks Plantation, 726 Owens Road, Yulee, Florida 32097, USA

* UK only
** Europe only

Appendix III

Cockatoo species reared by the author

Species reared at Loro Parque, Tenerife, 1987 and 1988, at Palmitos Park, Gran Canaria, 1989 to the present day, and in the author's collection.

Species	Hand-reared	Parent-reared
Galah (Roseate or Rose-breasted) Cockatoo	X	—
Triton Cockatoo	X	—
Moluccan Cockatoo	X	X
Umbrella Cockatoo	X	X
Western Long-billed Corella	X	—
Bare-eyed Cockatoo (Little Corella)	X	X
Goffin's Cockatoo	X	X
Red-vented (Philippine) Cockatoo	X	—
Banksian (Red-tailed Black) Cockatoo	X	—
Palm Cockatoo	—	X
Cockatiel	X	X

Epilogue

Many – perhaps even the majority of readers of this book – will not previously have been aware of the endangered status of about one-third of the cockatoos. In 1992 the International Council for Bird Preservation assessed them as follows:

Critical Citron-crested Cockatoo and Red-vented Cockatoo
Critical/Endangered Moluccan Cockatoo and Goffin's Cockatoo
Endangered Three races of the Lesser Sulphur-crested Cockatoo: the nominate (*Cacatua sulphurea sulphurea*), *C. s. parvula* and *C. s. abbotti*, and the Umbrella Cockatoo.

If you care about the future of cockatoos, help to conserve them in their natural habitat. There are two organizations which are sponsoring cockatoo conservation projects and which need your help with funding these operations. They are:

The World Parrot Trust
Glanmor House
Hayle
Cornwall
TR27 4HY
UK

International Council for Bird Preservation (ICBP)
Wellbrook Court
Girton Road
Cambridge
CB3 ONA
UK

References cited

Adams, M., Baverstock, P. R., Saunders, D. A., Schodde, R. & Smith, G. T. (1984) 'Biochemical Systematics of the Australian Cockatoos (Psittaciformes: Cacatuinae)' *Australian Journal of Zoology* **32**: 363–77.

Anon. (1991) [No title] *Parrotworld* **8** (5): 77.

Alderton, D. (1989) 'Aspergillosis' *Parrotworld* **7** (1): 28–31.

Allen, C. & Johnson, K. A. (1991) 'AFA Members Contribute to Success of TRAFFIC USA's 1990 Psittacine Captive Breeding Survey' *Watchbird* Apr/May: 15–20.

BKSDA (1989) *Laporan inventarisasi satwa liar. Katatua Cempaka* (Cacatua sulphurea citrinocristata) *di Kabupaten Sumba, Timur* Balai Konservasi Sumber Daya Alam, VII Kupang: 13 pp.

Atkinson, J. (1989) [no title] *Parrotworld* **7** (3): 38–9.

—— (1992) [no title] *Parrotworld* **9** (3): 40–41.

Bedford, Duke of (Lord Tavistock) (1954) *Parrots and Parrotlike Birds*, Fond du Lac.

Berry, R. J. (1979) *Breeding Cockatoos and Macaws* Paper presented at American Federation of Aviculture Convention.

Blakers, M., Davies, S. J., Reilly, P. N. (1984) *The Atlas of Australian Birds*, Melbourne University Press, Carlton.

Bloomfield, P. (1984) 'Breeding the Blue-eyed Cockatoo, *Catatua ophthalmica* at Chester Zoo' *Avicultural Magazine* **84** (3): 141–4.

Boswall, J. (1983) 'Tool-using and Related Behaviour in Birds: Yet More Notes' *Avicultural Magazine* **89** (3): 170–81.

Chapman, P. (1989) 'Yellow-tailed Black Cockatoos' *Queensland Aviculture* (2): 30–2.

Christidis, L. (1990) 'Animal Cytogenetics' In: *Chordata 3(B) Aves 4* Gebrüder Borntrager, Berlin-Stuttgart.

Christidis, L., Shaw, D. D. & Schodde, R. (1991) 'Chromosomal Evolution in Parrots, Lorikeets and Cockatoos (Aves: Psittaciformes)' *Hereditas* **114**: 47–56.

Christidis, L., Schodde, R., Shaw, D. D. & Maynes, S. F. (1991) 'Relationship among the Australo-Papuan Parrots, Lorikeets, and Cockatoos (Aves: Psittaciformes): protein evidence' *Condor* **93**: 302–17.

Coates, B. J. (1985) *The Birds of Papua New Guinea* Vol. 1. Dove Publications, Alderly, Australia.

Collar, N. J. (1989) 'Red Data Birds: the Cockatoos' *World Birdwatch* **11** (2): 5.

Connors, N. & Connors, E. (1988) 'The Glossy Black Cockatoo' *Australian Aviculture* **42** (5): 116–18.

—— (1991) 'Black Cockatoos in Australia' *Magazine of the Parrot Society* **XXV** (1): 16–21.

'Country Aviculturist' (1991) 'Breeding the Long-billed Corella' *Australian Aviculture* **45** (3): 55–7.

Courtney, J. (1986a) 'Age Development in the Glossy Black Cockatoo' *Australian Bird Watcher*.

—— (1986b) 'Age-related Colour Changes and Behaviour in the Northern Funereal Black Cockatoo' *Australian Bird Watcher* **11** (5): 137–45.

——(in prep.) *Australian Parrots in Aviculture*.

CSIRO (1982) *Division of Wildlife Research Report* 1980–82: 50–52.

Dawley, C. A. (1991) 'Cyrano's Story' *Parrotworld* **9** (2): 28–34.

Day, R. & Day, G. (1991) 'Goffins 1990 (*Cacatua goffini*)' *Magazine of the Parrot Society* **XXV** (3): 94–7.

Diefenbach, K. (1985) *The World of Cockatoos* TFH, New Jersey, USA.

Dosser, G. (1989) 'Gang Gang Cockatoos' *Australian Birdkeeper* **2** (10): 374–5.

Elgas, B. (1992) 'Hybridization, a Blight upon Aviculture' *The Majestic Macaws* **3** (4): 7, 20.

Emison, W. B. (1991) *Interim Report to the World Parrot Trust on the Threatened Population of Red-tailed Black Cockatoos in South-western Victoria, Australia*. Unpublished.

Evans, M. (1992) 'Work continues to perfect vaccines against PBFD and Pacheco's' *Cage & Aviary Birds* Feb. 22: 7.

Finch, B. (1982) *Newsletter of the Papua New Guinea Bird Society* Jul.–Aug.: 29.

Foreign Bird Federation (1990) *Register of Birds Bred in the UK under controlled conditions for the years 1987–1990*. (1991) *Register of Birds Bred in the UK under controlled conditions for the years 1988–1991*.

Forshaw, J. M. (1981) *Australian Parrots* 2nd (revised) edition. Lansdowne Editions, Melbourne.

—— (1989) *Parrots of the World* 3rd (revised) edition. Blandford Press, London.

—— & Cooper, W. (1989) *Parrots of the World* 3rd (revised) edition. Blandford, London.

Gedney, C. W. (1879) *Foreign Cage Birds* Vol. II. The Bazaar, London.

Graham, D. L. (1990) 'Feather and Beak Disease: its Biology, Management, and an Experiment in its Eradication from a Breeding Aviary' *Proceedings of the Annual Conference of the Association of Avian Veterinarians* 1990: 8–11.

Grazier, H. & Spouse, T. (1991) 'The Unexpected Event of 1990: the Breeding of a Red-tailed Black Cockatoo' *The Magazine of the Parrot Society* **XXV** (1): 2–3.

Greene, W. T. (1884–87) *Parrots in Captivity* Vols. I–III, George Bell & Sons, London.

Griffiths, A. V. (1965) 'Breeding the Blue-eyed Cockatoo' *Avicultural Magazine* **71** (4): 109–11.

—— (1966) 'News and Views' *Avicultural Magazine* **72** (2): 90.

Holyoak, D. T. (1972) 'Adaptive Significance of Bill Shape in the Palm Cockatoo (*Probosciger aterrimus*)' *Avicultural Magazine* **78** (3): 99–100.

Jones, M. J. & Marsden, S. M. (1992) *The Conservation of Threatened Birds and Their Key Forests on Sumba*. Draft report to ICBP.

Joseph, L., Emison, W. B. & Bren, W. M. (1991) 'Critical Assessment of the Conservation Status of Red-tailed Black Cockatoos in South-eastern

Australia with Special Reference to Nesting Requirements' *Emu* 9: 46–50.

Joshua, S. K. (1992) *A Study of Avian Cytogenetics and Psittaciform Taxonomy*, Ph.D. thesis, QMW University of London, England.

Joyner, K. L., Swanson, J. & Hanson, J. T. (1990) 'Psittacine Pediatric Diagnostics' *Proceedings Association of Avian Veterinarians* 60–82.

Kaal, G. T. (1986a) 'Practical Experiences with the Ultrasonic Nebulisation Therapy' *Proceedings, 1st International Parrot Convention* Loro Parque, Tenerife.

—— (1986b) 'Diagnostic Endoscopy in Psittacine Birds' *Proceedings, 1st International Parrot Convention* Loro Parque, Tenerife.

Kerr, N. (1991) 'Psittacine Beak and Feather Disease' *Australian Birdkeeper* 4 (11): 522–5.

King, C. E. (in press) 'Influence of Social and Physical Environment on Feather-picking of a Female Blue-eyed Cockatoo *Cacatua ophthalmica* at Rotterdam Zoo' *Zoo Biol.*

Künne, H.-J. (1992) 'Erhaltungszuchtprojekt Goffin-Kakadu' *Die Voliere* 15 (4): 104.

Lambert, F., Wirth, R., Seal, U. (in press) *Parrots, An Action Plan for their Conservation and Management* ICBP/IUCN.

Lendon, A. H. (1951) In 'News and Views' *Avicultural Magazine* 57 (5): 191.

—— (1979) *Australian Parrots in Field and Aviary* Angus and Robertson, Sydney.

Lofto, D. R. (1992) 'Breeding parrots at −40°: Moluccan Cockatoos at Prairie Aviaries' *Proceedings, 3rd Canadian Parrot Symposium* pp. 44–7, Silvio Mattacchione and Co.

Low, R. (1972) Abnormal Feathering in Cockatoos' *Cage & Aviary Birds* Aug. 3.

—— (1979a) 'An Insight into Cockatoo Lore' *Cage & Aviary Birds* Jul. 21: 1 & 3.

—— (1979b) 'An Extrovert Charmer of High Intelligence' *Cage & Aviary Birds* Sept. 15: 3.

—— (1980a) 'Breeding Goffin's Cockatoo' *Avicultural Magazine* 86 (4): 195–201.

—— (1980b) 'Goffin's Cockatoo Provides an Important Opportunity for Aviculturists' *Cage & Aviary Birds* Oct. 4: 3.

—— (1980c) 'Breeding the Citron-crested Cockatoo' *Cage & Aviary Birds* Mar. 29: 3.

—— (1984) *Endangered Parrots* Blandford Press, Poole.

—— (1988) 'Moluccan Cockatoo has Few Equals' *Cage & Aviary Birds* May 7: 5, 7.

—— (1991a) 'Time for a More Scientific Approach' *Australian Birdkeeper* 4 (7): 311–14.

—— (1991b) 'Indonesian Cockatoos in Aviculture: a Warning' *PsittaScene* 3 (2): 3–5.

—— (1992a) *Parrots – Their Care and Breeding* 3rd (revised) edition. Blandford, London. 416 pp.

—— (1992b) 'Indonesische Kadadus in der Vogelzucht – eine Warnung' *Gefied. Freund* 39 (4): 98–104.

—— (1992c) 'Indonesian Cockatoo Survey' *PsittaScene* 4 3: 4–5.

Macgillivray, W. (1914) 'Notes on Some North Queensland Birds' *Emu* **13**: 132–86.

Marshall, R. & Crowley, A. (1992) 'A Field Study for the Control of PBFD Virus in Wild-caught Cockatoos' *Proceedings Annual Conference of the Association of Avian Veterinarians* 1992: 37–41.

Messer, A. (1982) *Report* for PHPA.

Milton, R. R. & Marhadi, A. (1987) *An Investigation of Parrots and Their Trade on Pulau Bacan (North Moluccas) and Pulau Warmar Aru Islands* WWF/ IUCN.

Mudge, G. P. (1902) 'On the Myology of the Tongue of Parrots, with a Classification of the Order Based upon the Structure of the Tongue' *Trans. Zool. Soc.* London **16**: 211–79.

Muller, K, (1975) 'Propagation of the Palm Cockatoo', *International Zoo Yearbook* **15**: 103–111.

Murphy, J. D. (1989) 'A Look at Pellets in the Lab' *Parrotworld* **7** (3): 15–19.

—— (1990) 'Work in Progress: Nutritional Research' *Parrotworld* **8** (2): 17–19.

—— (1991a) 'Sarcosporidiosis' *Parrotworld* **9** (1): 19–22.

—— (1991b) Psittacine Beak and Feather Disease, *Parrotworld* **9** (2): 23–6.

—— (1991c) 'A Vaccine for Pacheco's' *Parrotworld* **8** (3): 57–9.

Nott, H. (1992) 'Bird Nutrition (Part 2): Parrots can be Fussy over Their Food' *Cage & Aviary Birds* Aug. 1: 15.

Pass, D. (1991) 'Research on Psittacine Beak and Feather Disease (PBFD)' *Australian Aviculture* **45** (3): 71.

Paul, S. (1991) [Letter to Editor] *Magazine of the Parrot Society* **XXV** (5): 167.

Peters, R. (1989) 'The Palm Cockatoo' *Australian Birdkeeper* **2** (8): 296, 297, 299.

Pfeifer, C. (1983) 'Breeding and Hand-Raising Slender-billed Cockatoos' *AFA Watchbird* **X** (2): 6–9.

Prestwich, A. A. (1951) *Records of Parrots Bred in Captivity, Part II*. Prestwich, London. 33 pp.

Riffel, M. & Dwi Bekti, S. (1991) *A Further Contribution to the Knowledge of the Birds of Sumba, Indonesia*. Unpublished report.

Ritchie, B. (1990) Beak and Feather Disease, *Proceedings, 2nd International Parrot Convention* Loro Parque, Tenerife.

—— (1992a) 'Test System Ensures Correct PBFD Diagnosis' *Cage & Aviary Birds* Mar. 28: 5.

—— (1992b) 'Vaccination Programme could Eradicate PBFD in Captive Birds' *Cage & Aviary Birds* Apr. 4: 5.

Rosskopf, W. J. & Woerpel, R. W. (1990) 'Psittacine Conditions and Syndromes' *Proceedings, Association of Avian Veterinarians* 432–59, Lake Worth, Florida.

Rosskopf, W. J., Woerpel, R. W., Fudge, A. M. *et al.* (1992) 'Iron Storage Disease (Hemochromatosis) in a Citron-crested Cockatoo and Other Psittacine Species' *Proceedings Annual Conference Association of Avian Veterinarians* 1992: 98–107.

Rowley, I. (1990) *Behavioural Ecology of the Galah* Surrey Beatty & Sons, NSW, Australia.

—— & Chapman, G. (1991) 'The Breeding Biology, Food, Social Organisation, Demography and Conservation of the Major Mitchell or Pink Cockatoo,

Cacatua leadbeateri, on the Margin of the Western Australian Wheatbelt' *Aust. J. Zool.* **39**: 211–61.

—— , Russell, E. & Palmer, M. (1989) 'The Food Preferences of Cockatoos: an Aviary Experiment' *Australian Wildlife Research* **16**: 19–32.

Saunders, D. A. (1976) 'Breeding of the White-tailed Black Cockatoo in Captivity' *Western Australian Naturalist* **13**: 171–2.

—— (1979) 'The Availability of Tree Hollows for Use as Nest Sites by White-tailed Black Cockatoos' *Aust. Wildl. Res.* **6**: 205–16.

—— (1982) 'The Breeding Behaviour and Biology of the Short-billed Form of the White-tailed Black Cockatoo *Calyptorhynchus funereus*' *Ibis* **124**: 422–55.

—— (1991) 'The Effect of Land Clearing on the Ecology of Carnaby's Cockatoo and the Inland Red-tailed Black Cockatoo in the Wheatbelt of Western Australia' *Acta XX Congressus Internationalis Ornithologici* 658–65. New Zealand Ornithological Congress Trust Board, Wellington.

Schmutz, S. M. & Prus, S. E. (1987) 'A Cytogenetic Study of Four Species of Cockatoos and Amazon Parrots' *Genetica* **74**: 69–71.

Schodde, R. (1988) 'New Subspecies of Australian Birds' *Canberra Bird Notes* **13**: 119–22.

Schooley, M. (1988) 'Smuggling' *Australian Birdkeeper* **2** (8): 300–302.

Schubot, R. (1990) 'Black Palm Cockatoos' *AFA Watchbird* **XVII** (1): 4–9.

—— Clubb, K. J. & Clubb, S. L. (1992) *Psittacine Aviculture*, Avicultural Breeding and Research Centre, Loxahatchee, Florida.

Schulte, E. G. B. (1990) 'Breeding Goffin's Cockatoo, 1974–1989' *Avicultural Magazine* **96** (4): 171–3.

Serventy, D. L. & Whittell, H. M. (1976) *Birds of Western Australia* 5th edition. Perth: Univ. W. A. Press.

Shephard, M. (1989) *Aviculture in Australia* Black Cockatoo Press, Prahran, Victoria.

Sheppard, C. & Turner, W. (1988) 'Handrearing Palm Cockatoos' *Parrotletter* **1** (1): 14–17.

Sibley, C. G. & Ahlquist, J. E. (1990) *Phylogeny and Classification of Birds*, Yale University Press, New Haven – London.

Sindel, S. & Lynn, R. (1989) *Australian Cockatoos*, Singil Press, New South Wales.

Smiet, A. C. (1985) 'Notes on the Field Status and Trade of Moluccan Parrots' *Biol. Cons.* **34**: 181–94.

Smiet, F. (1982) 'Threats to the Spice Islands' *Oryx* **16** (4): 323–8.

Smith, G. A. (1975) 'Systematics of Parrots' *Ibis* **117**: 18–68.

Smith, G. A. (1985) 'The Palm Cockatoo (*Probosciger aterrimus*)' *Magazine of the Parrot Society* **XIX** (2): 32–40.

Stennet, D. (1988) 'Short Cuts to Pairing of Cockatoos' *Parrotworld* **6** (3): 38–41.

Tabaranza, B. (1991) 'Bestandsaufnahme des Rotsteisskakadus auf den Philippines' *Mitteilungen: Zoologische Gesellschaft für Arten und Populations-schutz* **7** (2): 5.

—— (1993) 'Status des Rotsteisskakadus auf den Philippinen', *Mitteilungen: Zoologische Gesellschaft für Arten- und Populationsschutz* **9** (1): 16–18.

Tavistock, Lord *see* Bedford, Duke of

Taylor, J. B. (1991) 'Die Papagein von Ceram' *Papageien* **4** (5): 149–55.

Thompson, D. W. (1900) 'On the Characteristic Points in the Cranial Osteology of Parrots' *Proc. Zool. Soc. Lond.* **[1899]**: 9–46.

Van Dongen, M. W. M. & de Boer, L. E. M. (1984) 'Chromosome Studies of Seven Species of Parrots Belonging to the Families Cacatuidae and Psittacidae (Aves: Psittaciformes)' *Genetica* **65**: 109–17.

Wegner, B. (1984) 'Breeding and Raising White-tailed Black Cockatoos' *AFA Watchbird* **XI** (4): 36–8.

Wilkinson, R. (1991) 'Chester Zoo Notes – 1990' *Avicultural Magazine* **97** (3): 147.

Wilson, K. (1992) 'The Magnetism of Major Mitchell's Cockatoo' *Australian Birdkeeper* **5** (1): 34–9.

Wirth, R. (1990) 'Moluccan cockatoos and other Indonesian Parrots' *Proceedings, 2nd International Parrot Convention* Loro Parque, Tenerife.

Wood, G. A. (1984) 'Tool Use by the Palm Cockatoo *Probosciger aterrimus* during Display' *Corella* **8** (4): 94–5.

—— (1988) 'Further Field Observations of the Palm Cockatoo *Probosciger aterrimus* in the Cape York Peninsula, Queensland' *Corella* **12** (2): 48–52.

Zieren, M., Yus Rusila Noor, Baltzer, M. & Najamuddin Saleh (1990) *Wetlands of Sumba, East Nusa Tenggara: An Assessment of Values, Developments and Threats.* PHPA/AWB Indonesia, Bogor, August 1990.

Index of common names

Page numbers in *italics* denote main text reference.
Page numbers in bold type denote illustrations.

Index of scientific names

(Main text reference only)

General index

aggression, male 66–7
alarm, baby 75
aspergillosis 119–20
aviary
   construction 45–6
   hygiene 43, 47
   security 44
   siting 46–7

banding 76–7, 79
beak 15–17
'beak ball' 67
berries 57
bond, pair 64–5, 68
breeding, colony 77–8
brooder 84

cage
   construction 48–9
   indoor 43, 44, 48–9
   suspended 43
camera, observation 65, 66
candidiasis 76, 93
CITES 24, 35, 202, 234, 245, 253–4
compatibility 64–5, 67
containers, food 60

disease
   detection 113–16
   iron storage 57
   kidney 53
   Pacheco's 117–19
   prevention 116–17
   psittacine beak and feather 41, 42, 124–9
   signs of, in chicks 92–3
   treatment of 117–22

drinking 25–6

environmental enrichment 109–10
evolution 13–14

feather plucking 100, 102, 109–10, 125
feathers
   cheek 17
   crest 14–15
feeding, behaviour of wild birds 24–5
feet 17–18
food
   captive birds 50–60
   chick rearing 86–8
   commercially prepared 52–4, 86–7
   containers 60
fruits 56–7

hybrids 26, 79–80
hygiene 93, 117

imprinting 41, 97, 110, 112, 173–4
incubation
   artificial 72–4
   humidity 73
   periods 72
   problems 74
incubator 72
intelligence 108
ionizers 44–5
iron-storage disease 57

karyotypes 132–5

This book belongs to
Joanna Whitelaw